The Quick and the Dead

Electronic Combat and Modern Warfare

Neil Munro

St. Martin's Press
New York

First published in the United States of America in 1991

Printed in the United States of America

ISBN 0-312-04802-5

Library of Congress Cataloging-in-Publication Data

Munro, Neil.
The quick and the dead : electronic combat and modern warfare / Neil Munro.
p. cm.
Includes index.
ISBN 0-312-04802-5
1. Electronics in military engineering. 2. Command and control systems. 3. Military intelligence. 4. United States—Armed Forces—Communication systems. 5. Soviet Union—Armed Forces—Communication systems. 6. Military intelligence—United States. 7. Military intelligence—Soviet Union. I. Title.
UG485.M79 1991
623'.043—dc20   90-8983
                                                                                                              CIP

Contents

*To my wife Yvonne, without whom I could not
have written this book.*

List of Figures

--- ◆ ---

Acknowledgments

First, I must recognize the contributions of many Defense Department and industry officials that I have talked to during my years as a defense reporter. I also need to thank the experts who have helped guide me through these very complex technical and military issues. Also those who kindly read the manuscript and gave me their views, including Julian Lake, John Rosado, Stephen Cimbala, Thomas Rona, and Don Gordon, whose book *Electromagnetic Warfare: Element of Strategy and Multiplier of Combat Power* got me started in the field.

Clearly, errors of omission or commission in this manuscript are completely mine.

I also need to thank in advance another set of people—the readers who send me their comments, whether they be complimentary or critical, pleased or outraged.

INTRODUCTION

It is also likely that sophisticated Western forces like USCENTCOM [U.S. Central Command] can exploit the technical advantages they will gain from superior C³I organization and technology and could use a combination of electronic warfare, targeting, and strike systems that massively degrade the C³I assets of Third World forces. The experience of Iraq and Iran indicates such strikes might cripple many Third World air forces and critically weaken their regular armies, particularly if they hit at both military and civil C3I links.

> From **Anthony Cordesman** *and*
> **Abraham Wagner,** *The Lessons of Modern War*

As this introduction is being written, U.S. and allied forces are girding for their greatest test since the Second World War. The outcome of the crisis will help shape the fate of many nations and peoples, but could also reveal how well the U.S. military has prepared itself for modern war.

War is being smothered in the affluent world by nuclear weapons, the growing attraction of liberal democracy, and by the slow but by no means universal decline of nationalism. But such optimism is of no use to troops scanning a hostile horizon in the Saudi desert or any other country of the developing world.

The Kuwaiti disaster clearly shows that despite the glorious prospects for peace wrought by the revolutions of 1989, the persistence of war and the uncertainty of the future mean that the Western world will need strong military forces for the foreseeable future, forces ready to handle any violent conflicts that will appear as the people of the world continue toward their uncertain futures. Most unlikely yet most important, the Western armies must also be ready for the catastrophic collapse of international relations as happened 1789, 1914, and 1939 and as might happen if the continuing Soviet revolution spins violently out of control.

In these peaceful circumstances when the public burden of military spending is more onerous than before, United States military forces have no choice but to prepare themselves for a new era in which they must be small but strong, cheap but capable, controllable but powerful.

This book explores how the U.S. military is coming to understand how electronic combat — the struggle for use of the electromagnetic spectrum to collect and distribute information, while denying information to the enemy — can determine who wins tactical firefights, large scale engagements, theater-wide campaigns, wars, and possibly even international crises. Also, the struggle for use of the electromagnetic spectrum effects the likelihood of nuclear war breaking out, and the ways in which it would be fought.

Skillful conduct of electronic combat will produce information that will allow targets to be speedily destroyed without wasted effort, allow commanders to quickly make wise decisions, allow the swift wrecking of enemy strategies, and allow relatively speedy victory without crippling losses of life.

But the principal point about information is that even a little can have enormous consequences. Unlike traditional warfare where a few extra oar-powered galleys, cannon-armed men o' war or battleships made no great difference to the outcome of wars, even a little scrap of information can change the course of history — if properly exploited. Tsar Nicholas II of Russia would well understand this because a poorly encrypted Russian radio message was intercepted and read by the Kaiser's troops in 1914. This German success led to the collapse of the Russian offensive, probably to the collapse of the

Russian monarchy and arguably to the communist domination of the USSR that lasted for over seventy years.

Moreover, some modern weapons are reaching their maximum possible level of mechanical efficiency. For example, stealthy cruise missiles are cheap, difficult to shoot down, have essentially unlimited range and can destroy nearly all targets night or day even with a non-nuclear conventional warhead. The only way such weapons can be improved is with additional information that allows them to be aimed faster or to let them find their own targets.

Because information is so central in modern warfare, every little technological or tactical issue that affects the speedy gathering, sharing and exploitation of information is of great importance. This fact creates an enormous burden for modern armies who must make themselves strong in nearly every area of modern technology as well as strategy, training, organization, and courage to effectively carry out their duties without gross errors in the chaos, confusion, fear, and unprecedented violence of modern warfare.

For such demanding tasks, there is no alternative to smart soldiers able to wisely use the advanced technology placed in their hands by modern scientists.

This means that military skill and clever soldiers will decide more battles than numbers or fancy technology. And perhaps the most important military skill is how best to wage this struggle for information.

The struggle for the control of the electromagnetic spectrum is called electronic combat because the spectrum is the channel through which information must pass. Just as control of vital sea lanes allowed Britain to dominate the world for most of the 1800s, so will control of the electromagnetic spectrum allow armies to dominate local wars now and in the future.

Skill at electronic combat is the touchstone of modern armies; without it, every army is vulnerable to an enemy who invests time, thought, and money in the preparations for electronic combat that allow him to dominate the struggle for information.

Without such skill, military establishments will pour billions into expensive but obsolete weaponry, tactics, and training as some elements of the U.S. military have done for many years.

Luckily for the West, the collapse of the Warsaw Pact greatly reduced the likelihood of warfare with the Soviet Union's powerful military and massive nuclear forces. This victory gives Western armies the time they need to prepare for a future in which electronic combat will be more important than ever in conventional combat.

But whatever the turbulent state of Soviet civil-military relations are today, this evening, or tomorrow, examination of the intellectually advanced Soviet concepts for electronic combat benefits those seeking to control conflict in peacetime or wartime.

Although many mid-level officers in the U.S. military are aware of the vital importance of electronic combat, the U.S. armed services have failed to grasp its fundamental importance. Despite the lessons of the Vietnam War, the 1973 Arab-Israeli War, and the 1982 Bekaa Valley battles, electronic combat gets too little attention from the Defense Department's bureaucracy which favors spending money on impressive aircraft or fine-looking ships.

According to one electronic combat official, "The pecking order is not going to change. First, platforms [such as tanks, aircraft, and ships], then weapons and then support. Electronic warfare is in that third category... The only way it changes is when we get into a fracas. That's when everybody needs us."

In a war out over Kuwait, we shall see a ferocious and bloody war, in which the side with the greatest combination of weaponry, skill, and willpower shall win the military victory. In all likelihood, we shall see how skillfully U.S. forces use their armory of electronic jammers, long range missiles, laser-blinding systems, deception decoys, as well as highly classified weaponry. No doubt there will be a sudden increase in electronic combat once soldiers' lives and leaders' reputations are clearly in the balance.

This book concentrates on ground warfare because ground troops are the bearers of final political power. It first describes the technology so that the reader can comprehend the complexity and breadth of technological preparations required. The book next discusses the basic tactics and techniques of electronic combat, including the Soviet military's view of electronic combat.

After preparing the technological and tactical ground, the book describes how peacetime conflict is shaped by electronic combat. Then readers are offered a discussion of Soviet strategies for electronic combat in conventional war, and a discussion of the varying successes of the United States' military services in coming to terms with this vital element of modern warfare. Then follows a chapter on how electronic combat effects nuclear deterrence. The final chapter ties the previous chapter together and shows how electronic combat is fundamentally changing the nature of political conflict.

Hopefully, wars will someday be universally regarded as vulgar and destructive. But until then, armies that fail to understand and invest in electronic combat will find themselves repeating the experience of the brave but useless attacks of Polish cavalrymen who were effortlessly destroyed in 1939 by the Nazis' Panzer divisions.

One

---◆---

THE ELECTROMAGNETIC SPECTRUM AND SURVEILLANCE SENSORS

You can never do too much reconnaissance.
Gen. George S. Patton, *War As I Knew It*

Bullets are the ammunition of guns; electromagnetic energy is the ammunition of electronic warfare.

Electronic warfare is intended to shut the ears, stop the voice, close the eyes and freeze the nervous system of enemy soldiers. Deaf, dumb, blind, and paralyzed soldiers do not live long in battle.

There are, broadly speaking, four different ways to use electromagnetic energy for war. It is now used for communications, surveillance, and weapons guidance. It will soon be used in the fourth way: to carry destructively powerful bolts of energy.

Although the technology of electronic warfare is growing more and more astonishingly complex, only an understanding of its basic principles is needed to appreciate its central role in modern war. After all, it matters little what type of radar-guided missile destroys an aircraft if the aircraft is destroyed. Indeed, the technology is so complex that it is hopeless to try to understand all of it, not just because the technology is constantly advancing, but because it is wielded by soldiers who are skilled at finding new and surprising ways of using military technology.

How the technology is used is just as important as what it can do. A soldier may see his enemy coming, but if he cannot control his trembling arm, he will soon be dead. This lesson in the control of military force is condensed into a simple maxim: move faster than the enemy can react, and his sword will not penetrate your shield nor will his armor stop your spear. And everything you do to confuse and blind your enemy can only help.

The two most important technologies to understand are sensors and communications systems. This first chapter describes the eyes and ears of armies — their sensors. The next chapter describes the voices and ears of armies — their communication systems.

ELECTROMAGNETIC ENERGY

In battle, electromagnetic energy is fired, reflected, absorbed, suppressed, magnified, and used for a great number of military purposes.

We do not have to imagine some forms of electromagnetic energy, because we can see it with our eyes in the form of light, we can feel its effect with our skin as heat, and we can hear sounds that have been carried over the air by electromagnetic energy.

We have learned how to produce a great variety of electromagnetic signals, which differ by two fundamental characteristics: wavelength and frequency.

WAVELENGTH If electromagnetic energy is visualized as ocean waves, the length of an electromagnetic wave is the distance from one wave peak to the next peak, or from one wave trough to the next trough. The actual wavelength of electromagnetic waves vary from hundreds of kilometers on one end of the electromagnetic spectrum to billionths of a single meter and even less on the other end. Most of the electromagnetic energy used by the military has wavelengths from a few tens of meters to a few thousandths of a meter.

FREQUENCY   Another characteristic of electromagnetic energy is frequency or how often complete waves pass a point. Because all electromagnetic energy travels at the speed of light, the shorter the wavelength, the more frequently waves pass an observer at a fixed point. In other words, the shorter the wavelength, the higher the frequency, and correspondingly, the longer the wavelength, the lower the frequency.

Frequency and wavelength determine some of the behavior of electromagnetic energy, such as the distance it can travel in the atmosphere, whether they can go around corners or penetrate water.

For better understanding, each frequency and wavelength can be placed on the electromagnetic spectrum. Long wavelength, low frequency energy is represented on the left by extremely low frequency radio signals. Very short wavelength, extremely high frequency signals are represented on the right by visible light and ultraviolet energy.

The different frequency and wavelength characteristics of radiations across the electromagnetic spectrum result in radiations that have different capabilities and properties. For instance, X rays can penetrate a great deal of matter, while visible light is blocked by a thin piece of paper.

The difference in energy properties have prompted scientists to subdivide the electromagnetic spectrum into various regions. These regions are defined by wavelength and frequency, but are often referred to by the name of the most prominent radiation in that region. Thus there is a visible light region, an infrared region, a radiowave region, among others.

These regions are further broken down into many distinct bands, each of which usually shares the same general properties as its parent region. For instance, when the wavelengths of white light are dispersed by a prism or by moisture in the air, an observer can see the colors of the rainbow. Each of these color bands have similar properties as the others, and when combined they make up the visible light region of the spectrum.

For military purposes, one of the most important properties of energy in any particular region or band is how well it travels through the atmosphere. For example, some radiowave signals can travel all the way around the world despite rain or wind, while infrared energy is absorbed before it can travel far.

There are four primary methods of propagating electromagnetic energy through the atmosphere.

The first and most common method of propagation is by line of sight. Just as light travels in a straight line from the sun to the human eye, electromagnetic signals travel straight from the transmitter to the receiver. Signals travelling by line of sight are relatively short ranged, and are blocked by hills and other obstacles. Only in space can signals travel unimpeded by line of sight.

Another type of propagation path is the groundwave path, in which signals travel through the earth's surface. For example, some of the radio signals received by an ordinary radio travel through the ground. Such signals are short ranged but have the advantage of being able to travel around hills and obstacles.

The next type of propagation path is the waveguide path, in which signals are channelled between outer space and the earth's surface by the earth's ionosphere. The ionosphere is a layer of electronically charged air high above the earth's surface which has the ability to absorb, reflect or divert various types of signals. For example, very long wavelength signals transmitted by low frequency radios are contained within the earth's atmosphere by the ionosphere, allowing them to propagate to great distances by the waveguide path.

The ionosphere is also important for the fourth or skywave path, where, unlike the channelling of signals in the waveguide path, radio signals are bounced back and forth between the earth's surface and the ionosphere. This means that a high frequency radio signal might be impossible to hear up at a range of 1,000 km because it has bounced away from the earth's surface, yet easily heard at 1,500 km range where it has bounced back down to earth. The areas where the signal cannot be heard at ground level are known as "shadow zones."

Another propagation path is the tropospheric scatter path. In this infrequently used method, signals are bounced off the earth's troposphere, which lies only a few kilometers above the ground. When the signal strikes the tropospheric layer at a shallow angle of 4 degrees or less, it can be detected at a distance of 70 km to 700 km. However the power loss is usually very high, so these radios need to be large and powerful.

Another potential way of bouncing signals out to long range is to use the thousands of small meteor trails that occur every day. As each meteor, small or microscopic, burns its way through the atmosphere, it leaves a tiny trail of electronically charged atoms, which can reflect radio waves just as the ionosphere does.

But because of the very short life of the meteorite trails, a radio using the meteor scattering path must be able to rapidly transmit large amounts of information during the few seconds each trail exists. However, there are so many meteorites that signal links averaging 100 words per minute can be established.

The distinct properties of each of the various electromagnetic regions and their associated bands allow scientists to design electronic systems to exploit the particular region of the electromagnetic spectrum best suited for a specific purpose. Almost the entire electromagnetic spectrum is utilized in electronic warfare equipment and techniques.

The radio-frequency or radiowave region, from very high to extremely high frequencies, is the most important for the military because it is used by radar, radar jamming, radio communications and radio-interception equipment. But most regions and bands of the electromagnetic spectrum are important in electronic warfare. For example, the visible light region is exploited by the human eye (still the most important target acquisition device), as well as by some lasers.

SENSOR SYSTEMS: RADARS, TELESCOPES AND INFRARED SCANNERS

The eyes and ears of any army are its electronic sensors. These sensors can track and identify targets, reveal approaching enemies or display friendly locations. They use most of the spectrum, including the radio-frequency, infrared, visible light and ultraviolet regions.

Some of these sensors can detect targets at hundreds of miles range, although few with a great range can also distinguish an enemy from a friend or can guide weapons to the target. This identification and guidance task can better be performed by other, shorter range systems.

Thus there are two general types of sensors: surveillance systems used to detect targets and weapon-guidance sensors used to help attack targets.

This chapter shall discuss the wide variety of military surveillance systems, leaving the targeting sensors for the next chapter.

SURVEILLANCE SENSORS IN THE RADIO-WAVE REGION

Active Sensors

The most important surveillance device in the radiowave region is radar because it can spot even small targets some thousands of miles away and measure their range with great accuracy in all weather, day or night.

Radars of various kinds are used for a myriad of purposes including surveillance, fire control, collision avoidance, terrain mapping, navigation, altitude control, air traffic control, vehicle detection, and tracking artillery shells in flight. But there are problems with the use of radar.

The main problem is that radar is an active sensor and so emits radiowave energy, much like a searchlight emits visible light energy, which allows the enemy to locate the radar and counterattack. So unless the designers and operators are very careful, the radar's signals will betray its existence and even its position, making it vulnerable to an enemy attack.

A radar system sends out a pulse by line of sight and analyzes the echo to determine target range and bearing. Range is determined by measuring the time between the moment a pulse is emitted and the moment its reflection returns. Direction is determined from the angle at which reflections are received.

Fundamental to all radars are a radar antenna, a radar signal, and a signal processor.

The radar's antenna usually serves as both a transmitting antenna and a receiving antenna. Ideally, it will maximize output power and will pick up the faintest echo of the returning signal.

The particular signal used in the radar depends on its task. Often called a waveform, the radar signal is varied by frequency and other features. Different waveforms are chosen for such tasks as maximizing detection range or picking out targets hidden in the clutter caused by reflected signals from hills and trees.

When the reflected signals are received by the radar antenna, they are analyzed by the radar's signal processor to determine the location of the target. In effect, the signal processor is really the brains of the radar.

Radar Bands

Just as the spectrum is divided into various electromagnetic regions, the radio-wave region is divided into radar bands. The bands go from A to M, with the lowest frequency band in the A band. There are very few military systems that use anything above the M band.

The differing radar bands all have their own characteristics which are exploited by radar designers. So when choosing an operating frequency for a radar, designers must take into account the characteristics of the particular frequency and the nature of the expected targets. Radar developers must strike a compromise on the particular waveforms, signal processors, antennas and propagation paths they choose to use.

Of the numerous trade-offs to be made when designing a radar, the most important is the choice between the high target resolution permitted by high-frequency radars and the great range allowed by low-frequency radars. Resolution is the ability to distinguish clearly between details. The higher a radar's resolution, the better it can detect and distinguish between small and closely spaced targets.

This long wavelength versus short wavelength problem has resulted in two general types of radars, low-frequency surveillance radars to alert friendly units of distant enemies, and high-frequency radars to guide weapons onto a collision course with nearby targets.

The HF and VHF Bands: OTH-B Radars

Over-the-Horizon-Backscatter (OTH-B) radars exploit the skywave propagation of the high frequency radio band (3 to 30 MHz) to detect targets from 1,000 to 4,000 kilometers (600 to 2,500 miles) range. But their great range is offset by several disadvantages.

Because OTH-B radars use relatively long-wavelength signals, they can only distinguish separate targets that are several kilometers apart. For this reason, the radars are only used to alert other defenses to an incoming danger.

OTH-B radars must also have very large antennas to transmit their long-wavelength high-power signals and to maximize sensitivity to the tiny fraction of the original signals that return to the receiver from the target.

OTH-B radars are vulnerable to disturbances in the atmosphere, especially near the North and South Poles where strong magnetic fields disrupt the radar signals. They are relatively easy to jam and there is a minimum distance short of which the OTH-B cannot detect targets.

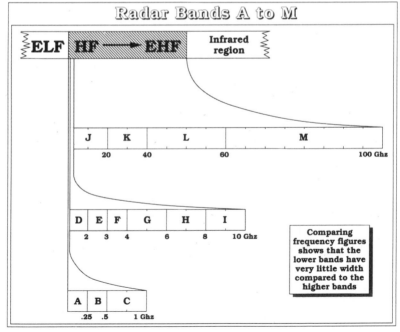

Fig. 1

But these limitations are balanced by the ability of OTH-B radars to see over the horizon to enormous distances. Thus OTH-B radars are used in strategic defense and surveillance roles. For example, the United States is building OTH-B radars located within its borders to detect incoming aircraft, cruise missiles and ships at sea. The Soviets already have four OTH-B radars in service.

Bands A to F: Surveillance Radars

Traditional radars can search for targets in two dimensions: altitude and direction. A typical two-dimensional radar is the ASR-9, used for air traffic control in the United States.

However, in modern military applications, two-dimensional radars are being replaced by three-dimensional radars able to track targets in three dimensions — range, direction, and altitude. For example, the British Martello radar operates in the D band, has a moving target indication capability, and uses eight elevation beams to determine target altitude.

Another increasingly common type of radar system uses a phased-array radar. This type of antenna looks like a flat panel, but consists of hundreds or thousands of small emitters, all controlled by computers.

By turning on and off the many small emitters in various patterns, the computer can concentrate a radar beam on any target in front of the radar panel. Because the computer can change the beam's direction practically instantaneously, a single phased array radar can simultaneously watch several aircraft, steer several antiaircraft missiles, and search the sky for undetected aircraft in microseconds.

The earliest phased-array radars were very large systems built to give warning of an incoming nuclear attack. These large phased-array radars typically exploit the lower bands to maximize power and long-range detection. For example, the extremely powerful American Pave Paws radars use B-band transmissions and has a range of up to 5,000 km (3,100 mi). But the shipboard Aegis phased-array radar uses the higher frequency E and F bands to combine the benefits of long range detection with relatively high resolution.

Phased-array radars are versatile and powerful, but very expensive. However, the U.S. military is investing heavily to reduce the cost and size of phased-array antennas. During the mid-1990s, the Pentagon plans to deploy extremely small phased array antennas, which can emit signals in frequencies as high as the M band, on various types of missiles and helicopters.

A recent development is the use of ground-wave signals to detect targets over the horizon. These OTH-Surface (OTH-S) radars are claimed to have ranges of up to 350 km (230 mi). However, few if any, OTH-S radars have been placed in service yet.[1]

Bands E to G: Target Acquisition Radars

Most radars in the E to G bands are target acquisition radars, which combine some surveillance capability with limited weapons guidance capability.

In air defense, the targets to be destroyed are small, swiftly moving aircraft. Thus any failure of coordination between wide-beam surveillance radars and narrow-beam guidance radars could allow the fast-moving attackers to destroy their own targets before they could be spotted by the weapon guidance radars.

To avoid this coordination problem, antiaircraft weapons typically carry short-range target-acquisition radars as well as weapon-guidance radars. With better target-tracking capabilities (but less range) than surveillance radars and greater range (but poorer target-tracking capability) than weapon-guidance radars, these target-acquisition radars are a compromise between the long-range surveillance radars and the short-range weapon-guidance radars.

This compromise is chosen because they are used to tell guidance radars where to look for targets. For example, the Soviet SA-8 system reportedly includes a G/H-band acquisition radar to lock on its two J-band tracking and missile guidance radars.

The E to G bands are also used by terrain-avoidance radars which are intended to prevent aircraft from crashing into the ground when flying very fast at very low altitudes or in bad weather. These radars watch the ground ahead of the aircraft and give warning of any dangerous obstacles to the low flying aircraft, such as a hill or forest.

Bands H to J: Short-range Surveillance Radars

As the operating frequency is increased, radar antennas are reduced in size and target resolution is increased, although range is progressively reduced. Because of the increased resolution but shortened range, the higher frequency bands are used most by shorter-ranged targeting radars.

However, there is a strong demand for compact surveillance radars. Nearly all airborne surveillance radars operate in the I and J bands, because the advantages of a small radar and high resolution are more important for pilots than extended ranges.

For example, an aircraft's terrain-mapping radar uses short range high-frequency radar waves to map out the terrain immediately in front of and below an aircraft. The linkage of an automatic pilot to the resulting radar image allows the aircraft to be flown automatically as low as is safely possible, thereby reducing pilot fatigue and aircraft vulnerability.

On the ground, soldiers use man-portable surveillance radars operating in the I or J radar bands to detect enemy troops or vehicles hidden among houses, trees, and other objects.

Radars have also been developed to detect and track artillery rounds in flight up to 30 km away. This enables the artillery gun to be located and attacked before many rounds can be fired. One U.S. Army artilleryman told the author that the U.S. Marine Corps was able to hit Arab mortar sites in Lebanon even before the first slow-moving mortar shell struck. This achievement was made possible by instantly communicating information gathered by a PQ-37 mortar-locating radar to the Marines' high-velocity artillery guns.

Bands K to M: Millimeter-wave Surveillance Radars

One of the main military advantages of millimeter-wave radars, which use frequencies from 30 to 300 GHz in the K, L, and M bands, is that they use only a small antenna. For example a narrow beam of only one-sixth of a degree wide at 94 GHz requires a dish only 38 centimeters (15 in) wide, whereas at 9.4 GHz the antenna would need to be ten times wider — 3.8 meters (12.5 feet) wide — to get the same narrow beam.[2] But this advantage requires precise and expensive engineering.

Much of the millimeter wave band suffers from extreme absorption by the atmosphere, sharply limiting the range of millimeter wave radars. But this problem of atmospheric absorption is a boon for covert operations. For example, it is very hard to intercept 60 GHz transmissions because they are very rapidly absorbed even in good weather.[3] Moreover, there are currently relatively few interception devices able to detect millimeter transmissions, because most detectors only operate up to 18 GHz. Thus aircraft or special forces using 60 GHz communications would be hard to detect.

Millimeter-wave radars also have good anti-jamming capabilities and excellent discrimination capability, despite smoke or dust. "However, as in all matters of electronic warfare, it would be wrong to be complacent" about millimeter wave radar's resistance to jamming, according to the editors of one volume.[4]

Impulse Radars

Impulse radars are not deployed yet. But proponents claim that they will help reduce radar costs, minimize the size of radars, detect small targets, defeat enemy jamming, help recognize targets, and see through vegetation. This long list of desirable features will supposedly result from repetitive transmission of a single powerful pulse of very wide bandwidth, perhaps using frequencies from the A to M bands. These claims have prompted the establishment of a research effort in the United States, so the next few years should show whether the radar is technically possible. Depending on how many of these attributes are possible, this type of radar could have an enormous effect by greatly increasing the numbers and quality of radars — and therefore smart weapons — on the battlefield.[5]

Laser Radars

Above the radiowave region of the spectrum, laser light can be used in radar-like devices called lidars which stands for light imaging, detection and ranging. In the same way that a radar uses radio-frequency signals, a lidar signal processor uses the laser light reflected from targets and received by an optical lens to locate the targets. Lasers can also emit frequencies in the infrared region.

A few lidars are in use for airborne target detection. In operation, a deliberately widened beam is used to first acquire targets by rapidly scanning the area. Once a target is detected, the laser can be greatly narrowed to a pencil beam in order to get improved targeting calculations or to increase the power on target. Such lidars have been used by the Soviets to examine U.S. satellites over the Arctic and to temporarily blind American pilots. A few U.S. lidars are known to exist, and are used in various tests and probably for tracking Soviet satellites.

PASSIVE SENSORS

The most characteristic feature of all the sensors discussed so far — be they radars or lidars — is their *active* nature. All emit energy and then collect the reflected echoes for detailed analysis. Like visible light searchlights, they broadcast their presence openly to all who can listen with the aid of appropriate equipment. However, there are also various *passive* surveillance devices that are harder for the enemy to destroy because they do not emit any energy, they merely listen for it.

The great advantage passive devices have over active devices is that they are very difficult to detect. This makes passive sensors very difficult to detect, destroy, or disrupt. Also, it is often easier to surprise a victim by using passive sensors because the victim will be unlikely to know he is being tracked.

A passive receiver can often measure angle better than can an active radar. Thus when radars are jammed, they can often be used to determine the direction of the target by simply disconnecting the transmitter and using the radar antenna and processor to determine the direction from which the jamming is coming.

Passive receivers can also detect targets at longer range than can active surveillance devices. The signals they detect have only to travel from the target emitter to the passive receiver, while the energy of an active system must travel from the radar to the target and then back to the radar receiver. Thus, in an active system, the distance over which the signal is attenuated, absorbed, reflected or diverged is twice that of a passive system. And under the inverse square law, if the distance is doubled, the power of the echo is reduce to a quarter of its original strength. This means that if the range to the target is doubled, the active radar's power or sensitivity must be increased by a factor of 16 since the radar signal is reduced to one-quarter strength on the outward trip to the target and to one-quarter of that on the return trip. However, a passive device need only have a factor of four increase in sensitivity to compensate for twice as much target distance or for a halving of the signal emitted by a target at any given distance.

The great disadvantage of passive receivers is that they normally rely on the enemy to work. If the enemy tries to minimize his signals or even to suppress them entirely, the passive receiver will find it difficult or impossible to operate. Of course, the enemy will regret not being able to use active radio, radar, infrared or visible light, so the passive receiver — if effectively linked to a useful weapon — will weaken enemy capability by reducing his free use of the electromagnetic spectrum.

Another disadvantage is that although passive devices have better angle resolution and greater detection range, they cannot easily measure the range to an emitter, because they cannot determine how long it took for the radiation to travel to the receiver.

But advanced passive sensors — such as the Infrared Search and Track System to be mounted on U.S. Navy F-14 fighters — can use computers to make rough estimates of range. Also, several passive receivers can triangulate the direction of received signals and so precisely locate the enemy transmitters, but only if the receivers are in constant contact with each other. However, if radio is used for such constant contact, the passive receivers are not really passive anymore!

Passive surveillance devices can monitor all regions of the spectrum. For example, radio receivers can detect signals in the radiowave region, infrared sensors can detect infrared energy and so on. But in general it becomes more difficult for passive sensors to detect signals as the frequency increases.

In the lower frequency radiowave region it is very easy to detect radiation because it propagates over the horizon. Even at the ultrahigh-frequency band, a passive receiver need only have a line of sight to the emitter. But at the extremely high frequency band where signals can be transmitted in narrow beams, a passive detector must be located between the emitter and the intended receiver. Passive radiowave detection is a major source of targeting information on the battlefield, as any imprudent soul who chooses to broadcast for too long without moving will discover.

Passive Radiofrequency Sensors

Modern weaponry emits vast quantities of signals. For example, armored vehicles will often transmit radio messages, while various electronic on-board devices leak radio-frequency signals from computerized navigation and fire-control systems, spark plugs and other sources.

Deliberately produced radio-frequency signals are relatively easy to detect, and correspondingly easy to suppress. Thus an aircraft can turn off its radars, navigation systems, radios, and identification systems if it wishes to minimize its radio-frequency signature. But accidental signals are much harder to suppress. Many modern aircraft use fly-by-wire control systems in which commands are transmitted from the pilot's joystick through computers and wires to electric motors at the flaps, elevators, ailerons and rudder. There is no particular reason why sensitive radio-frequency receivers could not detect these signals at a militarily useful range, although the inability to determine range would probably mean that the signals could only be used for warning of possible friendly or enemy aircraft.

Passive Infrared and Microwave Sensors

The major fact of life for radio-frequency passive sensors is that they are normally reliant on enemy cooperation. However, this limitation does not always apply to the shorter ranged, higher frequency microwave to infrared regions.

All objects release some amount of microwave and infrared radiation. The higher the temperature of an object, the greater the relative amount of higher frequency radiation that is emitted. Thus ice emits very little radiation but anyone can see the visible light radiation emitted by a red-hot piece of metal. This naturally emitted radiation is called blackbody radiation.

The easiest blackbody radiation to detect is infrared radiation; it can be detected by passive infrared or thermal viewers. The classic example is the clear infrared signal of an aircraft propelled by a very hot jet engine.

Importantly, blackbody radiation in the microwave bands can also be detected even when the target is at a very low temperature. Most military aircraft and vehicles emit 100,000 times less microwave radiation than infrared radiation, but "aircraft have been detected at a few kilometers against the background of a 'cold' sky and tanks at a few hundred meters against the much 'hotter' background of vegetation."[6]

The U.S. Department of Defense's *Critical Technologies Plan* reported that "microwave radiometry is emerging as an important sensor given its resolution and its range in poor weather," when compared to infrared. However, the DOD's research program in passive microwave sensors is at a very early stage. The DOD's goal in 1989 was to develop an antitank and antiship microwave sensor by the year 2000, according to the report.[7]

If appropriate battlefield technology is developed — and that is largely a matter of time and money — then these natural microwave signals could be detected by passive sensors, opening up many new target detection opportunities.

Already in wide use are many passive surveillance devices able to detect infrared radiation.

One basic infrared sensor is the human body, which can detect infrared radiation when it heats the skin. But a more useful infrared surveillance method is to actively illuminate targets or terrain with great amounts of infrared energy, so allowing even simple infrared receivers to detect targets by the reflected infrared energy —just as an eye would detect targets if the terrain were illuminated with a visible-light searchlight. For instance, infrared "searchlights" can be used to actively illuminate an area for the passive infrared cameras mounted on antitank weapons. This method was first used by German tanks in World War II against Soviet tanks, and has since been greatly improved. But the active infrared searchlight can be detected easily by enemy infrared sensors, and so destroyed.

This problem prompted the development of more modern passive infrared devices called thermal imagers or forward-looking infrared (FLIR) devices. These rely on the various levels of blackbody infrared energy to build up a TV-like picture of the scene. These more complex thermal viewers can allow users to detect cold targets against hot backgrounds or to track many targets hidden in trees or smoke.

In general, the hotter the target, the easier it is to detect. Thus the average jet engine stands out against the cold sky like a beacon in a dark night. But the relatively low temperature of cooler objects, such as human bodies, makes them more difficult to track, especially when they are hiding in rough terrain or among trees.

Thus, for ground troops, infrared is largely limited to short range tactical applications. In the air, the Soviets have led the way by mounting infrared sensors on MiG-29 and Sukhoi-27 fighter aircraft for passive infrared detection and tracking. At sea, infrared sensors are becoming more attractive as the danger posed by rocket-propelled, sea-skimming antiship missiles is realized.

VISIBLE WAVELENGTH ENERGY SENSORS

After infrared, the visible or light region is next on the electromagnetic spectrum. Energy in this region is exploited by the most important passive surveillance device on the battlefield, the human eye.

The eye allows soldiers to identify and destroy targets independently. It is the best short-ranged sensor in existence, able to detect small variations in tone or color and able to track targets despite a confusing background. Also, the eye relies on an indestructible source of light, the sun.

But sunlight is not available twenty-four hours a day. And unlike some other radiation, light — whatever its source — cannot penetrate terrain, water, mist, or smoke nor can it travel unaided over hills and around corners.

Various devices exist to overcome these natural and man-made limitations. Telescopes and binoculars extend the capability of the eye by enabling it to detect or identify smaller or more distant targets. The U.S. F-14 Tomcat fighter carries a powerful TV camera under its chin that can allow it to identify targets at up to 32 km (20 mi) range in daylight.

The eye can only be truly passive when the sun is above the horizon. When the sun goes down, alternative light sources such as search-lights, flares, and star shells are needed, so revealing in a most obvious fashion the presence of humans.

But modern technology offers an alternative. Soldiers can see clearly at night when they use telescope-like devices called image intensifiers. These magnify the brightness of what little light there is even during the darkest night. Image intensifiers can be small enough to fit on a rifle, and powerful enough to reveal human figures at several kilometers on an overcast night.

ULTRAVIOLET RADIATION

The ultraviolet region is not used very much in surveillance tasks. Although the level of emitted or reflected ultraviolet radiation is normally orders of magnitude lower than other signals, so too is the ultraviolet background. However, the relatively constant contrast between the target and background can permit passive ultraviolet devices to construct images even from the normally very low levels of ultraviolet energy available. Probably the most important of ultra-violet surveillance devices are the U.S. early warning satellites which watch for the fiery launching of nuclear-tipped missiles.

As a practical matter, the low level of ultraviolet energy emitted by low-temperature targets such as people and vehicles and high atmo-spheric absorption greatly reduce the usefulness of ultraviolet.

Humans have aggressively exploited the spectrum from extremely low radio frequencies to optical frequencies for surveillance. With current technology, the most important long range system is radar because radiowaves can travel immense distance and penetrate rain, clouds and the night.

However, like all active sensors, radar broadcasts its presence making it potentially vulnerable to enemy attack. Because of this shortcoming, military forces are making increasing use of shorter range passive sensors, especially for systems intended to guide weapons onto targets. These guidance sensors are the subject of the next chapter.

Notes

1. *International Defense Review*, December 1987, p. 1620.
2. A. L. Rodgers et al., *Surveillance and Target Acquisition Systems*, (Oxford: Brassey's, 1983). p. 152.
3. D. Curtis Schleher, *Introduction to Electronic Warfare*, (Norwood, Mass: Artech House, 1986), p. 288.
4. Rogers et al., *Surveillance*, p. 152.
5. *Defense News*, 16 March, 1990.
6. Rogers et al., *Surveillance*, p. 152.
7. U.S. Department of Defense, *Critical Technologies Plan*, (Washington, D.C.: Government Printing Office, March 1989), p. A-41 and p. A-44.

◆

Two

GUIDANCE SENSORS

The means of destruction are approaching perfection with frightful rapidity.

Antoine Henri de Jomini, *Précis de l'Art de Guerre, 1838*

Alongside communication and surveillance tasks, electromagnetic signals are also used to guide weapons to strike enemy soldiers, vehicles, and aircraft. Energy from extremely low to ultraviolet frequencies is used in various active and passive ways for such weapons guidance.

Unlike surveillance systems, guidance sensors are not able to detect targets at long range. But armed with information supplied by surveillance sensors, they are able to steer weapons to their targets.

Guidance sensors can also identify targets better than can surveillance systems. A surveillance radar may spot a mobile target thousands of miles distant, but without additional information it cannot tell whether the target is friendly or not. Reliable identification is especially important in the case of aircraft: is the target an incoming enemy aircraft intent on destruction or a friendly bomber returning to base? This identification problem has a major consequence: targets usually cannot be attacked with very long range sensors because only short range systems can identify them. But sooner or later, technologies will be invented to allow long-range target identification, allowing targets to be destroyed at heretofore unprecedented ranges.

As with surveillance systems, radar is the primary active guidance sensor. However, passive infrared systems are becoming increasingly important, especially because they have longer ranges and work much better at night than the oldest and most important sensor of all, the human eye.

GUIDANCE SENSORS

If targets are to be destroyed, then guidance sensors to carry the explosives to the target are vital. But guidance sensors — especially narrow-beam guidance radars — must often have target locations handed-off to them by active or passive surveillance sensors, most often radar.

Once precise target location information is provided to a guidance system, there are several ways for the system to ensure the target is hit.

The first way is by simple prediction, just as a hunter aims his gun at the spot where he predicts the duck will be by the time his shotgun pellets arrive. Thus automatic cannon firing simple explosive shells are aimed by tracking radars, whose computer analyses target speed and direction to determine where the aircraft will be by the time the shell reaches it. But unlike ducks, pilots like to shoot back and to maneuver — making the shooter's task much more difficult.

To overcome the problem of evasive maneuvering, radars and infrared sensors are often used to guide antiaircraft missiles until the moment of impact with the target. There are roughly three different types of guidance: command, semiactive, and active.

The simplest guidance system is the command guidance system, in which the target and missile positions are continuously tracked by eye or radar so the crew can order the missile to intercept the maneuvering target, much as a driver endeavors to collide with other vehicles during a demolition derby.

A somewhat better method is semiactive guidance, in which the missile homes in on radar signals reflected from the target. For example, the U.S. Navy's Aegis antiaircraft missile system uses a central large phased-array radar to detect and track targets, but also has four separate illumination radars that are used to paint the target so the missiles can keep heading towards the radar echoes until they hit the target.

However, semiactive missile guidance has disadvantages, the most obvious being that each target must be illuminated by a radar until final impact, which ties up a radar until target destruction. This problem is alleviated by modern technology; the Aegis illumination radars switch from target to target so that twelve missiles can be guided by four illumination radars. Another problem is that the missile launcher must keep its radar firmly illuminating the enemy, so placing sharp restrictions on its own movement.

A still better method is fully passive guidance, in which the missile contains all the computer power it needs to home in on energy emitted by the target. An example of this passive homing guidance technique is the continually upgraded AIM-9 Sidewinder heat-seeking antiaircraft missile, which has been responsible for 90 percent of the aircraft destroyed by Israeli, American, and British air forces since the Vietnam War.

Because the Sidewinder missile can track the heat emitted from a target by itself — out to a range of more than 32 kilometers (20 mi) in good conditions — it needs no additional instructions after being fired. Once the trigger is pulled, the pilot can forget about the missile and concentrate on the next problem.

Another form of guidance is active radar, in which autonomous missiles have an integral radar to track and guide them to a collision with it. There are many large, active homing antiship missiles, but only one homing antiaircraft missile — the U.S.'s Advanced Medium Range AntiAircraft Missile (AMRAAM) — and a few homing antitank missiles.

Like the heat-seeking Sidewinder missile, the main advantage of such active homing weapons is they require little or no communication with outside sensors, eliminating vulnerable communications links and freeing the missile shooter to escape or to attack again. Although these autonomous missiles are expensive, their likely effectiveness has prompted increasing efforts to develop them.

Given the variety of guidance systems, the particular sensor and guidance technique chosen for each weapon depends on what the weapon is supposed to accomplish.

Active Weapon Guidance

Radar is the only active guidance sensor capable of helping destroy targets at relatively long range. While the lower frequency A to F radar bands are used by surveillance radars, the guidance radars use the bands from G to M and beyond. Because the atmosphere absorbs so heavily signals at high frequencies, many radars use the I and J bands to guide antiaircraft missiles such as the Soviet SA-8 Gecko missile.

There are many varieties of radar-guided antiaircraft missiles, including the U.S. Patriot, the Soviet SA-10 Grumble, and the British Rapier. There are also many radar-guided antiship missiles, such as the Israeli Gabriel, the French Exocet, and the Chinese Silkworm. Nearly all radar-guided antiaircraft missiles use semiactive guidance, but the much larger antiship missiles carry their own active radar guidance system.

However, the most impressive radar-guided missile is the American Longbow radar and its improved Hellfire antitank missile planned for deployment in the mid-1990s. Carried on the AH-64 Apache armored attack helicopter, the Longbow radar operates at 95 GHz, where there are very few intercept devices to detect its very narrow beam. The radar operates at such a high frequency that it produces a TV-like image of its target that can be easily understood by a missile gunner. Moreover, once a target is found by the radar, the Hellfire missile can use a similar radar to guide itself to impact with an enemy tank or helicopter at ranges of at least 10 kilometers. The short range of such extremely high frequency radar signals does not pose a problem for the short ranges of antitank warfare, but would probably preclude their use for longer range antiaircraft and antiship weapons.

Despite the dominance of radar frequencies for long-range antiaircraft and antiship weapons, many other guidance systems use other frequency bands, such as the infrared band.

Infrared searchlights mounted on tanks — similar to visible search-lights — enjoyed a briefly important role in the 1950s and 1960s. But the growing availability of passive infrared sensors made the search-light obsolete. After all, no tank crew wanted to make a target of themselves by being the first to turn on their infrared searchlight.

The primary nonradar active sensor system is the laser, often used to semiactively guide weapons to impact. First used to guide laser-homing bombs onto North Vietnamese bridges, this semiactive guid-ance technique is also exploited in the American Copperhead artillery shell, designed to passively home onto light reflected from a target "painted" by a laser-equipped forward artillery observer. Although expensive, the Copperhead shell gives artillery guns unprecedented accuracy and gives the power to destroy targets with very few shots — but only if the soldier aiming the laser can avoid being killed while staying in communication with the artillery unit.

Active lasers are also widely used to improve the accuracy of gunfire by precisely measuring target range. Such rangefinders are widely used on tanks, antiaircraft guns and artillery fire-control vehicles. For instance, the AH-64 Apache helicopter uses a laser to measure range for its on-board 30 mm cannon, which significantly improves the chances of a quick kill.

Passive Guidance

Although active radar is the primary means of guiding weapons to their targets at long range, passive sensors are dominant at shorter ranges.

The simplest and the most important passive sensor is the human eye. Whether helped by artificial means or not, the eye is the only way of aiming a rifle or an antitank gun, redirecting artillery fire, or guiding a short-range antitank missile.

With the increasing danger of the battlefield and the rapid rate of improvements in guidance systems, more and more weapons are being guided by passive systems.

In the radiowave region, the most important passive guidance system is signal direction finding and location. By comparing the direction of arrival of a radar or radio signal, several dispersed radio stations can obtain an accurate location fix on a transmitter, although accuracy will be reduced at very long ranges. Each direction finding station can fairly easily fix the direction within two to three degrees, so a target 32 km (20 mi) away could be localized within an 0.8 km square area without too much difficulty.

Obviously, if the direction finding systems are in contact with artillery, missiles or aircraft, the survival of the enemy radar or radio is a matter of some doubt — unless it is so heavily protected that it cannot be damaged, or is moving so fast that weaponry cannot be delivered quickly enough.

But radio location is not as easy as it sounds. For instance, a ground-wave radio signal may propagate to the receiver by multiple paths, so arriving from several different angles. Another difficulty is caused by "ghosts" which appear when two or more receivers compare the direction-of-arrival angles of several emitters. When these factors are combined with the normal confusion of war, fearful crews, normal wartime communications problems, deceptive measures, and the unceasing movement of many emitters, one can understand that quick and accurate direction finding is not as easy as it sounds.

Passive location is especially important at sea because even one stray emission may betray the location of an entire battle fleet. If an enemy task force is located by the detection of an emission — be it accidental radio transmission, leaking signals from an electrical device or the serendipitous interception of communications — then numerous antiship missiles could be aimed at the particular piece of ocean occupied by the enemy. In this case, the missiles will guide themselves to final impact by using active radars or by homing onto radio or infrared emissions.

When there is no friendly artillery available to attack any radars or radios, often the best form of combined direction-finding and attack system is the increasingly deadly antiradiation missile.

The most common antiradiation missiles are air-launched missiles released to home on the signals emitted by antiaircraft radars. For such purposes, destruction of the enemy radar by the antiradar missile is not its primary goal; merely suppressing radars and intimidating the enemy radar operators from turning on their radar is enough to allow a bombing raid to slip through enemy defenses.

Modern antiradar missiles are becoming increasingly more complex and effective. Some are designed to fly faster so as to hit emitters before they can react, and some can stay aloft for hours to prevent an enemy from turning on his radars. Some missiles are designed to home onto a target even after the target stops emitting, while most missiles can home onto a radar by following accidental leakage of its signals.

The United States has at least four types of antiradar missiles in service, including the 1960s-era Shrike, the 1970s Standard, and the 1980s HARM and SideARM. All of these are rocket-powered air-launched missiles.

The new jet-powered Tacit Rainbow miniature aircraft is slated to enter service during the 1990s, if it overcomes technical and budgetary obstacles. In action, the Tacit Rainbow is intended to be launched either from the air or from the ground, and to loiter over a battlefield until it detects a radar that it can attack.

Many radar-guided missiles have backup antiradar capability. For example, if radar-guided antiship missiles are hit by enemy jamming, they can use their radar antennas as a radiation-homing guidance system, effectively turning the missiles into antiradar missiles.

Moreover, there are reports that the Soviet military has developed missiles that home onto aircraft-carried radars, thus greatly reducing the value of the U.S. armory of radar-equipped aircraft and radar-guided antiaircraft missiles. If the reports are true, the Soviets have succeeded where the U.S. failed with the Seekbat and Brazo antiradar missile programs in the 1970s.[1] However, next-generation U.S. antiaircraft missiles are expected to combine active radar homing as well as passive homing, making life just that much more difficult for enemy pilots.

The role of antiradar and antiradio missiles can only grow more important. According to one U.S. congressman, a joint report by the Central Intelligence Agency and the Pentagon's Defense Intelligence Agency paints a far grimmer picture of the Soviet military's antiradar missiles than previously acknowledged. Because the Soviets fielded a new anti-radiation missile every two years, the report "should be required reading" for proponents of fighter aircraft armed with radar-guided missiles, other radar systems such as the AWACS early-warning radar aircraft, "and all our other costly systems that have been rendered potentially obsolete by this family of relatively simple

Soviet missiles.... The only way that [the U.S. Navy's radar-equipped] CG-47 and DDG-51 destroyers can avoid being seriously damaged or sunk is to turn off the radar," according to congressman John. D. Dingell (D. Michigan).[2]

Although Dingell overstated the case — and underestimated the potential ability of radar-equipped forces to defeat radar-homing missiles — the effect of these missiles is to increase the advantage of an attacker by restricting use of the defender's radars. Also, the increased role of antiradar missiles increases the value of passive sensors, such as infrared detectors. Antiradar missiles will have an increasingly powerful effect in war, especially when used in combination with other friendly infrared, optical, and radar-guided weaponry.

Despite the growing importance of antiradar and antiradio missiles, it is unsurprising that the first passive guidance system outside the radiowave region exploited the highly-detectable infrared radiation emitted by the very hot exhausts of jet aircraft.

However, these early infrared detection systems could only home onto the very hot jet engines and were easily confused and so frequently tried to home in on the hottest object visible — the multimillion degree sun. However, electronic miniaturization has ensured more sensitive sensors, allowing modern missiles to ignore the sun and lock onto the thermal signals from an aircraft's fuselage.

The modern infrared-guided weapon is perhaps best personified by the fifteen pound shoulder-fired Stinger antiaircraft missile. Easy to carry and shoot, the Stinger was put to very effective use by the Afghan resistance against Soviet helicopters and aircraft. Not even the hot background of sun-baked mountains prevented the Stinger from destroying large numbers of Soviet aircraft and their crews. The quality of the Stinger's passive seeker was such that the Soviets could not field a technical defense, and they had to replace the helicopters with less useful artillery. This was to no avail, for the Soviet military was eventually driven out of Afghanistan.

The deadliness of infrared missiles is somewhat overshadowed by expensive radar-guided systems, but infrared missiles — especially the continually modernized AIM-9 Sidewinder and shoulder-launched Stinger — have been responsible for the vast majority of aircraft kills since the 1950s. However, it is well to remember that radar-guided weapons are frequently used to help their shorter range heat-seeking brothers by disorganizing enemy aircraft formations and forcing enemy pilots into positions where they are shot down by the infrared killers.

New types of advanced infrared sensors are being developed that will allow small missiles to home in on relatively cool targets. These new computer-controlled sensors are called infrared focal plane arrays and can stare constantly at their targets, greatly helping them to defeat countermeasures. When these new arrays are built into anti-aircraft missiles, it will be extremely difficult for pilots to dodge the bullet.

Long used against aircraft and ships, infrared sensors are now finding increasing use in ground warfare. American M1A1 tanks use a thermal viewer to find and destroy targets hidden in a dusty and smoky battlefield, day or night. Thermal viewers are now being placed on aircraft to track other aircraft, on ships to track incoming missiles, and on helicopters to help find and kill targets hidden by dark, trees or smoke. As the costs of infrared technology are reduced, more and more weapons will be equipped with infrared sensors to keep them fighting twenty four hours a day, under all weather conditions.

Despite the important role played by radars as well as passive radio-frequency and infrared homing weaponry, the human eye is clearly the primary battlefield sensor, and with improving technology, more and more devices are being used to multiply its power. Thus telescopes, binoculars, long range cameras, and image intensifiers are already widely deployed for all kinds of purposes, both as primary sensors and as backups to radar or infrared. Sometimes, these eye-enhancing devices will not be able to use the sun, so they must create their own light using searchlights or flares, which may give away their positions.

Naturally, visible light sensors can be relatively small, simple, and cheap, because the image is already at the right frequencies for eyes to see.

The relatively new technology of fiber-optic cable will further increase use of optical frequencies. Fiber-optic cable can carry pictures from a TV camera in a missile's nose back to the missile's operator sitting in a reasonably safe location. Simply by steering the missile to the target, as in a harmless video game, the operator can destroy targets at ranges of tens of kilometers. The U.S. Army tried to develop a very promising fiber-optic guided missile called FOG-M to attack helicopters and armored vehicles out to 30 km, but failed in late 1990 because of financial problems. However, German and French military scientists are cooperatively developing a missile called Polypheme, intended to be fired from a submerged submarine at its most dangerous hunter, the antisubmarine warfare aircraft.

Electromagnetic energy from the ultra-violet region is used to a limited extent by passive guidance sensors. Reportedly, advanced versions of the Stinger antiaircraft missile use ultraviolet as well as infrared radiation to track targets.

There will be greater future use for ultraviolet guided weapons if plans for space-based interceptors are converted into reality because the extremely hot rocket motors of long-range missiles emit a great deal of ultraviolet radiation — probably more than enough for a sharp contrast with the earth.

TARGET IDENTIFICATION

Unless a target can be correctly identified, there is every chance that friendly weapons will accidentally destroy friendly forces during battle. Even during peacetime errors occur; the Soviets shot down a Korean Boeing 747 passenger aircraft over Sakhalin in the dark of night partly because they failed to distinguish it from an electronic eavesdropping version of the Boeing 707 used by the U.S. Air Force.

In the heat and chaos of battle, such destructive accidents will be routine, especially given the limited time available for defeating enemy aircraft — as the tragic 1988 destruction of an IranAir airliner by the U.S.S. Vincennes during a skirmish with Iranian gunboats so graphically showed.

The core of the problem is that while modern weapons and sensors can detect and attack targets at great ranges, they cannot identify targets easily except at short ranges.

The lack of a reliable identification system will cause each side to destroy a significant number of friendly or neutral ships and aircraft, pass up opportunities to shoot at enemy targets, and generally constrict the use of long range weapons until targets approach close enough to be identified.

Thus Egyptian air defenses shot down roughly as many Egyptian as Israeli aircraft during the 1973 war, while the U.S. pilots only rarely used their long-range radar-guided Sparrow antiaircraft missile during the Vietnam War for fear of shooting down their own aircraft.

The lack of a front line for fast-moving helicopters, aircraft and ships means that no one can be sure whether the target is friendly or hostile. Moreover, the problem is worsened during limited war by the confusing presence of neutral ships and aircraft — such as the unfortunate IranAir jet shot down by the U.S.S. Vincennes in the Persian Gulf.

Clearly, the Kuwaiti conflict in the Persian Gulf in late 1990 strained identification systems even further, as both the Iraqis and allied forces possessed much similar equipment, including various types of Mirage fighters, Hawk antiaircraft missiles, as well as tanks supplied by the United Kingdom and Soviets. Worsening the situation further is the fact that most of the allied forces — including Syrian, Egyptian, Saudi, and NATO forces — had trained little together, and had no well-established means of communication or identification. However, the various NATO armies, including France, the United Kingdom, and the United States, had the benefit of much experience gained in prior military exercises.

Although there are no easy solutions, there are roughly five ways to tackle this persistent and serious problem.

The first technique is to muddle along by placing strict rules on who can shoot at what, and when. For example, during any war, U.S. Air Force aircraft would avoid U.S. missiles defenses by flying through a temporary no-fire corridor. Such corridors would be opened for the twenty to twenty-five minutes needed to get an air strike out and back.

Another solution is to equip aircraft and ships with Identification Friend or Foe or IFF systems. These radiodevices operate by automatically giving a correct response to an interrogation signal from another IFF device — electronically exchanging a password, so to speak. Thus an antiaircraft radar might send an interrogation signal to an incoming aircraft; if the correct response is given, then the aircraft is most likely friendly and the antiaircraft unit will not shoot.

But this technique is vulnerable to enemy mimicking of the identification signals — despite sophisticated encryption techniques — so allowing his aircraft to attack without being shot at. Secondly, the enemy may use the IFF emissions to track and attack the friendly aircraft — just as the Germans and the British did to each other's aircraft during World War II.

The most technologically ambitious identification technique is to try and keep track of all targets at all times and pass the information to all friendly forces that can use it. For example, modern computerized radars can track hundreds of aircraft from their take-off bases until they land, thus theoretically allowing easy identification of enemies and friends. Also, radar information could be combined with information from short range infrared sensors, long-range radio-interception stations, and other sensors. Aside from the very high cost, the main problem with this technique is that it needs a very complex communications system that could well be destroyed or disorganized during combat.

Another possible identification technique is to order weapon crews not to fire until they identify targets by sight, as U.S. pilots were forced to do during the Vietnam War. But eyesight is unreliable in the confusion of battle; more importantly, it is also very short ranged, so allowing enemy forces equipped with long range weapons to get the first deadly attack before friendly troops can reply.

A more sophisticated version of this technique is to design advanced sensors capable of identifying enemy targets at very long ranges. For example, the U.S. F-14 fighter carries a long-range telescope, allowing the pilot to identify aircraft at roughly twenty miles range — but only if the weather is clear. More advanced methods are under study, including the identification of electronic emissions, or the analysis of radar echoes to determine an aircraft's shape or the speed of its rotating engine blades. Although this method of identification is theoretically the most satisfactory, the long-range, all-weather technology does not yet exist, unless it has been kept well classified.

Because of the many problems with these various methods of identification, armies will rely on a combination of methods for the foreseeable future. As technology develops, armies will be able to extend their identification range, but it remains to be seen whether identification technology will catch up with detection and killing technology.

CONCLUSION

Technology continues to advance at a dizzying pace, allowing mankind to ruthlessly exploit the electromagnetic spectrum from extremely low frequencies to visible light.

Current trends in sensor technology include development of longer range and sharper-eyed sensors. But perhaps the greatest trend is the computerized integration and combination of several types of sensors in one weapon to allow them to compensate for each other's weaknesses. Thus modern antiship missiles carry active radar, passive infrared as well as antiradar guidance capabilities and can also receive guidance instructions from distant headquarters. This combination of sensors will make these missiles very difficult to defeat.

Such powerful technology can only have a powerful effect on tactics. Faced by waves of British bombers attacking German cities at night, the Luftwaffe adopted a new tactic that allowed ground controllers and radars to guide night fighters onto the tails of lumbering British bombers. Similarly, the British developed new antisubmarine tactics to exploit the ability of radio direction-finding systems to locate German U-boats for loitering antisubmarine aircraft.

But long-range sensors can have a much more powerful effect on war than just changing military tactics. Now, long-range sensors can change the nature of higher level military operations and theater strategy.

Changes in operational and theater warfare are caused by powerful communications systems able to exchange sensor information between far-flung combat units. For example, modern navies will try to disperse and hide themselves in the vast oceans until distant friendly radars and communications satellites tell them where they should shoot their massed antiship missiles to destroy an enemy fleet that the ships will never see.

In the next few years, we shall see great numbers of long- and short-range sensors being closely tied together by global communications networks, theoretically allowing top commanders to survey the world much as television viewers switch between channels.

The enormous impact of these communications networks and the problems they face is the subject of the next chapter.

Notes

1. Doug Richardson, *Techniques and Equipment of Electronic Warfare*, (London, Salamander Books, 1985), p. 126.
2. *Philadelphia Inquirer*, 7 December 1989, p. 32.

Three

———————————— ◆ ————————————

ELECTROMAGNETIC INTERFERENCE AND ELECTROMAGNETIC WEAPONS

Technology always delivers less, arrives later and costs more than forecast.

Col. Jonathan Alford[1]

Electromagnetic energy can be used to destroy or damage targets. The difference between a radio, a jammer, and an electromagnetic weapon is basically power. Turn up the power on a radio and you have a jammer. Turn up the power on a jammer, point it at an enemy, and you have a crude directed energy weapon.

The technical problems are many; but when adequate power is concentrated by some type of weapon, it can be converted into powerful bolts of electromagnetic energy that can jam signals, upset computers, frazzle sensitive electronics and even inflict physical damage.

As far as is known, there are basically two types of directed energy weapons in service or on the drawing board: laser and radio frequency weapons. These weapons will be directed against two types of targets — computerized electronics, and sensors, including the human eye.

Directed-energy weapons bridge the gap between the traditional "hard kill" inflicted by explosive weaponry and the "soft kill" caused by electronic jamming. Such weapons may eventually blur the technological differences between electronic warfare and explosive warfare.

LASERS

Laser Properties And Characteristics

Laser beams are beams of electromagnetic energy whose frequency is so pure that the peaks and troughs of the signals are precisely in step. This purity is what gives lasers so much power. A typical laser in a high-school physics lab produces only one-thousandth of a watt, but with a beam one millimeter in diameter, its intensity is comparable to sunlight.[2]

In practice, the frequency of the laser beam depends heavily on the way in which the energy is converted into the laser beam. The various types of lasers include solid state, gas dynamic, free electron, chemical and nuclear devices, each of which gives its name to its associated beams.

The method used to create the laser beam largely determines the frequency and wavelength, and some laser frequencies are more useful than others. For example, the beam from a laser using a mixture of hydrogen and fluoride gases suffers heavily from atmospheric absorption, while a mixture of deuterium and fluoride produces a laser beam that can travel long distances through the atmosphere.

There are some general problems that limit the effectiveness of all lasers, including removing excess heat, beam aiming, atmospheric absorption, and packing the power supply into a small enough package. But the main problem is simply getting sufficiently powerful pulses to hit enemy targets at long range. Because of these technical problems, the first laser weapons will be low power lasers used to blind enemy sensors at short ranges on the battlefield.

The most obvious target for the laser is the human eye, because the eye automatically focuses visible light into a narrow spot in the center of the eye. For example, the eye can focus lasers even as weak as one ten millionth of a watt — a tiny fraction of the energy put out by a 60 watt household lightbulb — into a beam powerful enough to damage the cornea, the central spot of the retina where sharp images are focussed.

However, soldiers are not defenseless against lasers; they can move, shoot back, attack, or wear protective visors, special anti-flashblindness goggles can darken in a few thousandths or millionths of a second; ordinary glass in spectacles absorbs strongly at ultraviolet wavelengths frequencies. But the only visors that can fully protect against all lasers at optical frequency are impossible to see through; handing out blindfolds on a battlefield will not increase battlefield effectiveness.

Most electronic sensors operating at the infrared, optical, or ultraviolet frequencies are tougher than the eye, and would be blinded or burned if hit by a laser beam of 100 watts for one-tenth of a second. Burning soft materials such as aircraft canopies requires 1,000 watts for a tenth of a second, while burning through metals requires from 10,000 to one million watts every tenth of a second. Clearly, eyes are the most vulnerable target — and are the first victims of laser weapons.[3]

For example, a tank's laser range finder similar to that on the American M-1 Abrams tank can burn eyes out to a range of 500 meters, or 2.4 kilometers if the victim is using binoculars.[4]

Burning through metal requires even more energy; about one thousand times the power required to damage a sensor.

The Impact On The Battlefield

Battlefield laser weapons will have a powerful impact in combat when they are introduced alongside conventional weapons such as artillery, tanks, and infantry.

Crude laser weapons — actually lasers used for rangefinding and to designate targets for laser-guided weapons — have already been used to blind enemy soldiers in combat. Nearly every army in the world already has crude laser weapons because most modern tanks are equipped with laser rangefinders that will blind soldiers unfortunate enough to be hit deliberately or accidentally by the beam.

These lasers have already caused casualties; Chinese soldiers were reportedly blinded during Sino-Vietnamese clashes in the late 1970s[5] and Afghan guerrillas frequently reported they had been hit by lasers mounted on Soviet vehicles.

But real, if very basic, laser weapons are already in service; during the Vietnam war, the U.S. reportedly used a laser to flashblind North Vietnamese antiaircraft gunners; and in September 1987 and late 1989, the eyes of two U.S. aircrew were injured when hit by a laser from a Soviet Navy ship.[6] Also, after press reports in early 1990 broke a veil of secrecy, the British Navy admitted to the world's first publicly acknowledged laser weapon — small and simple low-power lasers on board many of its destroyers, intended to dazzle incoming bomber pilots at a range of 2.4 km (1.5 mi). Some subsequent reports said the British lasers had been used to dazzle Argentinean bomber pilots during the 1982 Falklands war.[7]

These are but straws in the wind, largely inconsequential by themselves, but strong indications of what is coming. The future was made clear by Denis Kloske, Defense Department deputy undersecretary of defense research and engineering, who testified to a congressional committee that "blinding on a tactical basis is something everybody has to deal with in the 1990s."[8]

Despite the current lack of publicly deployed laser weapons, the danger of laser beams is sufficiently great for the U.S Army to warn its troops moving to Saudi Arabia in September 1990 that "with the increased use of laser equipment, eye casualties will increase....issue the laser protective goggles to the fighting and observing troops...emphasize the reporting of confirmed and/or suspected enemy laser use."[9]

It will be a very long time before laser weapons replace machine guns, artillery, and missiles in the armies of even the most technologically advanced countries. But it will not take more than ten years before the difficult technical problems are overcome and the military's use of lasers expand beyond rangefinding and target designation to attacking sensors and destroying relatively vulnerable targets such as attack helicopters.

The first such expanded uses of laser weapons will be as adjuncts to traditional weapons. For example, the rangefinding lasers used in antiaircraft weapons will become more powerful in the hope of occasionally blinding or dazzling a pilot, possibly causing him to crash.

And the first targets of lasers will be sensors such as those mounted in television-guided missiles, but especially the most important sensors of all, human eyes. According to the former head of the Defense Intelligence Agency, "Use of low-energy lasers in combat, even though their power outputs are not very high, would result in a significant amount of jamming and sensor blinding."[10] Thus at a cost of over $2 billion, the Army has issued laser protective visors to soldiers, tanks crews and helicopter pilots. And in late 1988, the U.S. Air Force ordered a supply of special visors to protect pilots from some lasers while ensuring clear vision. The manufacturer was reported to have said, "Work is continuing on newer technology in anticipation of greater protection needs from next generation lasers."[11]

The fear of laser blinding — whether from powerful laser-rangefinders or from crude anti-eye weapons — will surely further restrict the ardor of combat troops, and would force increased emphasis on indirect-fire weapons such as artillery as soldiers spread out over more territory to hide from the new weapons. Although bad weather and smoky conditions can severely restrict their battlefield uses, lasers would give soldiers more reasons to be less adventurous and would prompt commanders to rely more on attacking the enemy with long-range artillery fire. Of course, friendly laser weapons would restrict the operations of enemy laser weapons, for surely the crews of laser weapons would have the same fears and the same reluctance to expose their eyes to the battlefield as all other soldiers.

Once lasers are deployed, new methods of defeating them will be developed. For example, tank crews could use television cameras to detect targets, artillery barrages could lay new types of smokescreens impenetrable by lasers and infantry could use antilaser goggles specially matched to filter out enemy laser weapons.

It is very unlikely that lasers will be used to attack anything except sensors and eyes for many years yet. For the immediate future, directly destroying hard targets simply requires too much power for any laser weapon to be kept mobile or survivable. But high-power lasers could find prominent uses as immobile antisatellite and strategic defense weapons. However, technological trends argue strongly that at some point in the distant future, armies will field very powerful laser weapons capable of smashing enemy armored vehicles to pieces.

Widespread use of lasers will eventually sweep unprotected infantry, sensors, and vehicles from the high-technology battlefield. They will have to be replaced by heavily protected soldiers and complex weaponry utilizing laser-resistant television cameras as sensors.

U.S. And Soviet Laser Programs

Both the Soviet Union and the United States have laser development programs. Obviously, much more is known about U.S. programs than about Soviet programs, most news of which is released through the Pentagon.

In the West, research into the tactical uses of lasers has received little funding because much attention has been given to exotic high-power laser weapons for strategic defenses. The main reason for this emphasis on long-term high power systems is the formation in 1983 of the Strategic Defense Initiative Organization (SDIO).

When it was established, SDIO absorbed several ongoing laser research programs, only to later cut their funding to concentrate on nearer-term kinetic energy weapons. SDIO has concentrated on a megawatt power hydrogen–fluoride chemical laser and a radio-frequency free-electron laser intended for a strategic defense mission.

But throughout the 1980s the Soviets appear to have taken a different path: "the Soviets are using their technological capability to move toward rapid deployment of low-power laser weapons" for tactical use, according to a 1988 Pentagon report.[12] Soviet weapon designers have always stressed early fielding of weapons, with gradual upgrades once they are in service. However, the economic and political collapse of the Soviet Union will probably severely retard Soviet progress in this field.

High Power Lasers

Most of the U.S. laser effort has gone into the SDIO's program to develop high-power lasers to shoot down enemy satellites and nuclear warheads.

The primary chemical laser program is the 2 million watt Alpha laser. Powered by the burning of hydrogen and fluoride, the laser is slated to be launched into space in the late 1990s as the Zenith Star experiment. Because the satellite is 24 meters (80 feet) long and some 45,000 kg (50 tons), it will be launched in two pieces on two rockets and will have to be joined together in space.[13] The SDIO is also sponsoring the upgrade of the Navy's 2.2 million watt mid-infrared chemical laser. The purpose of the upgrade is to test it against a space satellite about 240 km (150 mi) up.

But despite budget cuts that significantly scale back the power output, the SDIO's free electron laser promises to be the most powerful Western laser when built at White Sands Missile Range, New Mexico, by the mid-1990s. Although the laser's power and frequency range are classified, the Pentagon has said it uses magnetic fields to convert the speed of high-velocity electrons into electromagnetic energy, which then greatly amplifies the laser light from an auxillary laser.

However, a desire for quick results from other programs and cutbacks in funding for the SDIO program is delaying development of these powerful directed energy weapons. But this delay, whether wise or not, does not greatly affect the long-term potential of these weapons.

While the U.S. is emphasizing careful research, it seems the Soviet military hopes to soon field some powerful laser systems, including several possible antisatellite lasers.

According to the DOD, "the Soviets have built high-energy laser devices to the 10-megawatt level and generally place more emphasis on weapons applications of lasers than does the West." However, the Soviets have not done as well in chemical lasers as the West, according to Pentagon documents.[14] The Soviets have long used lasers for satellite tracking from sites in Estonia, in the northwest USSR, and from Georgia in the southwest.

The chief of the U.S. Space Command, General John Piotrowski, told reporters that existing Soviet ground-based lasers could knock out spy satellites up to an altitude of 560 km (350 mi), where nearly all surveillance and spy satellites are based. The General also said the Soviet lasers could damage those at 1,200 km (745 mi), adding that satellites at thirty times that altitude could suffer from "in-band" damage, presumably by visible light or infrared lasers attacking optical or infrared sensors.[15] One report written by an Air Force captain in the hawkish Defense Intelligence Agency, claimed the Soviets are also developing an airborne laser that could be used in a space attack role.[16]

There is open photographic evidence which shows that the Soviets are building a laser facility at a mountaintop site called Nurek, 50 km (31 mi) southwest of Dushanbe in the southernmost portion of the USSR. The high altitude of the summit ensures less absorption by the atmosphere and the southern location of the facility gives a better view of space satellites parked over the equator. These factors indicate it is intended to be used to track and probably attack satellites in geosynchronous and low earth orbit. According to the *Chicago Tribune*, the CIA is unsure of the facility's purpose, but the Defense Intelligence Agency is leaning toward viewing it as a weapon center.[17] The official DoD view is that the Nurek site "may in fact be used to generate high-energy laser beams for antisatellite missions."[18] It remains to be seen whether this Soviet laser program will survive the political turmoil in the USSR.

Tactical Laser Programs

Both the USSR and the U.S. are also developing tactical laser weapons; obviously, less is known about Soviet developments than about U.S. developments.

As far as available information indicates, the Army has the clear lead in tactical laser research, possibly because the low power requirements for short-range battlefield lasers are less than for Navy or Air Force weapons. Army power requirements are lower because of the relatively short battlefield range to the most important target — the human eye. This leaves the Army as the pioneer of directed energy weapons in the U.S. Department of Defense.

The most important of the several current Army laser programs is the Stingray system, intended to find and wreck enemy vehicle sensors. Operationally tested in 1990 on a Bradley armored fighting vehicle, Stingray combines surveillance, targeting, and destruction roles in one weapon; it uses a wide-angle laser beam to broadcast low-power laser light which is reflected back to the Stingray by enemy optical systems. These reflections tell the Stingray crew where the enemy optics are, allowing it to fire a high-power laser shot in the enemy's direction, with the intent of blinding sensors and any crew looking through periscopes.

"You would put something like this on a tank and you would have the capability to scan about 45 degrees. You could do that at the same time that the tank main gun would be firing at another tank," said Lt. Gen. James Merryman, Deputy Chief of Staff for Research, Development and Acquisition, told Congress.[19] According to another senior Army official, the Stingray would have a very valuable reconnaissance role because it could reliably detect enemy vehicles by reflection from their optics.

But at a price of about $300,000 to $500,000 each, the Stingray lasers would only be issued to a small proportion of the Bradleys, most probably to reconnaissance troops. Also, users would have to be careful to prevent the Stingray from attacking friendly as well as enemy optics.[20] In September 1990, the program office declared it would award a contract that would lead to the procurement of forty-eight weapons in the mid-1990s.

A poor cousin of this system may be deployed much earlier. Developed by the Loral Corp., the Hardhat system is simply a powerful infrared lamp mounted on a tank, and intended to jam infrared signals transmitted from Soviet antitank missile launchers to their missiles while in flight. When tested in September 1990, Hardhat's bright light captured the attention of the guidance system inside the antitank launchers, causing the missiles to crash into the ground before they could hit the tank. Other Army programs include special ammunition for the infantry's 40mm grenade launchers; when fired, the ammunition creates a short but powerful laser beam intended to dazzle and blind enemy tank crews. Also, the Army has tested two handheld laser weapons called Dazer and Cobra, intended to flashblind troops and armored vehicles.[21] The Army also began development of tank- and helicopter-mounted laser systems but canceled them in the late 1980s because of technical and cost obstacles.

The Air Force has put less effort into the development of tactical laser weapons, as far as is publicly known. However, the Air Force reportedly fielded a classified flashblinding laser during the Vietnam War in limited numbers with publicly unknown success. Reportedly, the most advanced laser weapon now under development by the U.S. Air Force is an upgraded version of the Vietnam War weapon used to flashblind antiaircraft gun crews. Presumably, it will flashblind gunners and jam television sensors. If not canceled during budget cuts, it is scheduled to be ready for production in the early 1990s. Another reported Air Force laser weapon is called Have Glance; tests of its ability to burn out the heat-seeking sensors of incoming infrared guided missiles are reportedly scheduled for 1992.[22]

Both these programs are classified, so their progress is uncertain. But the 1991 Senate Defense Appropriations Act cancelled Air Force laser-blinding programs, as well as similar airborne laser programs under development by the Army and Navy.

The U.S. Navy seems to have lagged behind the other services in laser weapons. In the early 1970s the U.S. Navy tested a laser designed to shoot down incoming antiship missiles. It was abandoned in 1973 for lack of money and probably for lack of success because destruction of a missile requires a very powerful laser. The Navy's only known laser is the 2.2 megawatt deuterium-fluoride mid-infrared chemical laser which was quickly taken over by the SDIO as a potential strategic defense and antisatellite weapon.

The latest effort was in the 1989 budget request when the Navy asked for $90 million to begin development of a ship-based antisatellite laser. However, control of the program and the funding for it was quickly handed over to the Army, which instead decided that the urgent need to destroy Soviet radar and observation satellites required an accelerated schedule, in turn requiring use of well-understood missiles to destroy the satellites.

Other Western countries are also working on laser weapons. A German and a French company are jointly developing a 1 million watt laser to be mounted on a armored vehicle to shoot down helicopters at five km range, and to damage optics and aircraft canopies at 20 km (12.5 mi).[23] The French are also planning to test in 1991 a 40 megawatt laser intended for use against aircraft and helicopters. Although the British Navy has deployed a low-power weapon on some warships, nothing is known of any British research.

Meanwhile, the Soviets have pushed forward with development of tactical lasers. A Pentagon study of critical technologies for future wars said the Soviets "have made significant progress in the development of novel pumping methods for 10-micron lasers, and are quite advanced in this area relative to the U.S....Their use of medium-power laser rangefinders in tactical applications is well documented, as is their development of short-wavelength transmitters for anti-sensor applications."[24]

The DoD has declined to elaborate on the power output or purposes of these Soviet "short-wavelength transmitters." The DoD typically limits what it says to protect its sources of information; thus unofficial leaks can be more informative, if less reliable. An unidentified intelligence source cited by the respected *Armed Forces Journal International* said the Soviets have several types of potential laser weapons already deployed with codenames assigned by NATO. These apparently include a ground-based laser designator incorporating millimeter-wave radar technology which caused one expert to ask "what's to keep the Soviets from simply turning up the power on such a device and using it as a weapon?"[25]

A good candidate for the first Soviet laser weapon is the curious turret on *Sovremenny* class destroyers. Mounted where main gun turrets were placed on previous generations of destroyers, the purpose of this likely laser weapon is unclear, but it is possibly intended to flashblind pilots and perhaps damage aircraft. It could probably blind infrared or television sensors on incoming antiship missiles. However, a very high power output would be required to shoot down antiship missiles.

Another laser system was reportedly seen on a Soviet next generation tanks. This Stingray-style weapon was reportedly intended to detect and blind enemy armored vehicles, including tanks. Armor expert Phillip Karber, vice president of BDM Corp., in McLean, Virginia, said these "counteroptic" lasers could severely reduce Western advantage in tank-mounted sensors and are "sure to change dramatically the designs and tactics for the current generation of U.S. and Western tanks."[26]

RADIO-FREQUENCY WEAPONS

Laser weapons are not the only directed energy weapons working their way onto the battlefield. Research in the U.S. and the Soviet Union is creating tactical, conventionally-powered radio-frequency (RF) and high-power microwave (HPM) weapons that use electromagnetic pulses to upset, jam, and even destroy enemy electronics.

While radio frequency weapons would use a broad range of radio frequencies to attack targets over a wide area, high power microwave weapons would use a concentrated beam of microwave signals to attack targets. Both types of weapon can be powered by stored electricity or by a conventional explosion — which also destroys the weapon as it blasts its targets.

According to John A. Rosado, a radio-frequency weapons expert who led the research effort at the Army's Harry Diamond Laboratories in Adelphi, Maryland, these weapons could first be used for jamming and fooling enemy electronic systems. With the addition of higher power emitters, they could burn out electronic components, integrated circuits, electronic amplifiers, electro-optical sensors, radars, electronic fuses, and command and control systems as well as computer-controlled "smart" munitions.[27] According to testimony by the head of the U.S Defense Advanced Research Projects Agency, electronic systems have already been destroyed in laboratory tests by crude radio-frequency weapons.

Rosado suggested that radio-frequency weapons could be carried on aircraft, missiles, satellites, tracked vehicles or ships to destroy incoming missiles, enemy radars, helicopters, fighter aircraft, radios, and command centers.

Given the demonstrated critical vulnerabilities of computerized weapon systems to self-inflicted interference and even low-power peacetime emitters, and the potentially revolutionary impact of these electronics-destroying weapons, there is clearly a great incentive to examine the technology to see if it can be militarily effective.

The Value Of Radio-Frequency and HPM Weapons

Radio-frequency weapons could cause a military revolution by sharply limiting battlefield use of advanced electronics. If defensive techniques do not keep pace, they would quickly destroy computer-controlled smart missiles, advanced radars, infrared sensors, aircraft, as well as sophisticated fighter-bombers — and anything else electronic in line of sight to the microwave weapons.

According to a DoD report, "because of the growing weapons systems reliance on microelectronics and electrical subsystems technology by U.S. adversaries, the high-power microwave weapon offers a revolutionary means of defeating enemy weapons in mass. It may also provide means of severely interrupting enemy communications ... without resorting to the nuclear arsenal. Protection against such weapons in the Soviet inventory, especially laser blinding or dazzle weapons, can have an equally profound impact for U.S. weapons platforms and sensors."[28]

Of course, no military revolution is instant, complete or permanent. While high-power microwave weapons might greatly reduce the role of computerized technology, the battle would still have to be won by rugged tanks and brave infantry.

Moreover, many computerized systems could be effectively used on the battlefield even if vulnerable to such weapons. For example, if a bomber has partially effective antiradio-frequency defenses, the range and destructiveness of enemy radio-frequency weapons will be reduced. Thus the bomber will be able to get closer to the radio-frequency weapons, so increasing its chances of destroying its target. And if the aircraft is hit by a radio-frequency weapon, its defenses will improve its chances of getting back to base.

Even partially effective defenses will push the radio-frequency weapon designer to build a more powerful weapon which will be less mobile, more visible and more vulnerable to enemy attacks.

But even if inexpensive and absolutely perfect defenses are developed to foil radio-frequency weapons, the weapons will still be extremely useful. Despite the uselessness of machine guns against tanks, they are still extremely valuable weapons because no army wants to immobilize their infantry with enough heavy armor plate to stop a bullet. Thus the procurement of even a few radio-frequency weapons could force the enemy to spend much more money incorporating expensive antiradio-frequency defenses into most weapons or to adopt defensive tactics that reduce overall effectiveness.

This logic applies even if the radio-frequency weapons cost much more than the cost of hardening targets, because the defender has many more targets to defend than the attacker has radio-frequency weapons.

Also, not all countries will have the advanced technology to defeat radio-frequency weapons, ensuring a massive slaughter by the technologically richer army of the enemy's poorly protected computerized electronics. This will give the most technically advanced countries that deploy these weapons a massive advantage over those countries that did not spend the money to protect their electronics.

And even when it cannot kill targets, radio-frequency technology will create very high-power jammers, radars and radios, all of which would be very valuable to modern armies.

When combined with conventional weaponry, these radio-frequency and high-power microwave weapons could have a powerful impact on the battlefield, weapons expert Rosado said. "Radio frequency weapons should not be thought of as a stand-alone weapon but rather as part of a layered defense,"[29] with conventional missiles and armored vehicles.

Research

Both the U.S. and the USSR are hard at work developing radio-frequency and high-power microwave weapons. Although by no means an unbiased source, the U.S. Defense Department has the best intelligence gathering systems. According to the 1988 edition of the annual *Soviet Military Power*. "Recent Soviet developments in the generation of radio-frequency energy could lead to fundamentally new types of weapons systems that could jam or destroy electronics equipment or be used in antipersonnel roles. The strong Soviet technology base in electromagnetic sources makes Soviet prototype short-range radio-frequency weapons highly feasible."[30]

The previous year's edition of the report said that "the USSR has conducted research in the use of strong radio-frequency (high-power microwave) signals that have the potential to interfere with or destroy critical electronic components of ballistic missile warheads or satellites. The Soviets could test a ground-based radio-frequency weapon capable of damaging satellites in the 1990s."[31]

The Soviets are world leaders in some of the basic technology involved in high-power microwave and radio-frequency weapons. According to an expert on Soviet technology, "High-power relativistic microwave electronics is one of the most successful areas of Soviet R&D,"[32] because it has a very high priority in the Soviet Union. "A typical Soviet research program is confined to a single institute, while most of the time only programs of major national importance are supported by a coordinated effort involving several research organizations. This is clearly the case with the high power microwave program where the tie between the Institute of Applied Physics in Gor'kiy and the Lebedev Physics Institute in Moscow proved to be especially fruitful."[33]

Not much more information is available on U.S. research into radio-frequency and high-power microwave weapons. Dr. Robert C. Duncan, assistant secretary of defense for research and development, told Congress in 1988 that U.S. research in high-power microwave weapons is "intended to develop a comprehensive understanding of the effects of [high-power microwave weapons] on tactical weapons systems to help assure the survivability of U.S. and Allied assets and to place vulnerable enemy systems at risk."[34] According to a DoD report, total unclassified DoD funding for research into these weapons in 1990 is about $50 million.[35]

The DoD's stated goal is to achieve a power output of 100 joules per pulse by 1990, 1,000 joules per pulse five years later, and 10,000 joules per pulse by the year 2000.[36]

However, 1989 budget cuts ended Pentagon plans to test a high-power microwave emitter against targets in 1992, possibly leading to the start of an effort to build a weapon.[37] Also, Army research chief Brigadier General Malcolm O'Neill said in late 1989 that the technology was not mature enough to justify commitment of research dollars to a weapon development program.[38]

But the Pentagon's multi-billion "black" budget hides many progams, including some radio-frequency and high power microwave development efforts, according to DoD officials. Information about these secret weapon systems will gradually leak out after their use in action, or after they are replaced by more advanced technology.

What Does an HPM/RF Weapon Look Like?

No one has determined what a battle-ready microwave weapon will look like. However, there are several candidates vying to be the primary high-power microwave generator needed by any weapon.

One of these possible generators is the free electron laser, in which electrons are passed through a chamber called a "wiggler" where their kinetic energy is converted into an electromagnetic beam by the twisting force of strong magnets.[39]

Another possible beam generator is the gyrotron, which produces energy in a similar way to the free electron laser. Other generators that might graduate into weapons include vircators, klystrons, magnetrons and beam-plasma devices, as well as "backward-wave oscillators."

Another promising type of generator is the explosive generator, in which explosive energy from a high-explosive charge is used to create a short pulse of radio-frequency energy. These one-shot weapons would be used in aircraft bombs and the tips of missiles or artillery shells to attack targets hidden behind hills or at very long range from friendly lines. Indeed, the U.S. tested radio-frequency artillery shells in the mid-1980s. Although the shells could produce adequate amounts of energy, they could not squeeze the energy into a short enough pulse to cause any damage.

However, the technology is at too early a stage to know the type of generator any weapon would use.

Problems

These electromagnetic weapons are by no means wonder weapons. They suffer from enough problems to prevent the military from easily converting laboratory models into workable weapons. Some DoD officials believe these problems can be solved by the mid-1990s.

The greatest problem is getting adequate power into a small enough package to be carried around on the battlefield, according to DoD and industry officials. The required power depends greatly on the target. For example, radio-frequency weapons in a strategic defense system would need vastly greater power to smash hardened warheads hurtling through the atmosphere than would short range tactical weapons intended to jam enemy sensors. Yet the short-ranged tactical weapons must be small enough to fit into a vehicle while the strategic defense systems can be hooked up to a nearby nuclear power station.

Brute power is not the only solution; the head of the Defense Advanced Research Projects Agency, Dr. Craig Fields, told the U.S. Congress in March 1990 that careful design of the microwave signal allowed testers to destroy radar receivers with "orders of magnitude less power" than before. "The consequences will be dramatically smaller microwave sources for tactical use," he said.[40]

Another problem is that the air will break down at higher powers than 1 million volts per square centimeter, resulting in a gigantic spark at the transmitter. But research suggests that this barrier can be broken by transmitting the pulse so quickly that the air molecules have no time to react.

Another obstacle facing radio-frequency weapons is the poorly understood vulnerability of targets.[41] Tests show that extremely high power pulses can cause physical damage to targets, while even very low power pulses can cause major disruptions to computerized electronics which are at the heart of smart weapons, radars, sensors and aircraft. But determining what frequencies at what powers do the most damage to which targets is a complex and expensive research problem. And until a weapon can be trusted to reliably damage or destroy a target under normal conditions, no army will rush to buy one.

With modern computers as a target, even quite low power pulses can cause great upset; software errors in unshielded computers leading to glitches and freeze-ups can be inflicted at 0.00001 to 0.0001 joule per square centimeter at a frequency of 1 GHz.[42] Low power pulses can destroy or damage computer chips, diodes in radars and radios, even semiconductors in electronic ignition systems and "very high fluence [power] levels might even detonate missile warheads, bombs, or artillery shells," said one expert. Only .000001 to .01 joules of radio wave frequencies per square centimeter can cause ignition of detonators, current overloads and spurious signals in electrical circuits.[43]

Even if a target cannot be destroyed, it might still be jammed. When used on targets outside lethal range, radio-frequency weapons could act as effective jammers by drowning out the target's signal. And if the radio-frequency pulse is powerful enough to induce electrical noise into the target's computer systems, then the target will be unable to hear any signals.

However, even with good understanding of vulnerabilities, "it will still be impossible to guarantee any system's immunity to high-power microwave attack. It would cost far too much to test a single system against more than a sample of all the possible combinations of microwave frequency, bandwidth, pulse width, peak power, beam direction and beam polarization," according to H. Keith Florig, a civilian expert on microwave systems at Carnegie Mellon University in Pittsburgh.[44]

The U.S. Defense Department is only slowly realizing the vulnerability of modern computerized systems to even commonplace peacetime electromagnetic transmitters. For example, the U.S. Army has lost 22 soldiers and five of its modern UH-60 Blackhawk transport helicopters when computerized flight controls were temporarily disrupted by low-power peacetime microwaves emitted by ordinary civilian microwave towers. According to Jerry McVey, a former Army major who investigated one of the UH-60 crashes, "We've got a very sophisticated electronic aircraft, and if the radiation we're putting up in peacetime — microwaves, antennas, TVs — is causing the aircraft to flutter and wobble, then — and I don't like to talk about this because of it is kind of a breach of security — we're going to have problems in wartime." McVey's accident report concluded: "The Army's required specifications for the protection from electromagnetic interference forces are much too low for the high-tech systems that are now coming into the inventory.... A large gap exists in the Army when it comes to electromagnetic interference studies and tests to prevent system degradation from electromagnetic interference."[45] Since the report, the Army has strengthened the protection on newly built helicopters to help avert similar accidents.

Another critical problem facing radio-frequency weapons is the efficiency of defenses against them.

Potential defenses include several techniques, such as wide-band limiters, which allow only a relatively narrow set of frequencies to pass through a circuit; extensive radio-frequency gasketing, which prevents pulses sneaking through plugs, sockets or other backdoor entrances; complete "Faraday cage shielding," which effectively places a metal shroud around the target to prevent any radiation reaching sensitive components; and wire screen shielding, which protects components from a chosen set of frequencies.

One possible new defense technology is microvalve technology, which aims to shrink the electrical valves (glass vacuum tubes seen inside old television or radio sets) until thousands can be packed onto a small computer chip. Because these valves are much more resistant to microwave pulses than are the semiconductors now used in all computer chips, they hold out the possibility of defeating microwave weapons.

CONCLUSION

Most of the technical developments described in this chapter do not presently exist in finished form, but lie in the future.

However, the directed energy weapon technologies beginning to emerge from the laboratories will have a revolutionary impact.

These technologies will take many years to mature, even in this rapidly advancing age. Yet the problems are not so much technical as bureaucratic. If it wished, the Pentagon could find the money to accelerate development of these directed energy technologies. But there is no doubt that these weapons will find a place in the inventories of the technologically advanced armies, long before any army will choose to publicize possession of them.

Notes

1. Quoted in Timothy Garden, *The Technology Trap* (London: Brassey's, 1989).
2. Jeff Hecht, *Beam Weapons: The Next Arms Race* (New York: Plenum, 1984), p. 62.
3. Freidrich Lindner, "Laser Weapons For Tactical Operations," *Military Technology*, 1987, 5, p. 125.
4. Maj. Charles Kinney, "Directed Beam Weapons Open 21st Century Warfare," *Military Electronics/Countermeasures*, February 1983, p. 26. Kinney cited figures prepared by the U.S. Army's Ocular Hazards Division of the U.S. Army's Letterman Institute of Research in San Francisco, California.
5. *Pacific Defense Reporter*, August 1985, p. 35.
6. *Navy Times*, 19 October, 1987. p. 37, *Washington Post*, 10 November 1989, p. 3.
7. *Jane's Defense Weekly*, 13 January. 1990, p. 48.
8. U.S. Senate, Committee on Armed Services, 11 April, 1988, p. 847.
9. U.S. Department of Defense, *Winning in the Desert: Tactics, Techniques and Procedures for Maneuver Commanders*, (Fort Leavenworth: Center for Army Lessons Learned, September 1990) p. 1.
10. *Signal*, December 1990, p. 37.
11. *Signal*, December 1988, p. 102.
12. U.S. Department of Defense, *Soviet Military Power*, [1988] (Washington, DC: Government Printing Office, 1988), p. 146.
13. *New York Times*, 3 January, 1988, p. 1.
14. U.S. Department of Defense, *Soviet Military Power, [1987]* (Washington DC: Government Printing Office, 1987), p. 112.
15. New York Times, 26 October, 1987.
16. Capt. Gregory Radabaugh. "Soviet Antisatellite Capabilities," *Signal*, December 1988.
17. *Chicago Tribune*, 22 June 1987, p. 1.
18. Department of Defense, *Soviet Military Power* [1988], p. 56.
19. *Pacific Defense Reporter*, August 1985, p. 34.
20. *Defense News*, 14 August 1989, p. 11.
21. *Defense News*, 5 March, 1990.
22. *Defense News*, 11 December 1989.
23. *Signal*, March 1990, p. 12.

24. U.S. Department of Defense, *Critical Technologies Plan* (Washington DC: Government Printing Office, March 1989). p. A40.
25. *Armed Forces Journal International*, June 1987, p. 26.
26. *Defense News*, 17 October, 1988.
27. Paper prepared by John Rosado in 1989.
28. Dept. of Defense, *Critical Technologies Plan*, March 1989. p. A-71.
29. *Defense News*, 24 August 1987, p. 1.
30. Dept. of Defense, *Soviet Military Power*, 1988. p. 146.
31. Dept. of Defense, *Soviet Military Power*, 1987. p. 51.
32. Simon Kassel, *Soviet Development of Gyrotrons*, Pub. No. RAND/R-3377-ARPA, (Santa Monica, Ca: RAND, May 1986). p. 45.
33. Ibid., p. 46.
34. U.S. Department of Defense, "*Statement on Defense Agency Research and Development*," made to the House Defense Appropriations subcommittee, 22 March, 1988, p. 4.
35. Department of Defense, *Critical Technologies Plan* [1989], p. A-72.
36. Department of Defense, *Critical Technologies Plan* [1989], p. A-72.
37. *Defense News*, 9 October, 1989, p. 52.
38. Ibid.
39. Henry Freund and Robert Parker, "Free Electron Lasers," *Scientific American*, April 1989, p. 84.
40. Testimony before the House Armed Services Committee, 1 March, 1990.
41. Rosado.
42. Keith Florig, "The Future Battlefield: A Blast of Gigawatts?" *IEEE Spectrum*, March 1988, p. 53.
43. Taylor, p. 38.
44. Ibid.
45. *Philadelphia Inquirer*, 8 November 1987, p. 1.

Four

COMMAND, CONTROL AND COMMUNICATION

...if the British march,
By land or sea from the town tonight,
Hang a lantern aloft in the belfry arch
Of the North Church tower as a signal light,
— One if by land, two if by sea,
And I on the opposite shore will be,
Ready to ride and spread the alarm...

Henry Wadsworth Longfellow,
Paul Revere's Ride

Modern armies and navies face two critical dilemmas. First, the combat units must hide and disperse to survive the hellish fire of modern weaponry, yet must combine their firepower to win. Second, the commanders must constantly make correct decisions on the best ways to defeat enemy units, yet must do so faster than the enemy commanders.

Historically, the only answer to these twin dilemmas of dispersion and timing has been to rely upon the genius of commanders to quickly make the best decisions on how to foil the enemy's strategy, and when to disperse and when to combine. Thus faith is placed in top-level leaders such as Alexander the Great, or lower-ranking leaders such as the thousands of mid-level officers who were at the heart of the Wehrmacht's military successes in World War II.

But without some means of communicating with and controlling their forces in the chaos and fog of war, these leaders can only command their desks.

Before motorized vehicles and wire or radio communications, the traditional means of ensuring battlefield control was to have a well-organized force that could be divided or united into relatively independent units without too much difficulty, horse-messengers to activate a reserve force, and a good hillside from where the general could view the battle and lead a thunderous cavalry charge at the critical moment of decision.

But technology has changed the nature of war; massed columns of men can be casually destroyed with only a moment's thought, so soldiers must now rely on being almost constantly in motion to avoid being targeted in the radar-directed gunsight of long-range armor-killing weapons. Napoleon could view his entire battlefield from the back of a horse, and his closely packed soldiers could shout orders at each other over the noise of the short range cannons; modern armies are so dispersed that they need many types of advanced long-range radio systems to stay in touch with each other.

Thus while battlefield movement and dispersion help survivability, they make control of even well-organized forces very difficult because information is difficult to gather, orders are hard to communicate, and there is so little time to respond to fast, destructive enemy attacks.

The only solution to these dilemmas is to combine modern radios, computers and sensors with a flexible military organization manned by well-led and well-trained soldiers into a Command, Control, Communications, and Intelligence (C^3I) network.

By democratically sharing information with all who need it, such a modern C^3I network can help each commander know his or her situation and circumstances. This would help commanders of platoons, battalions, divisions and corps better fight their own battles. Also, the networks could help each commander understand what help every other unit needs, helping units to better combine their strengths, to compensate for weaknesses, and to exploit enemy errors.[1]

Thus, by distributing the intelligence needed by commanders to exercise autonomy and initiative, even while increasing the likelihood of coordination, such C^3I networks could dramatically increase combat effectiveness, allowing numerically weaker forces to vanquish clumsier enemies.

This type of electronic C^3I network is radically different from the traditional arrangement, where information and orders flowed through the same paths from commander to subordinates. Now information can reside in a central computerized pool, readily available to all friendly forces, even as orders are transmitted from the leaders to subordinates through radios.

A C^3I network is intended to help even mediocre leaders speedily gather and combine information about enemy and friendly actions, evaluate it quickly, and promptly make a decision. It also helps rapidly transmit orders to widely dispersed combat units so they can concentrate firepower from fast moving and long-range weaponry. It is hoped that the C^3I network will survive enemy electronic combat attacks and, most importantly, help friendly forces shoot more quickly and accurately than the enemy, whose own C^3I system — it is hoped — has been crippled by electronic warfare attacks.

A C^3I system can also extend the commander's ability to control a battle in the same way that highly mobile and destructive weapons have extended the ability of men to destroy each other at ever-increasing ranges. Thus the Soviet military believes a C^3I network could allow a Moscow-based commander to quickly concentrate reserve forces spread all over Europe to help an offensive in Germany or Norway.

C^3I networks are changing tactics as well as war plans at the operational, campaigns, and worldwide levels.

For example, while Napoleon's cavalry charged stirrup to stirrup, C^3I systems allow tanks to disperse across the countryside and converge speedily only at the moment of attack. Moreover, commanders no longer have to physically destroy the opposing army to win. Instead, C^3I systems allow commanders to combine attacks on the enemy front line with attacks on rear areas, headquarters, and support forces at the same time, possibly inflicting such shock that the enemy army collapses without suffering heavy casualties, as the French army collapsed before the blitzkrieg of ten Panzer divisions and several hundred dive bombers in 1940.

C³I networks can also allow armies, navies, and air forces to build a broad and powerful force out of several types of specialized combat units designed for maximum effectiveness against a narrow variety of threats. For example, the U.S. Navy's antisubmarine frigates can hunt submarines well but cannot deal with enemy aircraft. Similarly, antiaircraft cruisers can destroy aircraft at long range but cannot easily defeat submarines. Yet modern C³I networks allow the frigate to cooperate with the nearby antiaircraft cruiser so they can protect each other from both menaces. Thus the Navy can use a C³I system to create a broad and powerful military fleet out of several types of specialized warships.

The networks can also help reduce the fog and friction of war. The Prussian general Karl von Clausewitz in the 1820s described the fog of war as the chaos and confusion that surrounds all military decisions. With precious little time to make a decision, and threatened by the danger of violent combat where "the light of reason is refracted in a manner quite different from that which is normal in academic speculation,"[2] commanders must quickly divine the truth from a torrent of false, incomplete, or irrelevant information. Fundamentally, nothing has changed since Clausewitz wrote that "many intelligence reports in war are contradictory, even more are false, and most are uncertain."[3]

But well-designed and skillfully operated C³I networks can help reduce this fog of war, which obscures not only knowledge of enemy capabilities and locations, but also creates a psychological fog around the commander's understanding of what is happening and what must be done to win in the "dreadful presence of suffering and danger." If a C³I network can survive enemy electronic warfare, and can collect, sort, analyze, and distribute information, it can help reveal enemy intentions, capabilities, and weaknesses, and fortify commanders' courage as they lead their troops into battle.

The fog of war plays its role in the larger problem of wartime friction. Clausewitz wrote that although everything in war is very simple in concept, everything is always very difficult to accomplish. The reason for this is friction, "the only concept that more or less corresponds to the factors that distinguish real war from war on paper."[4] Partly caused by fear, physical effort and plain bad luck, friction is the cumulative effect of all the things that can go wrong in war such as delayed attacks, poor intelligence gathering, or reduced mobility. "The difficulties accumulate and end by producing a kind of friction that is inconceivable unless one has experienced war," he wrote. "Action in war is like movement in a resistant element. Just as the simplest and most natural of movements, walking, cannot easily be performed in water, so in war it is difficult for normal efforts to achieve even moderate results." He added that the answers to friction are "iron willpower" of the commander and combat experience of the soldiers.

The idea of friction helps explain why the inexperienced and slow-moving Iraqi army fared so badly against the unorganized Iranians during the first months of the bloody Iran-Iraq War. Eight years later, the Iraqi army had so improved in quality, and its officers were so efficient, that it was able to sharply reduce the problems of friction so effectively that it launched several successful offensives.

In the modern age C³I networks can have a role in overcoming friction — by automating many actions heretofore carried out by tired, frightened and hungry soldiers, by minimizing the difficulties and delays in correctly exchanging information, and perhaps by acting as a critical medium through which commanders can use their iron willpower to push combat units forward through the fires of combat.

But despite the obvious military advantages of great leaders and of high-quality C³I networks, few armies are so blessed as to be have an adequate supply of either.

It is very difficult in peacetime to identify the Napoleons, Rommels, Pattons, or Zhukovs, because their unique qualities are difficult to nurture and exercise in a peacetime army.

Moreover, building C³I systems superior to the enemy's has proven to be far more difficult than hoped for, partly because all C³I systems use appallingly complex technology that is ultimately dependent on the quality of their human operators; but mostly because war is so chaotic that brave and aggressive leadership by front-line commanders is still the vital ingredient of success. In combat, armies often resemble wet spaghetti, which can only be led, never pushed.

COMMUNICATION SYSTEMS

Almost the entire electromagnetic spectrum can be exploited to communicate messages, no matter how complex the message is or how distant the listener may be. The principle is simple; one simply modifies the signal according to a pattern the intended listener can understand. The better the communication system is, the faster it can transmit more data accurately.

A central fact of electronic communication is that there is only limited room on the electromagnetic spectrum. It is not an infinite resource, as anyone whose radio reception has been ruined by interference from other transmitters can attest. Although each of the various regions of the electromagnetic spectrum can carry large amounts of information, it is important to have exclusive use of a small frequency band. Otherwise, rival messages will interfere and sometimes destroy each other.

Because the spectrum is a limited resource, electronic communication involves trade-offs between accuracy, transmission speed and quantity. For example, the larger the message transmitted, the less likely it will be received completely accurately. If the message is made shorter but transmitted over the same length of time, more care can be taken to ensure it is completely accurate. However, there is an alternative: simply use more space on the electromagnetic spectrum.

Space on the spectrum is called bandwidth and is measured in Hertz. Both the available space in any particular electromagnetic region or band and the amount of space that any particular signal uses are measured in Hertz.

"The currency of communication is bandwidth ... the more you want out of communications, the more you have to pay."[5] The faster the transmission, the more accurate the message or the greater the amount of information transmitted at a given instant, the more bandwidth usually required.

A radio channel for a simple Morse code message only needs a band 10 Hertz wide, a teleprinter link takes up 100 Hertz, a phone or voice-radio link takes 4,000 Hertz, and a TV link of only moderate quality takes up to 4 to 6 million Hertz.

The shortage of available spectrum space forces radio designers to minimize signal bandwidth, often by clever techniques or more technologically advanced equipment.

The higher frequency regions and bands of the spectrum are much wider than the lower regions and this affects their capacity. For instance, the very low frequency band can only be used for a few radio conversations at a time, while the extremely high frequency band can convey thousands of similar conversations simultaneously.

Radio Frequency Regions

A large portion of the electromagnetic spectrum, from extremely low frequencies to visible light, can be used effectively for communication. Every region has its distinct properties that make it more useful for some communication tasks and less useful for others.

Extremely Low Frequency

Extremely low frequency (ELF) radio signals travel thousands of kilometers. They have two main advantages, the ability to penetrate water and to resist nuclear disruption.

Extremely low frequencies are used to communicate with submarines because they are able to penetrate several hundred feet of water before their energy — and so the information they carry — is absorbed. This allows submarines to move faster and hide deeper while remaining in communication with their bases.

Also, extremely low frequencies are only slightly affected by the electromagnetic disturbances in the atmosphere caused by nuclear explosions. This relative immunity greatly increases the military value of extremely low frequencies, especially for nuclear missile-launching submarines, whose main task is to remain hidden until a nuclear war breaks out, when they will receive and then act upon orders.

But there are several disadvantages of extremely low frequency communications that greatly restrict its usefulness. First, the very long wavelength of energy in this band permits only very slow transmission of information, so it can take several minutes for a three-letter word to be communicated. Although this limitation precludes detailed messages, it is not of great importance to nuclear missile submarines, which can easily be notified of which preplanned and printed orders are to be executed by a simple three-letter code.

A second disadvantage is that the transmitter needs to be very large. The U.S. extremely low frequency transmitter is based in two states, and has a antenna tens of miles long. Such an antenna is obviously expensive, immobile and somewhat vulnerable to attack. Importantly, it also means that there is no chance for extremely low frequency talk-back: transmitting equipment and antenna cannot be crammed into a submarine.

The combination of a slow rate of communication and a huge transmitter renders the extremely low frequency band largely useless for most soldiers, yet very useful for maintaining contact with submarines. Thus the Soviet military has built four extremely low frequency stations around the USSR and the U.S. has built one station.

Very Low Frequency

Next along the electromagnetic spectrum is the very low frequency (VLF) band. Signals in this band propagate out to a range of several thousand miles and are largely immune to the effects of nuclear explosions, but can penetrate only a few meters through water.

However, very low frequencies can transmit data somewhat faster than extremely low frequencies. They also use a somewhat shorter transmission antenna, which can be made mobile, although not with great ease. In the case of the U.S. C-130Q communications relay aircraft, the antenna is 10 km (6.2 mi) long; in use it hangs vertically from the circling aircraft.

Like extremely low frequencies, the size of the aerial and the comparatively low data-transmission rate makes very low frequencies unsuitable for tactical communications, so their main military use is for one-way transmissions to submarines and ships.

Low Frequency

Next on the electromagnetic spectrum is the low frequency band which has a relatively short transmission range of 900 to 1,700 kilometers (560–1,050 miles).

Low frequency signals need a smaller transmitter antenna than very low frequency — 100–200 meters long (325–655 feet) — and are largely safe from the effects of nuclear weapons. But they can penetrate only a few centimeters of water.

So, low frequencies are generally unsuitable for tactical operations, and are best suited for two-way communication in a nuclear war between bombers or submarines and their bases. One of the most important uses of low frequency communication is to transmit the go-code giving attack orders to U.S. bombers during nuclear war.

Medium Frequency

Medium frequency (MF) signals combine short range and relatively low bandwidth to render them largely useless for military communications. However, extremely high-power medium frequency Loran (Long Range Navigation) radio beacons are used to aid aircraft. Given its low military value, much of the medium frequency band is allocated to commercial AM radio stations.

High Frequency

The high frequency (HF) band, sometimes called short-wave, is very widely used by the military for long range radio transmissions. High frequency signals require only a few watts of transmitting energy to carry all the way around the world.

The high-frequency region is particularly valuable because of its large bandwidth and high data rate, which allows signals to be cheaply transmitted from a small low-power whip-antenna to receivers all over the world.

But because of its reliance on the ionospheric layer of the atmosphere for its long range, high frequency is very vulnerable to disruption of the atmosphere by nuclear explosions, sunspots, night conditions, humidity, and the seasonal effects that disturb the atmosphere.[6] Thus high frequency communications would be greatly degraded for hours to days in a nuclear war.

A second disadvantage of high frequency signals is the ease with which they are transmitted, allowing easy enemy eavesdropping and jamming, and possible wartime overcrowding of the band.

Nonetheless, despite its disadvantages, high frequency is a very favored form of long-range radio communication during peacetime and conventional war.

Very High Frequency

Next in the electromagnetic spectrum is the very high frequency (VHF) band. A range of a 40–50 km (25–30 mi)[7] is achieved by line of sight propagation, although an unreliable very short range skywave path is possible in the lower areas of the band. Meteor-scatter propagation is also possible in the lower half of the band.

The larger bandwidth in the very high frequency band allows a higher datarate and more channels than high frequency, while only a small antenna is needed for the very short wavelengths. Thus very high frequency is widely used for combat net radio networks that link ground units.

But most very high frequency signals are greatly degraded by intervening terrain and so cannot be easily heard behind obstacles. Although this has little relevance to aircraft, it is a major disadvantage for ground and naval units. This means ground troops are forced to maintain alternative communications links including unreliable cable telephones or radio-relay transmitters for use when very high frequency communication is blocked.

Ultrahigh Frequency

Ultrahigh frequency (UHF) signals can be transmitted up to a few tens of kilometers along a line of sight, and up to several hundred kilometers when bounced off the short-lived trails of ionized atmosphere created by hundreds of small meteorites that enter the earth's atmosphere every day. Because of their similar characteristics, ultrahigh frequency communications share many of the same advantages and disadvantages of very high frequency communications.

However, at ultrahigh frequencies a new capability appears: communication via a relay satellite in space which can receive the line of sight signal and rebroadcast it to listeners on earth. This artificial propagation path has the advantage of being largely independent of the fickle and ever-changing ionosphere, although satellites are very expensive and somewhat vulnerable to enemy attack in war.

Superhigh Frequency

The next radio frequency band is the superhigh frequency band, where there is a large bandwidth available for use.

Superhigh-frequency signals, often called microwave transmissions, travel by line of sight. However, the most important characteristic of these frequencies is that they can be focused by a small dish antenna into a narrow beam with a divergence of only a few degrees. The main advantage of this narrow transmission path is that an enemy will find it very difficult to intercept.

An important attribute of this band is that its wavelengths are so short that the air gradually absorbs its electromagnetic energy. Consequently, superhigh-frequency signals can be greatly reduced after only several kilometers passage through the air. With fog or rain, the problem rapidly becomes greater. These losses can be compensated for by the use of high-power transmitters and sensitive receivers, although at undesirable expense. The use of superhigh frequency relay satellites, which need only penetrate the depth of the atmosphere, helps minimize this atmospheric absorption problem.

Superhigh frequencies are often used in communications satellites, but also in microwave relay systems, where very high bandwidth signals are relayed across a country from tower to tower in chains stretching several thousand kilometers. High-capacity civilian microwave relays can carry 11,500 telephone calls simultaneously. The only limitation of this method is that each tower must be in line of sight to the next tower on either side, and not so distant that the signal might be absorbed by heavy rain, usually about 40–50 km (25–30 mi).

The narrow propagation path of superhigh frequency signals can protect against enemy eavesdropping, but it requires that antennas be pointed accurately in the right directions, which forces friendly units to keep track of each other's positions. This tracking problem largely rules out the use of superhigh frequency communication for aircraft, helicopters and armored vehicles, but not for periodically static units such as antiaircraft missile batteries, headquarters units, and logistics units.

Extremely High Frequency

Next on the spectrum is the extremely high frequency band, which propagates solely by line of sight. This region offers a huge amount of bandwidth for passing many high-bit-rate messages simultaneously without mutual interference. Its line of sight propagation path can be made so narrow that enemy interception (and thus enemy jamming, decryption and deception) is very difficult. Also, extremely high frequency signals are largely immune to the effects of nuclear explosions and require only very small antennas for transmission and reception.

However, the line-of-sight limitation sharply increases the difficulty of establishing a communications link, especially with a mobile receiver. Atmospheric absorption is also a problem, although this can be minimized by exploiting windows in the atmosphere through which particular frequencies in this band can pass without great loss.

The extremely high frequency band is an ideal match for communications relay satellites. Thus the U.S. Military Tactical and Strategic Relay Satellite — slated for launch in the mid-1990s — was designed to relay high-volume, classified communications between vital military assets, such as nuclear forces, regional headquarters and civilian command authorities. The additional expense of extremely high frequency equipment is compensated for by the vast increase in security, reliability, and communications capacity. However, like many other Pentagon programs, it may become a casualty of deep budget cuts in the early 1990s.

Infrared Frequencies

One of the earliest uses of the infrared region of the spectrum for communication was the German *Lichtsprecher* infrared radio in 1941.[8]

Because of its high frequency, infrared energy can easily be transmitted in extremely narrow beams, preventing enemy interception or jamming.

Nonetheless, there are major problems with infrared communications. Infrared beams can usually only penetrate 5 to 8 km (3–5 mi) through the atmosphere, and are easily blocked by clouds, dust, rain, and terrain. Also, infrared transmitters and receivers are expensive, especially when the pointing and tracking systems used to keep the narrow beam pointed at the receiver are taken into account.

These disadvantages sharply limit the usefulness of infrared, although there is probably a future for short-range infrared communications if the cost is reduced by new technology.

Visible Frequencies

Light, which is easily received by the human eye, has long being exploited to communicate messages. Semaphore, smoke signals, mirrors, flags and so on are the oldest methods, now rendered sometimes obsolete by exploitation of other regions of the spectrum. Of course, these visible messages are greatly affected by the availability of light, by terrain features, by atmospheric factors such as smoke and by distance. Moreover, their data transmission rate is slow and unreliable because they depend upon the human eye for detection, and the human brain for interpretation.

However, communication by light is still absolutely vital to military units — if only because the most versatile receiver of information is the human eye.[9] Thus hand signals, maps, operating instructions, flags and handwriting are vital to battlefield effectiveness. Other visible communication devices such as signal lamps still have their uses, especially if they can be kept hidden from the enemy. Flares can serve as a method of communicating simple messages concerning friendly location or the beginning of an attack. Simplicity is the chief virtue of reliance upon visible light and the eye, but easy detection and low-data rate are the chief drawbacks.

The electronic way to use light in communications is to modulate light-frequency laser beams, which travel by line of sight. Whereas most light sources broadcast light of many slightly different frequencies in a chaotic jumble, lasers transmit a beam of essentially single frequency in which the individual waves are in exact phase — or lockstep — with each other.

The light is collected at the communications receiver by a telescope-like device and then interpreted by a signal processor. The great bandwidth of the light region of the spectrum allows vast amounts of information to be rapidly passed, but the cost of the lasers and the tracking equipment limits its uses to only a few areas.

A few U.S. satellites are equipped with lasers to tell each other when Soviet missiles are being launched from their silos. The U.S. is also developing a laser system that will allow satellites to send lengthy messages to submarines hundreds of feet underwater. Also, some U.S. aircraft on covert transport missions can use compact lasers to exchange information without fear of enemy interception.

Fiber-optic cables can also be used to carry laser communications. These cables are made of a clear plastic that absorbs very little of the laser energy and so allows transmission of light over much greater distances than possible through the atmosphere. The cables are difficult to tap, carry an enormous amount of information, and weigh very little, properties that make them attractive to the military.

However, fiber-optic cable systems are largely useless on the mobile battlefield because they are vulnerable to enemy attack and are inconvenient to lay or repair. These problems sharply limit their use in war to communication between fixed bases or over short distances between vehicles in a temporarily static unit.

COMPUTER SYSTEMS

Altogether, many different communications systems can channel enormous quantities of information from one unit to another. But the information needs to be sent to the right people, at the right time, in the right format.

The communications networks must be coordinated by computers able to identify information and steer the information to the right destination. Otherwise, the networks will become hopelessly jammed with irrelevant, misdirected, surplus or even incorrect information, just as a city's roads will get jammed if there are no traffic cops.

For example, a single infrared scanner may collect some data on the location of a single enemy aircraft, in which many people are interested. Thus the data should be quickly transmitted through a communications network to antiaircraft missile units, friendly fighter aircraft, nearby ships trying to remain undetected, intelligence organizations trying to understand the enemy's strategy and so on.

The job is further complicated when many sensors collect a great diversity of information of vital concern to diverse audiences. Thus information on ammunition supplies is vital for logistics troops, information on enemy tank movements is vital for frontline commanders, information on intercepted enemy radio conversations is vital for intelligence officers, information on casualty rates is vital for medical units, and so on.

These pieces of information must be transmitted on different communications networks to many locations some of which are more important than others, using different levels of message scrambling techniques. Only computers using fiendishly complex software can keep track of who needs what type of information, when they need it, and how best to get it to the eventual users.

The military have had very great difficulty in creating the software needed to keep the messages flowing in the communications network. The problems have caused many military computer systems to cost more than budgeted, fall behind schedule, and still not do what was asked.

But traffic and routing software is not the most difficult part of computerized communications systems. At some point the electronic data must be processed and combined by computers into a form that can be understood by soldiers sitting at computer screens — the final and perhaps most difficult stage of communications.

Computerized data contain many different kinds of information. For example, information from logistics troops about ammunition supplies may arrive as long lists of numbers. Information from front-line reconnaissance troops about the position of an enemy unit may arrive as a set of map coordinates. Information from radio-interception units about the frequencies used by enemy radios may arrive organized by different periods of time. Information gathered by computerized radars about an enemy aircraft many come as distance, compass heading and vertical angle report.

In addition to diversity, some information is more reliable than other information, and some information directly contradicts other information.

Combining the many kinds of information into a single report, while minimizing the uncertainties and ambiguities, and then presenting the report in a understandable form for the commander is not at all easy. But it has to be done or the commander will simply have to ignore the tidal wave of information because there is simply no time to study it.

But if it can be done, every soldier and every commander would potentially have the marvelous ability to understand all the intelligence gathered by friendly forces. Chaos and fog would be (partially) dispelled, allowing friendly forces to launch coordinated and fierce attacks on critical enemy vulnerabilities.

C³I NETWORKS

Without organization, an army is only a heavily armed mob likely to be destroyed by the first coordinated force it meets.

What converts a mob into an effective modern army is a leader with a well understood plan, good organization, good training, good personnel and a computerized command, control, communications and intelligence (C³I) network that enables commanders to lead their widely dispersed troops.[10]

Although communications are central to C³I systems, the role of the sensors that collect the information and the computers that feed the commanders information cannot be forgotten. Frontline radio-interception units, reconnaissance troops, photographic satellites or radar-carrying aircraft produce the information about the enemy that the commander so desperately needs, and without which the communications systems would be largely pointless.

But a good C³I network is very difficult to create, because it needs much more than fancy radios and well-led and trained soldiers. The problems are not caused merely by the extreme complexity of the computerized technology, but largely by the difficulty of ensuring that the technology complements a well designed and flexible military organization.

So although a good C³I network is vital for military effectiveness on a high-technology battlefield, it is secondary to the basic factors of leadership, training and organization.

This was very evident during World War I in the British response to the new trench warfare brought about by the development of machine guns and long-range artillery bombardments. Because machine guns and artillery quickly destroyed all communications between frontline combat units, so instantly reducing any offensive to chaos, the British generals sought battlefield control by ordering their attacking infantry to advance straight ahead to a particular objective according to a particular timetable that matched the precisely calculated bombardment of friendly artillery. This straightjacketed command and control policy gave the generals a semblance of control and predictability but only by sacrificing all flexibility and any opportunities to exploit sudden — and fleeting — advantages that might open up before their lower level commanders in the frontline battles.

The Germans rejected this shortsighted policy and decided to make the best of battlefield chaos. They ordered their better trained and more independent "stormtroop" infantry units to exploit heavy artillery bombardments by infiltrating through the disrupted Allied front lines, leaving the task of eliminating any bypassed British units to the German follow-on assault forces. It mattered little to the German generals that they lost contact with the stormtroopers, or that those units became disorganized in the breakthrough, or that pockets of British resistance held out for a while behind them. It did not matter greatly because, far more importantly, the British defense lines were quickly destroyed, allowing the German main forces to break into the British rear. Thus by decentralizing battlefield leadership to their trusted stormtroop company, platoon, and squad leaders, the Germans constructed a military organization that achieved battlefield success, and they did so without any significant communications technology.

Thus, a combat organization and its associated command and control system can be built to create battlefield success, despite a lack of new technology or even the temporary lack of any communications. But combat strength can only be improved by combining a powerful C^3I network with good organization and training.

This lesson was also made clear by the Germans as they pioneered the development of the first ground combat units with an electronic command and control system — the highly-mobile and extremely effective Panzer divisions. Without such a C^3I network, the Panzer divisions with their well-balanced and complementary combat units of highly mobile tanks, infantry, artillery, and antitank guns, would have quickly become hopelessly confused, intermingled, and disorganized in the confusion of battle.

But once these units were kept in contact by radios, divisional commanders could use the information gathered by far-flung reconnaissance troops to combine fast-moving forces into compact battlegroups that could quickly smash through weak points in the enemy's defenses, tactics that crushed Britain's and France's armies in only six weeks.

In fact, without radios, the only way to control the vehicles of the Panzer division would have been either to split them up into small and independent, but relatively harmless, combat units or to concentrate all the vehicles so tightly together they would have resembled a herd of buffalo, so providing a fine target for enemy artillery.

The radio made the Panzer division possible, but not inevitable. The British and French had the same technology as the Germans but foolishly divided their armored units into small and ineffective penny packets that were quickly brushed aside as the Panzer divisions swept toward the English Channel. It was a superior understanding of warfare that allowed the Germans to combine the new technology of tanks, aircraft and radios in a new type of combat unit.

The Panzer division also elevated ground-based C^3I from tactics to operational level combat. Whereas the British only used radios to allow artillery to help infantry attack enemy bunkers, the Germans used radios to drive an armored stake through the heart of the Allied defenses.

But the Germans did not have a monopoly on intelligence; only a few months after the German invasion of france, the Royal Air Force successfully defeated the German Air Force by relying on a revolutionary combination of radar, fighter aircraft and communications systems. Just as the Germans' C^3I networks allowed them to concentrate their tanks, the Royal Air Force's C^3I network allowed it to concentrate its relatively few fighter aircraft where they could do the most good.

Navies and air forces have usually led armies in the development of far-flung electronic C^3I networks, largely because they must use technology simply to operate in their particular environments. Also, superior technology has traditionally given a much greater advantage in the air or at sea than on land. Compared to ships or aircraft operating in uncluttered environments, technologically outclassed troops can use bad weather, jungles, mountains, cities or marshes to hide from relatively short-sighted, slow-moving enemy units. The Afghan *mujaheddin* drove the Soviet Army out of Afghanistan not by relying on a technology-intensive force with aircraft or radar, but instead relying on rough terrain to shield their mobile infantry, which was armed with crude 122 mm rockets, sturdy Kalashnikov rifles and the relatively simple (but technologically sophisticated) Stinger heat-seeking missiles to fend off helicopters.

At sea or in the air, the only complicating factors are weather, and occasionally coastlines, so even small a technological advantage can yield speedy victory. Thus world navies pioneered radios and were the first to discover how C^3I systems changed their operational-level and even theater strategies. For example, in the huge naval battle of Jutland in 1916, radio interception and radio communications helped British officers control the tactics of their forces and also helped them keep track of enemy movements.

Twenty years later, the Allied and German navies built vast communications and intelligence-gathering systems to control their huge forces during the bitter battles over the Atlantic sea lanes from 1939 to 1945.

Since World War II, the U.S. Navy has built a global C^3I system to help direct the fire and movement of world-spanning aircraft and fast-moving carrier forces. It has also built a C^3I system that extends into space to control the launch of the longest range and most destructive of all weapons, earth-shattering nuclear missiles.

Thus C^3I systems have rapidly changed military ideas and actions at tactical, operational, theater and now global levels of conflict.

But it is all too easy to place too much faith in the value of C^3I networks, especially battlefield networks. Although C^3I networks will increase the chances for control, they also accelerate the pace of war, effectively reducing the chances for control. Perhaps C^3I systems will allow top-level commanders a broad view over the battlefield, but they are unlikely to allow those commanders to keep pace with what is going on in the front line.

Designing a C^3I network is not at all easy. Still more difficult is building a new organization that can allow the military to best exploit the possibilities of the new C^3I technology.

However, some general rules are obvious. Any C^3I network must be flexible enough to be repaired as its various pieces are destroyed by the enemy, be cheap enough to buy in adequate quantities and be simple enough to operate in the chaos of war. The C^3I network should quickly pass only the required information between troops so that commanders do not get deluged with useless information or suffer from micromanagement and interference from higher level commanders.

The C^3I systems should not be abused to allow a top level commander to interfere with the battle decisions of lower level commanders. Indeed, C^3I systems must give battlefield commanders the flexibility to lead from the front, even while they coordinate widely-dispersed forces.

It almost goes without saying that C^3I systems should be able to quickly link the radios and computers used by all elements of a nation's military or an alliance's armed forces. This goal of "interoperability" is actually very difficult to achieve, because the armed forces of every country — and the services within each national military — prefer to carry out operations in different ways, and to build separate C^3I that meet their own purposes. Thus the U.S. military has suffered from significant problems in this regard, most notably during the invasion of Grenada, where U.S. ground troops were unable to contact Navy ships because of poor communications planning.

Interoperability requires much more than radio systems capable of contacting each other; it also require a common command structure, as well as common communications practices and procedures.

For example, even if army troops and navy ships use an identical radio, they will be unable to communicate unless both are also equipped with the right codes used to scramble messages. Moreover, unless all services know and understand how the others handle information, then message will get delayed, garbled, or even lost in the complex C^3I systems. And the only way to ensure such coordination is to create a common command structure that will knock the services' heads together during peacetime.

To its credit, the DoD made great strides in this area in the years after Grenada. For example, there were few C^{3I} problems during the invasion of Panama in 1989. This was possible because the Congress and the DoD established a good command structure that skillfully planned and carried out the invasion. Also, DoD planners had the invaluable advantage of over a year's planning time to properly prepare a complex communications plan that ensured over 700 radio links did not jam each other, and that messages would quickly get to the right place.

But the DoD cannot afford to rest on its laurels. Like the Kremlin, it must always strive to control the separatist tendencies of its various services and communities, who will seek to build C^{3I} systems that suit their purposes, but not the purposes of other services or the DOD. Thus during the military buildup in Saudi Arabia, the allied forces established a special panel to coordinate the C^3I systems of U.S. forces, Saudi Arabia, the United Kingdom, France, and the other allies.

The C^3I network must also be flexible enough to permit wartime modifications and responsive enough to allow friendly units to act faster than the enemy so that enemy attacks can be foiled before they begin and friendly attacks can be completed before the enemy can react.

Thus, while engineers may decide the cheapest and most capable C^3I network would use a single commander at a single central message exchange, in reality this would be a disastrous decision because it would hand the enemy an invitation to wreck the C3I network by blowing up the central exchange.

Therefore it is not surprising that there are many types of C^3I networks for many types of military organizations, and that each nation builds different C^3I networks according to their own military heritage and needs.

For example, American C^3I networks are built to maximize the low-level initiative and flexibility deemed necessary to win in the chaos of battle. Thus a single American artillery observer can use his radio to control the fire of all of his division's artillery rockets and guns. But the Soviet military's C^3I networks are built to maximize the centralized control deemed necessary to push the main attack forward in the chaos of battle. Thus a Soviet artillery officer can only use his radio to control the artillery pieces allocated to him by his commanders.

Each of the many C^3I systems used by armies has its own advantages and disadvantages, which depend on the armies' purposes and the nature of the war. Like a hunter choosing a suitable weapon to strike down his intended victim, each army chooses a C^3I system according to how it wants to fight its wars.

For example, if — as the Soviet military thinkers expect — battlefield confusion and heavy radio jamming will make it impossible for artillery officers to communicate with anything except the nearest artillery guns, the Soviet's centralized control system would be much more effective than the de-centralized American system. The Soviet tank divisions would grind forward according to Moscow's plan while the American officer struggled vainly to direct the massive but blind American artillery firepower.

Speed and responsiveness are hallmarks of a good C^3I system because it is crucial that combat units react faster than the enemy if they wish to survive and win. This is much more true today than even fifty years ago because, compared to every previous generation, modern soldiers have much less time to organize themselves in battle. While in World War II, a tank regiment could travel about 80 km (50 mi) a day, now a much more destructive attack helicopter battalion can cover this distance in only twenty minutes — Clausewitz's friction permitting.

It might be assumed that modern communications and computers always quicken response time. But they can in fact slow down command and control times if the commander is overloaded with a torrent of information. Thus command and control systems — as well as computerized battle management systems — must be very carefully designed to filter out unimportant information and to combine a great deal of important information so the leaders can quickly and easily understand the situation.

It is well to understand that the information requirements of top leaders can be very different from those of staff officers. To perform their complex jobs, staff officers must keep track of numerous enemy and friendly units, the condition of the terrain, the state of friendly and enemy supplies and many other factors.

But to fight the all-important battle between the maneuvering armored combat units, the division commander really only needs to know the locations and strengths of friendly and enemy battalions, and of any possible opportunities or dangers. He should not be concerned with supplies, the locations of targets that could be attacked by artillery, next week's weather, or the thousands of other factors that his supply, artillery, helicopter, intelligence, electronic warfare, medical, tank and infantry officers care about. Thus his command and control needs are very different from the other parts of his division.

This difference between the needs of the commander and the needs of his many subordinates has in the past led to commanders bypassing normal communications channels, often creating communications systems purely for their own use.

For example, in World War I, U.S. general George Marshall armed his staff officers with homing pigeons and told them to accompany the forward battalions during American offensives. Thus frontline information flew straight back to the general, bypassing the slow route through battalion, regiment, division and corps headquarters. This scheme allowed Marshall to keep track of much of the forward battle, and then quickly respond to opportunities by telephoning additional attack orders to the frontline regiments. Similar tactics were used by the Soviets, British, Germans and by the U.S. general George Patton in World War II, and by General Don Starry in the late 1970s when commanding U.S. troops in NATO exercises.

In future wars, it is likely that such unorthodox "directed telescopes" will be established by commanders desperately seeking limited amounts of information about the front line battle. Sophisticated C^3I networks developed by communications officers may in war be firehoses of information for commanders who may only want a faucet of facts.[11]

Just as important as quickly getting the right information to the right place is the survivability of a C^3I network, and of any "directed telescopes" added by the field commanders.

In any war, commanders will be killed, radios will be jammed, and radars will be destroyed. Thus the winning army will probably be the one that is better able to continually reorganize its C^3I network and its combat units to compensate for the losses of leaders, communications, and sensors.

The endurance and resilience of the Wehrmacht's tactical command and control system was the primary reason it took so long for the Allies and the Soviets to drive the Germans back to Berlin during the Second World War. Even when German combat units were destroyed in brutal combat with the Russians on the Eastern front, their surviving fragments would repeatedly reform into adhoc organized battlegroups, complete with newly appeared combat leaders. The secret of this superior German endurance was not better communications or intelligence gathering, but a militarily effective tactical command and control system, a system created not by technology but by a well-thought-out military training program that taught the soldiers how to cooperate and fight in the most desperate of circumstances. Thus although technology can be a great help, it cannot be a substitute for well-trained soldiers.

This reflects the greatest potential dilemma with all C^3I systems; that the advantage of top-level direction and coordination can degenerate into top-level micromanagement. In the fear, uncertainty, and chaos of war, it will be difficult for top-level commanders not to try and use any effective command and control systems to minimize uncertainty on the battlefield by monitoring and directing the actions of their lower level officers.

According to one bomber pilot who chafed under excessive command and control during the Vietnam War, "In the interim between Korea and Southeast Asia [Vietnam War] the efficiency of communications channels improved vastly and their multiplicity increased dramatically, which was a mixed blessing. Since the ability to communicate was there, everyone in the chain of command seemed to feel they should be aware of minute details within units under their control. As a result the instant transmission of information became paramount, thus saturating those communications channels. The channels were always inadequate because the more information they relayed the more requirements they generated for even more detail. Enhanced communications made the highest commanders think they were in the cockpit or at the head of the platoon. Four star generals, appointed secretaries of defense, and even presidents make poor combat pilots or riflemen.... Access to real-time information begot an increased desire for control, which justified more headquarters with larger staffs, who created new reports, requiring further detailed analyses, which required additional information. I doubt that Arthur McArthur would have made it to the top of the hill with the flag in the Philippines or that Eddie Rickenbacker would have shot down a single German aircraft if they had had the benefit of all the help we had in Southeast Asia."[12]

Thus top-level micromanagement — sometimes known as forward leadership from the rear — threatens the lower level officer's initiative that is vital to deal with the routinely unexpected events and unique circumstances that arise on the battlefield.

The lesson is that the well-prepared Army should have a good top-level commander willing to tolerate wartime uncertainty because he trusts the battlefield judgments of his lower level officers. Thus the command and control system should be extensive enough to allow reliable communications between the commander and officers, but not so extensive that it chokes initiative and clogs maneuver.

Nor can C^3I systems provide motivation; they cannot replace good officers capable of leading brave troops into the murderous fire of enemy weaponry. Computerized C^3I systems allow coordination of different weapons and allow direction of forces, but they cannot convince soldiers to climb out of foxholes to defeat artillery and machine gun fire.

Today, the primary threat facing C^3I systems is electronic combat. If sensors are blinded by electronic jamming, then the combat commander will be starved for information. Worse still, if the men and women behind the sensors are tricked by electronic deception, then the commander will be fed false information. Even if correct information is gathered, the commander will be unable to counter enemy attacks if electronic communications are jammed or slowed. Few military organizations can survive destruction or disruption of their

C^3I network — unless the enemy is also suffering from the same distress.

Modern C^3I networks must be built on a foundation of well trained soldiers, and must be built to survive the worst form of electronic warfare that they could face.

Another must for modern C^3I network is that they help soldiers use the many types of weapons now in current armories. While field commanders during World War II had to organize relatively few types of forces, today they must coordinate logistics, artillery, tanks, missiles and infantry, electronic warfare aircraft, bombers and fighters, jamming, deception, intelligence and extensive communications systems, as well as nuclear weapons and chemical weapons.

Perhaps the most impressive C^3I systems entering service now are those for use by land forces. The reduced weight and cost of radios and computers is allowing armies to build C^3I networks that finally rival those used by their more technologically-oriented naval and air force cousins. Indeed, the very novelty of C^3I technology to the muddy soldiers seems to be helping the U.S. Army to make imaginative and militarily effective use of the new technology.

Partly because of their advanced technology, the American military seems to be leading the world in the development of advanced battlefield C^3I networks. Under development now for the U.S. Army is a battlefield C^3I system that uses three radio networks to tie together five computerized battle management systems.

The two primary radio networks are the SINCGARS and MSE. SINCGARS stands for Single·Channel Ground and Airborne Radio System, and is the standard very high frequency radio used by tanks, artillery units, infantry companies, and attack helicopters to talk among themselves.

MSE, or Mobile Subscriber Equipment, is the higher level battlefield telephone system used by larger units to exchange information with one another. It is based on small truck-mounted radio-telephone exchanges connected by microwave relays. With the addition of a planned upgrade, the MSE will be able to transmit some computerized information around the battlefield, so allowing quick exchange of intelligence information gathered by aircraft, spy satellites, and radars.

The third communications system is called the Army Data Distribution System or ADDS. If budget cuts and development problems are overcome, it will be deployed in the mid-1990s. Its first role is as a specialized radio system to be used by air defense troops to exchange computerized information about enemy aircraft between friendly fighter aircraft, surveillance radars, ground missile crews and commanders. ADDS's second role is to transmit information about targets to friendly artillery weapons.

These three communications systems tie together all five computerized battle management systems, the first and most important of which will be the All Source Analysis System (ASAS). To be deployed sometime in the 1990s, the purpose of the computerized ASAS is to help clear away what Clausewitz called the fog of war, allowing units to fight with accurate and up-to-date knowledge of the enemy movements, strength and purposes. The truck-borne system will allow intelligence personnel to combine all information sent in by ADDS, MSE, or SINCGARS about enemy units, actions and intentions. The ASAS will also use global communication networks to tap into information collected by far-distant Navy and Air Force units, as well as spy satellites.

Information sorted by the ASAS will be transmitted to the second management system, the computerized Maneuver Control System, which is to be used by the commander to control and direct his tanks and infantry battalions.

Information from the All Source Analysis System will also be passed to third battle management system, the Advanced Field Artillery Tactical Data System, to be used by the artillery units from the mid-1990s to keep track of targets to be destroyed. Once equipped with the new computer systems, an artillery crew's main concern will not be finding targets, but choosing the best ones to destroy with the relatively limited supply of high-technology ammunition, according to a senior Army official.[13]

The fourth battle management system is the Forward Area Air Defense Command and Control System which is intended to warn friendly antiaircraft troops when a enemy or friendly aircraft is heading their way. Slated for deployment in the mid-1990s, this computer system will be linked through ADDS to an Air Force communication system called the Joint Tactical Information Distribution System, which transmits airborne radar information about enemy aircraft to the ground troops.

The fifth computer system, called the Tactical Army Combat Service Support Computer System, is to be used in the late 1990s by supply troops to get the proper supplies in the right amounts to the troops at just the right moment. This computer system relies on SINCGARS and MSE for information.

The U.S. Army believes this C^3I network — based on three communications systems and five computer systems — will allow them to speedily exchange battlefield information and to react quicker than an enemy. However, all of the systems, except the MSE, have either fallen behind schedule or cost more than planned. As a result, it is very likely that several of the systems will be greatly scaled back or even cancelled.

The Army is not so foolish as to believe that even the full deployment of its planned C^3I networks will make everything visible to the commander. According to an Army 1982 field manual, "At the very time when battle demands better and more effective command and control, modern electronic countermeasures [such as jamming] may make that task *more difficult than ever before*. Commanders will find it difficult to determine what is happening. Small units will often have to fight without sure knowledge about their forces as a whole. Electronic warfare, vulnerability of command and control facilities, and mobile combat will demand initiative in subordinate commanders" to compensate for expected disruption of command and control.[14]

The U.S Air Force is also improving its C^3I networks by buying new computer systems to speed the collection, sorting and distribution of information.

Among the most important systems are new mission-planning computers, intended to quickly get pass intelligence information to pilots shortly before they begin an attack mission. First operationally employed during the 1990 Kuwait crisis, the mission-planning computers are to be based at every squadron and are intended to accept information collected by national intelligence agencies such as the Central Intelligence Agency, which manages spy satellites, but also from tactical intelligence systems similar to the All Source Analysis System. The mission planning system combines the information about weather, the locations, numbers, and capabilities of enemy antiaircraft weapons, the characteristics of aircraft to be used, and a description of the target it is supposed to destroy, with a computerized map, to allow the pilot to choose the best route to and from the target. In choosing the best route, the pilot can avoid enemy missile batteries or areas frequented by enemy fighters, and can also combine his attack with his colleagues so that the enemy will be suddenly faced with a coordinated attack by several aircraft arriving from different directions at the same time. Also, new computerized radios are being developed to point out new targets to pilots in flight.

The importance of such C^3I systems is hard to exaggerate; by greatly reducing the time needed to plan missions, more sorties can be flown, perhaps doubling the effective size of the U.S. Air Force for the cost of a fighter squadron. Also, by reducing vulnerability, fewer aircrews and aircraft will be killed. And by speeding responsiveness, more enemy units will be killed in less time, so shortening the war and reducing overall deaths.

The Navy has the most advanced tactical C^3I systems, including mission planning systems for its carrier-based aircraft. Moreover, the Navy plans to improve its tactical C^3I networks with the most advanced tactical C^3I systems yet developed — the Joint Tactical Information Distribution System.

This radio system operates at ultrahigh frequencies and can routinely pass large amounts of data over 100 radio channels simultaneously, even while it changes frequency thousands of times per second to sidestep enemy jamming. Thus the radio network can be simultaneously used by fighter pilots of one or many squadrons to warn others of enemy interceptors, by ground attack aircraft to point out new targets, by electronic warfare aircraft to coordinate jamming, by ships to identify targets, and by aircraft carriers to track movement of their aircraft.

Perhaps it greatest benefit is that it uses a small television display in cockpits to show pilots all information gathered by distant radar aircraft and other sensors. Thus this democratic network allows fighter pilots to look over the shoulders of the radar operators in the Navy's E-2 Hawkeye radar aircraft which can track hundred of aircraft and missiles for 300 miles in all directions. Such "situational awareness" will greatly reduce the chance of U.S. Navy aircraft being ambushed, and greatly increases the chance that fighter will be effectively concentrated to destroy approaching threats. Citing its high cost of up to $1 million for each aircraft, the Air Force has declined to buy this advanced radio system, preferring instead to spend the money buying a few extra underequipped fighter aircraft for its colonels to fly.

The Navy's C^3I system is greatly helped by super-high frequency satellites that can be used to gather information from radar-equipped ships, land-based intelligence gathering centers, and space-based spy satellites. Also, land-based low and very low frequency transmitting stations are available to send messages from top naval commanders to stealthy submarines hiding under the ocean waves.

Despite impressive modern technology, the value of C^3I networks depend fundamentally on the quality of the soldiers using them. Coordinating the many types of combat units, ensuring the continued survival of the C^3I network, and getting the intelligence information to the leaders as quickly as possible are as important as they are difficult — even in peacetime when soldiers do not have to cope with the chaos, fear, and destruction of war. In combat, only the very best educated and well trained soldiers will be able to properly organize themselves and their C^3I networks — even if they have the benefit of an excellent military doctrine that helps them realize what they must do.

But the greatest danger to technology-intensive C^3I networks is enemy electronic combat operations, which can destroy headquarters, jam communications, blind sensors, deceive intelligence analysts, slow decision-making and even cause a very swift collapse of the C^3I networks, bought so expensively in peacetime.

Notes

1.   Martin L. Van Creveld, *Command In War* (Cambridge, Mass: Harvard University Press, 1985); Clarence McKnight, ed., *Control of Joint Forces: A New Perspective*, (Fairfax, Va: Armed Forces Communications and Electronics Association, 1989); and Roger Beaumont, *The Nerves of War* (Washington DC: AFCEA International Press, 1986). See also Lt. Col. G Kenneth Allard, *Command, Control, and the Common Defense* (New Haven, CT: Yale University Press 1990). This analysis traces the separate development of the services' command and control systems, while calling for a new strategic vision that would combine the fighting power of all three services.

2.   Karl von Clausewitz, *On War*, ed. Michael Howard and Peter Paret (Princeton University Press, 1984), p. 113.

3.   Clausewitz, *On War*, p. 117.

4.   Ibid, p. 119.

5.   Lt. Col. Roger Cemm, "HF: New High Flyer In Communications," *Defense and Foreign Affairs*, June 1987, p. 31.

6.   See chapter 22 of *The Amateur Radio Relay League Handbook* (Newington, Ct: American Radio Relay League, 1986), p. 22-5.

7.   Ashton B. Carter, "Communication Technologies and Vulnerabilities" in Ashton B. Carter, John Steinbrunner and Charles A..Zraket, eds., *Managing Nuclear Operations* (Washington, DC:Brookings Institution,1987).

8.   Lt. Col. Richard Fitts, ed., *The Strategy of Electromagnetic Conflict*, (Los Altos, Ca: Peninsula Publishing, 1980), p. 152.

9.   In technical terms, "the eye is an extremely versatile optical system.... In normal circumstances it operates through binocular stereoscopic vision with nerve fibers between eye and brain providing the communication link for processing the perceived scene. The human eye has great powers of accommodation, high accuracy of alignment and can distinguish between colors and tones. It operates best in daylight conditions but will also work to a varying extent down to quite low light levels. The eye has moderate field of view approximately 30 degrees in elevation and 40 degrees in azimuth, a good circular field of about 10 degrees and a central best vision field of 1 to 2 degrees in diameter. Movement can be detected in peripheral vision out to nearly 180 degrees in azimuth." From A.L. Rogers

et al., eds., *Surveillance and Target Acquisition Systems*, 1983, (Oxford: Brassey's Defense Publishers 1983), p. 17.

10. Gen. William DuPuy, "Concepts of Operation: The Heart of Command, the Tool of Doctrine," in Lt. Gen. Clarence McKnight, ed., *Control of Joint Forces* (Fairfax, VA: Armed Forces Communications and Electronics Assoc., 1989).

11. Van Creveld, *Command in War.*

12. Jack Broughton, *Going Downtown: The War Against Hanoi and Washington*, (New York: Pocket Books, 1988), p. 79.

13. *Defense News*, 30 October, 1989.

14. U.S. Department of the Army, *Operations; Field Manual 100-5* (Washington DC: Government Printing Office, 1982), p. 1-3.

Five

◆

ELECTRONIC WARFARE

*To achieve victory we must as far as possible
make the enemy blind and deaf by sealing his
eyes and ears, and drive his commanders to
distraction by creating confusion in their minds.*

Mao Tse-Tung

So far we have discussed the possible ways of exploiting the spectrum for communication, surveillance, targeting, and attack. But in war, competition for the control of the spectrum is fierce and bloody. In 1904, barely a few years after radios appeared, a Russian sailor introduced electronic warfare by using a jammer to disrupt the Japanese Navy's radio-directed bombardment of Port Arthur.

In the military struggle for the use of the electromagnetic spectrum, various tactics will be used — such as passively listening for an enemy's messages, jamming enemy communications, destroying enemy emitters and so on. Since World War II, these standard tactics have been called "electronic warfare."

Two points must be emphasized. First, although the Soviet and Western militaries share many of the same electronic warfare tactics, they do not agree on how these tactics should fit into their overall war plans. Thus the Soviets fit the tactics under their doctrine of radio-electronic struggle and the U.S. fits the tactics under a series of

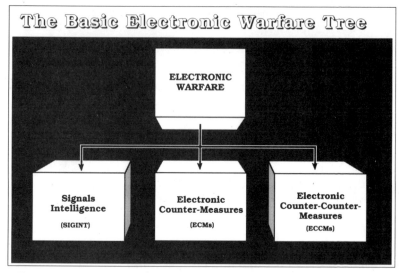

Fig. 2

doctrines called electronic combat or command, control, and communications countermeasures. These different doctrines incorporate electronic warfare tactics into military operations and military strategies, which help decide the victors of battles and wars. The broader doctrines and their expected impact on modern high-technology warfare are discussed in later chapters.

Second, despite all the electronic warfare technology, human factors cannot be eliminated from the picture. The shock of surprise, the fear of death, and the fog of war will be as vitally important in electronic warfare as in "ordinary" warfare.

ELECTRONIC WARFARE TAXONOMY

In the years after World War II, British and American observers named their wartime jamming and electronic eavesdropping tactics "electronic warfare."

A typical postwar definition of electronic warfare, written in 1969 by the U.S. Joint Chiefs of Staff said: "Electronic warfare is military action involving the use of electromagnetic energy to determine, exploit, reduce, or prevent hostile use of the electromagnetic spectrum and action which retains friendly use of the electromagnetic spectrum."[1] This traditional definition divides electronic warfare into three general missions. These are:

- Electronic countermeasures (ECM) intended to jam enemy radars and radios.
- Electronic counter-counter measures (ECCM) intended to overcome enemy jamming.
- Electronic support measures (ESM) intended to gather intelligence on enemy actions by the interception of signals from enemy transmitters.

Although not part of the threefold division of electronic warfare, the mission of Signals Intelligence (SIGINT) — learning about enemy purposes, capabilities and weaponry — is closely associated with electronic warfare. However, SIGINT is carried out by the intelligence services in peace and war, whereas electronic support measures are carried out by combat soldiers in wartime.

The traditional definition of electronic warfare is very narrow and restricted. Narrow because the electronic warfare tactics seems to have no connection to anything else, and restricted because it includes only wartime activities by excluding peacetime electronic warfare. More importantly, the traditional definition also restricts electronic warfare to only *electromagnetic energy*. Thus age-old combat tricks such as camouflage, surprise, and deception, as well as firepower appear to have no role in electronic warfare.

This narrow definition has severely stunted Western understanding of how electronic warfare tactics can be used to help win battles, campaigns and wars.[2]

However, the U.S. military has been cautiously looking beyond the traditional definition and in mid-1990 finally modified the traditional definition. Reflecting a formula suggested by a few Air Force officers as far back as 1978, the new definition says "Electronic warfare is military action involving the use of electromagnetic energy to determine, exploit, reduce, or prevent hostile use of the electromagnetic spectrum *thru damage, destruction and disruption* while retaining friendly use of the electromagnetic spectrum."

This somewhat confused definition simultaneously restricts electronic warfare to use of electromagnetic energy while endorsing physical destruction — presumably with bombs and other high explosives.

Bureaucracies usually make progress in small steps. So, presumably the contradictions and restrictions will eventually be removed. However, the new definition shows how slow the Department of Defense is in understanding how combat has swept past the traditional definition of electronic warfare.

In a subsequent chapter, we shall see how the U.S. services are attempting to prepare themselves for the new demands of electronic combat. First comes a discussion of the traditional vision of electronic warfare.

ELECTRONIC INTELLIGENCE GATHERING

Finding the enemy is the first act of combat. So electronic surveillance must be the first tactic of electronic warfare. Electronic support measures are intended to detect, identify, and find enemy emitters, while signals intelligence is intended to discover enemy capabilities and intentions.

Electronic support measures are usually under the direct control of a field commander and are intended to provide warning time to help defensive measures, such as activating friendly jammers or shooting down an attacking enemy. For instance, a shipboard electronic support measures system could detect the radar signals typical of an incoming antiship missile, or an aircraft-mounted radar warning receiver would warn a pilot he is being watched by enemy radars. Without electronic support measures, ships and aircraft are hopelessly vulnerable to the lighting-quick attacks of modern missiles.

By contrast, signals intelligence is usually associated with less hurried operations in peacetime and wartime, such as the analysis of enemy radar transmissions for subsequent use in developing jam-

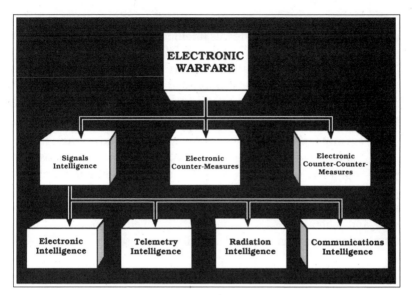

Fig. 3

ming devices, or the interception of enemy conversations. Signals intelligence is usually subdivided into attempts to gather information from enemy communications (communications intelligence, COMINT), from radars (radar intelligence, RADINT), or from enemy missile tests (telemetry intelligence, TELINT). Without signals intelligence operations performed prior to war, each side would be woefully unprepared to deal with the enemy's radars and sensors.

Mere detection of an enemy signal by ESM or SIGINT is not very valuable; it must be interpreted and responded to. For example, an unidentified signal could be an incoming aircraft's radar, a routine radio request for supplies, or a covert signal from a commando group. Signal classification will decide the response.

In combat, signal classification must be done as quickly as possible. Thus, computers are used to tell whether the signal is an attacking missile or nearby radio communications. If the computers decide the signal is a threat, then defense must be quickly activated — bombers may lose altitude to hide behind hills, ships may switch on jamming devices, and fighter aircraft may change direction to catch the enemy by surprise.

But signals intelligence is a noncombat activity, so there is much more time to react when a signals intelligence unit detects a signal. A signal's time of arrival, characteristics, direction of origin, and so on are passed along to any interested party for detailed analysis. Thus the Air Force would be most interested in new enemy antiaircraft radar signals, while the Army would be most interested by unexplained signals coming from an enemy ground unit.

For example, if a new enemy radar were detected, signals intelligence analysts would want to know the radar's maximum power, its pulse-repetition frequency, carrier frequency, modulation, antenna pattern, antenna scan and many other characteristics. They would also like to learn about operational procedures for using the radar, why and when it was developed and deployed, its associated communications patterns, and any and all weaknesses.

During World War II, the Allies' use of signals intelligence allowed them to discover the existence and capabilities of the secret German V-1 flying bomb, even before it had finished its flight tests over the Baltic Sea. By successful interception and decryption of the brief radio conversations held by the troops overseeing the test program, the British were able to deduce the range of the flying bomb and its speed.[3]

However, in wartime operations there is very little time for relaxed analysis. For instance, should an airborne electronics support measures receiver detect energy waves in the I or J radar bands, rapid classification is necessary, for they might well be from an incoming missile. If so, appropriate countermeasures must immediately be taken against it or disaster will strike.

Even more than signal classification, the tactic of decrypting the enemy's scrambled radio communications can reveal an enormous amount of information about the enemy. During World War II, the Allies scored a staggering triumph by breaking nearly all the major German message-scrambling systems, so allowing even the highest level German radio messages to be read almost as soon as the Germans could send them. These secret decrypts, codenamed Ultra, made a great contribution to Allied victory by giving a very detailed view of German war production, military movements, supply problems, combat plans, secret weapon testing results, and morale, as well as telling the Allies whether the Germans believed various Allied deception schemes. Indeed, the success of this tactic was so great that the Ultra intercepts helped shape Allied military operations and wartime strategy.

Similar strategic successes cannot be ruled out today, despite the progress in encryption techniques — as the Walker spy ring proved. So successful was the spy ring in providing the Soviets with details of American communication secrets that top-level Soviet defector Vitaly Yurchenko simply told his Central Intelligence Agency hosts that had there been a war, the Soviets would have won.[4] Given this example, it would not be too surprising if American experts have unscrambled a great many Iraqi messages during the Kuwaiti conflict.

It is usually easier to read lower level communications traffic than top-level messages because lower level messages usually are not scrambled.

Although each low level message may yield little information, they can be put together much as small stones are combined in a mosaic to form a wonderful picture. Thus for the signals intelligence specialist even the most apparently boring signals can be a gem, sometimes giving the answer to a difficult puzzle or suddenly pointing the way to an important new discovery. For example, during World War II, Allied intelligence analysts were at a loss to explain the inexplicably high priority in gasoline ration cards given to a unidentified base on the German peninsula of Peenemunde. The mystery was solved when a reconnaissance aircraft brought back pictures that identified the base as Germany's secret rocket research establishment. Shortly after this discovery, the Royal Air Force attacked and largely destroyed the secret base, setting back German rocket programs by years.

Moreover, even low-level messages can carry very important information. The complexity of modern armies offers many opportunities for communications intelligence gathering simply because there are numerous supporting units each with its own radios, any one of which can give interesting information. For example, during the Battle of the Bulge, German intelligence analysts monitored the radio messages of American rear-area traffic police, so learning of the approach of large armored regiments. This allowed the Fifth Panzer Army to avoid the initial American counterattack.[5]

But deliberate or even accidental deception by the enemy is a persistent danger for electronic eavesdroppers. To reject deception and extract correct information from enemy signals, intelligence analysts must be aware of the enemy's style of operations. Does he use deception? How are the important orders and information distributed? How are enemy radio operators trained? Do lower level officers lie to their superiors?

For example, "Iraqi and Iranian communications also presented another problem. Long before the [Iran-Iraq] war, Iraq and Iran had established a history of using their C^3I systems to 'lie to please' at every command level."[6] If believed by eavesdroppers, such deliberate lies could lead to serious errors or failures to exploit weaknesses.

Even if one cannot read the enemy's electronic mail, much valuable information can be gleaned by watching who is sending messages to whom. This black art is called traffic analysis. It is of very great importance for it can reveal the enemy's location, strength and purpose, even if the enemy codes and encryption systems are unbroken.

Traffic analysis is usually performed by recording and comparing each signal's origin, destination and timing. By comparing the position of numerous emitters, whom they communicate with, and how often, the relationship between the various emitters can be determined. Transmitters can also be watched as they move from location to location, perhaps betraying their identify and purposes.

Thus, heavy signal traffic to many units from a single transmitter moving around in the enemy's immediate tactical rear indicates a headquarters unit. Alternatively, the location of a logistic unit would be betrayed by many signals sent to many units, originating from a transmitter far in the rear that only infrequently changes location.

The information derived from enemy radio conversations can be combined with traffic analysis to provide very accurate and up-to-date information. This is obviously very useful to a commander, either on the defensive or the offensive. Thus Rommel was greatly aided in his desert battles by the 621st *Funkaufklarung* (radio-reconnaissance) company. This small but very well trained company was often capable of speedily telling Rommel the location, strength and intentions of numerous British units.

The information gathered by the company was trusted so much by Rommel that he concentrated his small forces on the most dangerous British units and ignored other units that his intelligence company told him were too weak or timid to attack. Thus Rommel's intelligence chief called the company "a very important factor in Rommel's victories."[7]

According to one of the German officers involved: "The battle of Sollum that raged from the 15th to the 17th June was a classic in the history of wireless intelligence. Not only had we deduced the timing of the start of the British offensive, but during the fighting the radio monitors kept Rommel's headquarters rapidly supplied with the most important enemy signals. These gave him an insight into how the enemy saw the situation, and revealed their concern about ammunition supplies. This in turn inspired Rommel's confidence in the correctness of his own orders, despite the fierceness of the enemy resistance in the tank battles."[8] It is no exaggeration to say that the *Funkaufklarung* was by far the most valuable company Rommel had.

However, still more important to Rommel was the theft of the diplomatic code used by the U.S. Embassy in Egypt, which gave Rommel copies of the very timely and detailed notes of a U.S. embassy official in Cairo, who frequently knew of British plans and strengths.[9]

When these electronic intelligence tactics were combined with good commanders, Germans efforts were handsomely rewarded by impressive operational successes against British armies in the Western desert. But neither success was enough to give Rommel a theater wide success which could only be won by driving the British from the Mediterranean.

Radio intelligence is clearly important in land warfare, but is critical in naval and air warfare. The single worst defeat of U.S. airpower in World War II occurred in 1944 when German air defenses successfully destroyed 53 of 178 bombers that attacked the German oil refineries at Ploesti in Rumania. The Germans had earlier been warned by an alert radio-interception unit that the bomber raid was incoming, even before the bombers were in radar range.[10] But despite this valuable experience, the U.S. Air Force resolutely failed to learn the need for deception, surprise and secrecy. During the Vietnam War, North Vietnamese troops and Viet Cong guerrillas were frequently able to vacate real estate shortly before the arrival of B-52 strikes because the strikes were advertised on Air Force radio warnings, intended to allow U.S. combat units to vacate targeted areas.

Another form of signals intelligence is radiation intelligence. This is the use of accidental transmissions to gather intelligence. For example, during the Vietnam War, North Vietnamese truck convoys

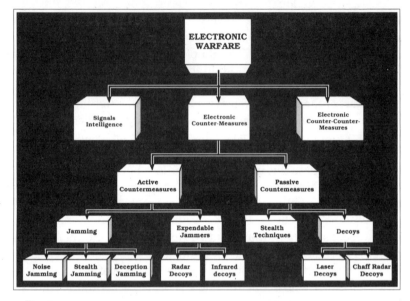

Fig. 4

frequently betrayed their location to U.S. Air Force aircraft equipped with Black Crow radiation intelligence systems, which detected leaking electrical interference from the trucks' spark plugs. After detection, the convoys frequently suffered damaging air attacks.[11] Clearly, there are many opportunities for similar radiation intelligence operations today. A simple example would be discovery of camouflaged headquarters units by the characteristic radiation leaking from their electrical generators or data-processing computers.

Good radio intelligence cannot rule out intelligence failures. To take one of many examples, German radio-intelligence officers knew the night before the D-Day invasion what was to happen at dawn. However, higher level officers did nothing about the warnings, not even to alert the troops defending the Normandy beaches.[12]

Despite these and many other failures, it is no wonder that Major General Ulrich Liss, chief of the German General Staff's Western intelligence branch during World War II, concluded that radio intelligence was the darling of intelligence chiefs. The German chief of staff, Fritz Halder, called radio intelligence the "most copious and the best sort of intelligence." And these officers never even knew of the

Allies greatest intelligence triumph — the Ultra decrypts of Nazi top-level Enigma signals, which allowed the Allies for years to gather amazingly detailed and up-to-date information about the continuing status of the Nazi war machine, its corps, divisions, and regiments, as well as the private concerns of its leaders.

Yet however accurate and timely, electronic intelligence is useless unless acted upon. This brings us to electronic countermeasures.

ELECTRONIC COUNTERMEASURES

The purpose of electronic countermeasures (ECM) is to reduce enemy use of the electromagnetic spectrum by jamming or deceptive transmissions. Broadly speaking, electronic countermeasures can be active or passive. Many types of countermeasures can be used alone or in combination to degrade the enemy's overall electronic warfare system.

According to the traditional definition, electronic countermeasures can only involve *electronic* means such as jamming, not physical or operational measures. However, this traditional definition is completely inadequate, because there is much more to electronic countermeasure than electronics. In the real world, real pilots learn to fly behind hills to prevent enemy radars detecting their approaching aircraft.

Once an enemy system is detected by electronic intelligence, there are many ways of crippling it. One option is to jam the enemy signals by spewing so much random "noise" energy into the electromagnetic spectrum that enemy receivers are unable to hear signals in the cacophony.[13]

These noise-jamming operations usually end up pitting the power output of the jammer against the power output of the radio in a brute-force battle. But many complicating factors, such as propagation paths, antennas and numerous tricks or devices make the situation very complex and confusing.

The noise-jamming approach usually concentrates on maximizing the jammer's power advantage over the receiver. Although it was the dominant electronic countermeasure from the 1940s to the 1980s, and remains the fundamental technique of electronic countermeasures, it has recently being complemented and sometimes replaced by "smart noise," and more importantly by deceptive electronic countermeasures.

Smart noise jamming was used by the Israelis to block a radio link between Syria and Egypt in the 1973 war. The radio link used an impossible-to-jam 500 kilowatt medium-wave radio antenna transmitting Morse code signals. The Israelis were able to so precisely mimic the dots and dashes of the Morse code transmissions that the radio signals were completely garbled, although they were still received by the Syrians and Egyptians.

Deceptive jamming includes manipulative and imitative deception. It is usually used by a single ship or aircraft to defend itself against one or two target tracking radars, whereas noise jamming is typically used to protect several aircraft against several search radars.

Imitative deception is the introduction of friendly signals disguised as enemy signals into enemy systems. One of the most common tactical uses of imitative deceptive countermeasures is the creation of numerous "ghost" friendly aircraft on an enemy radar screen, achieved by an airborne jammer retransmitting the same signal that the enemy radar reflects off the aircraft, but at a time when the radar is looking in another direction. This technique can fool the radar into believing that it sees another aircraft in that direction.

For example, the U.S. Navy is fielding an expendable deceptive jammer which is dropped by aircraft to broadcast a larger echo than the real target, hopefully capturing a tracking radar's attention for enough time to allow the aircraft to attack and escape. Several improved types of expendable device, some of which combine infrared and radar decoys, are under development. Another new jamming device in use by the Israelis and possibly by the U.S. Navy is the towed decoy which trails behind the aircraft trying to decoy missiles away from the aircraft.

Although imitative deception techniques may require only a relatively small power output, accurate signals intelligence must be available to ensure that the deceptive signals match the real signals. Otherwise, the enemy will easily recognize and reject the deceptive signals. This problem is very complex; aircraft must frequently know what the next enemy radar pulse will look like if they are to fool the radar. Thus the imitative jammer needs to know the precise nature of the radar's future transmissions, such as the number of pulses per second, when they will arrive, the duration of each pulse, their bandwidths and most important, their waveforms.

There is more to imitative deception tactics than jamming radars: In December 1942 a German submarine transmitted false orders to a convoy, so redirecting it homeward, after listening to and sinking one of its escorts.[14]

A subtler type of deception jamming is manipulative deception, which is meant to eliminate revealing, or convey misleading, indicators to confuse hostile forces. For example, a common tactic in air warfare is for aircraft to drop extremely hot flares intended to fool deadly infrared missiles into chasing a flare, not the real aircraft. In recent years TV news reports have shown low-flying Soviet or Israeli aircraft dropping a stream of burning magnesium flares to confuse Stinger or SAM-7 missiles.

Alternatively, radio silence could fool the enemy into thinking that no opposing force was present — possibly making him vulnerable to a surprise attack. For example, in the early 1942 Crimean offensive, German General von Manstein tricked a Soviet commander into massing his defenses at the wrong place by operating a false radio net simulating a Panzer division on a quiet sector of the front. The Panzer division then broke through another sector and spearheaded the total destruction of two complete Soviet armies of around 140,000 men. Needless to say, the Soviets have not forgotten how such a deception tactic ballooned into a German operational triumph.

Active deceptive jamming includes a wider variety of tactics than noise jamming. These include the feeding of incorrect height information to an aircraft's terrain following radar, the issuing of spurious signals to make the proximity fuzes of artillery shells explode long before they approach the ground, the distorting of navigation signals used by the enemy's guided missiles and so on. One of the most important attributes of deception jamming is that it is inherently smart, and not always obvious. Because it is more difficult to identify, deception jamming may continue undisturbed for a longer duration.

But while deception jamming needs more accurate intelligence than does noise jamming, it also needs much less jamming power. This reduction in power demands is important because aircraft cannot generate much electrical power. Thus noise jamming is typically used by specialized aircraft with powerful jammers designed to screen other aircraft from enemy search radars. The attack aircraft then use deception jammers to confuse tracking radars long enough to attack and escape.

Stealth is another type of jamming. One example is Israeli signals that caused Soviet-built radios used by Arab forces to reject all incoming signals. The Israeli signals actually tricked the radios into greatly raising their cut-off threshold intended to filter out normal background electromagnetic noise, so effectively blanking out all incoming signals. This feat ensured that Arab radio operators could hear nothing when they put on their earphones, despite working radios.

A related form of stealth jamming uses jamming signals that masquerade as background noise. This is difficult, because it requires that power levels be low enough to look like background static, but high enough to disrupt enemy signals. An early application of this technique occurred during the 1941 "Channel Dash," when the Germans transferred several large warships from France to Norway through the English Channel. By gradually increasing the level of radar jamming over a period of weeks, the Germans led the inexperienced British crews to conclude the jamming was just background noise. Thus when the Germans ships sailed rapidly one morning through the English Channel, the jamming concealed their approach until they were within sight of the coast and there was too little time for the British to respond.

A potentially new and revolutionary form of jamming is computer-virus countermeasures, suggested in an article by Myron Cramer and Stephen Pratt.[15] A computer virus is a small software program whose primary purpose is to replicate itself inside computerized systems, much as a virus replicates itself inside the human body. The computer virus can be designed to carry out some form of destructive action that erases or alters information inside its target computer, so preventing computerized weapon systems from doing their job properly, if at all. Cramer and Pratt suggest that such viruses could be forced into enemy computer systems by conventional radio transmissions, or by spies able to copy them into software programs where the virus could lie undetected until activated at the beginning of war.

These viruses could prove enormously destructive, because they might spread rapidly throughout computerized communications networks used to link radars, radios, computers, and command centers.

Once the viruses spread themselves, they could wreck entire networks before they could be detected and eliminated by antivirus software (computerized antibodies, so to speak). More dangerously, viruses could slightly alter data, causing errors to occur, missiles to miss their targets, and computer systems themselves to alter data. Such a subtle effect would be hard to detect and also hard to eliminate during a battle.

The danger of viruses was largely confirmed in a February 1990 U.S. Army document that said Army battlefield computers could be infected by viruses introduced over radio links. This means that the enemy will have many opportunities to introduce many types of different viruses into computer networks, in the hope that at least one type of virus will cause damage.

Also, if viruses can be introduced into computer networks by air, surely they can be introduced into computerized radars and radios.

Importantly, if — or more likely, when — a computer was infected, the destructive virus could quickly spread to many other frontline computers because of the tight links throughout the C^3I system. Also, the viruses would spread to higher level computers, including computers in the U.S.

From there, viruses could spread into the civilian telephone network and civilian computer systems, paralyzing military logistics centers, arms factories, banks, and other vital elements of the defense industry.[16]

The U.S. Army and Navy, as well as the super-secret National Security Agency, have begun to address these problems. Thus the agency is sponsoring development of virus-killing software — computerized antibiotics, so to speak — while the Army has begun to test its computers against radio-delivered viruses and has asked industry to study ways of attacking enemy C^3I networks with radio-delivered viruses.[17]

Little is known of the U.S. government's work on the virus threat because of strict secrecy. However, it is not at all implausible that the U.S. has already prepared viruses to attack an enemy's computerized systems, such as those operated by the Iraqis in the Kuwaiti conflict.

These various forms of active noise, deception, smart, and virus jamming are complemented by many passive deception jamming techniques.

Passive deception measures include smokescreens, radar reflectors, and dummy heat sources intended to hide or disguise friendly forces from enemy surveillance devices.

The most important passive jamming tactic is the dropping of chaff, which consists of clouds of small metal-coated strips. Chaff is normally used to protect aircraft and ships from targeting radars.

However, because the length of each chaff strip must correspond to the radar's wavelength, they are best used against high-frequency, shorter range radars. The lower frequency, longer range search radars can use such a long wavelength that chaff strips would be to long to use. A more serious problem with chaff is that radars using Doppler signal processing can see through the chaff clouds. Doppler radars are designed to only see fast-moving aircraft, not slow-moving chaff clouds.

Another potential passive jamming technique is changing the propagation properties of the air so that radar waves are bent and twisted in unpredictable directions. This is discussed in a book by Soviet authors Vakin and Shustov, although there is still no published evidence that a practical method has been developed.[18]

An increasingly favored passive deception technique is stealth design of aircraft, ships and tanks. The purpose of stealthy designs is to minimizes the radar, radio, infrared, optical, and acoustic "signatures" of vehicles, so making them harder to detect. Although nothing can be made invisible, a stealthy vehicle will often have the critical advantage of getting the first shot in.

Stealth techniques are as old as the first use of camouflage to hide from enemy eyes. But modern stealth technology began with the easiest and most urgent applications: reducing infrared emissions from aircraft to protect them from heat-detecting sensors. Thus during World War II, the Germans spread a chemical over submarine hulls to hide them from any Allied infrared detectors. This was a technical success, but also a gross intelligence failure because the Allies never did develop infrared detectors. More recently, Soviet designers tried to cool and dilute the hot engine exhausts of Afghanistan-based helicopters to prevent their destruction by heat-seeking Stinger missiles.

During the 1970s, the United States began an ambitious program to develop aircraft largely invisible to radar by relying chiefly on shapes that reflected radar echoes away from the radar, so minimizing the returning echo. This effort resulted in the development and production of fifty-nine F-117A Stealth fighters. Nothing in life is free, so the F-117A's stealthiness reportedly came at the price of being unable to dogfight or carry a large bomb load.[19] However, it is perfectly possible the fighter could sneak close enough during a confused battle to attack the enemy with medium range guided weapons.

Further research produced the B-2 Stealth bomber, 132 of which were planned to be built to penetrate the dense Soviet air defense system at a lifetime cost of $120 billion or more. Unlike the F-117A, which relies on sharp-angled radar reflectors, the B-2 relies more on a rounded shape and radar absorbing materials to reduce radar echoes.

The chief advantage of stealth technology is that it effectively reduces the range of enemy search radars, allowing the stealth-design aircraft to get close enough to the enemy to destroy him with a guided missile before he can react. Another profit from stealth technology flows from the fact that electronic warfare techniques are always synergistic — the effect of the combined parts is always greater than the sum of the individual parts. Thus the reduced radar cross sections of the B-2 and F-117A also reduce the jamming power required for the aircraft to blind search radars. This reduction in power output also increases the opportunity for stealthy noise jamming and reduces the chances that passive sensors could be used to track the jamming signal.

But stealth technology does not make the aircraft truly invisible to radar or other sensors. There are many powerful radars that can detect even very small nonmetallic targets such as insects or birds at long range, so even the best stealth aircraft will have to rely on a noisy and confusing electromagnetic battlefield to conceal their approach.

Also the extreme cost of building stealthy aircraft has forced a reduction of the Air Force's B-2 program from 132 bombers to 75 bombers. Almost certainly, Congress will reduce those numbers to as low as fifteen bombers — a poor result for $50 billion of investment in research, production and operating costs. Similar cost problems have forced continual reductions in the planned numbers of the U.S. Navy's two-seat A-12 tactical stealth bomber.

Aside from the obvious heavy financial costs, a critical problem with stealth aircraft is the fact that their sensors are limited by the need to be stealthy. This restricts them to using passive sensors or very modern and very expensive hard-to-detect radars if they want to find targets without revealing themselves. Moreover, why should stealth aircraft risk themselves by attacking targets? Would it not be better to use them to find targets for ground-launched long-range missiles?

However, stealth techniques are being employed in an increasing number of weapons, including warships, helicopters, and missiles such as the American advanced cruise missile. Certainly, stealth technology probably has an interesting and expensive future ahead of it.

One possible hint of this future appeared in the U.S. magazine *Aviation Week and Space Technology,* in an article describing how U.S. civilian researchers had discovered a special type of chemical called Schiff base salts that absorb radar waves. According to one of the discoverers, it would only cost around $30,000 to cover a combat aircraft with a special coating capable of absorbing 80 percent of radar waves across a wide bandwidth.[20] The story also said the Pentagon would test the new materials by the end of 1987. Although the technology was immediately classified after the article appeared, it should surprise no one if future research produced dramatically new technologies radically altering each side's ability to hide from or find each other.

The traditionally narrow definition of electronic warfare has been somewhat adjusted to cope with new technologies. One of the most obvious new technologies are antiradiation missiles, which passively home in on enemy radio and radar emissions, just as heat seeking antiaircraft missiles home in on the heat emitted by aircraft.

Antiradiation missiles are most used by air forces to scare enemy antiaircraft radars into silence, so greatly simplifying life for attacking pilots and jamming aircraft.

These missiles are not included in the traditional definition of electronic warfare and cannot be designated as active or passive, but are so useful they have been patched on as an electronic countermeasure.

Perhaps the earliest antiradiation missile was the German 200 kilometer (125 mile) range Hagelkorn, which was tested in 1943 as a means of attacking land-based aircraft navigation beacons. The U.S. Navy led the postwar development of antiradiation missiles, leading to their first use in 1966 against Soviet-supplied and -manned radars in North Vietnam.[21] The antiradiation missiles were also the principal armament of U.S. Air Force Wild Weasel electronic warfare aircraft, which hunted down radars by tracking their emissions and then attacked them with antiradiation missiles and ordinary bombs.

After the Vietnam experience, the U.S. continued with development of antiradiation missiles, creating the High-speed Anti-Radiation Missile or HARM missile, but the Soviets were not far behind and supplied the Egyptians with antiradiation missiles for use against Israeli command centers during the 1973 war.

Further development led to the Air Force's development of unmanned, suicide drone aircraft carrying a high-explosive warhead and an antiradiation guidance system. These Tacit Rainbow drones are intended to loiter over enemy forces until a radar begins transmitting, and then dive onto the target to destroy it.

Also, the Soviets have reportedly fielded an air-to-air antiradiation missile capable of homing onto radars in enemy aircraft. If true, these AA-10 missiles could scare NATO fighter pilots into turning off their radars, so largely blinding Allied pilots. Two similar U.S. systems, called Seekbat and Brazo, were developed in the early 1970s, but were canceled after successful tests.[22] Since then, the U.S. has not developed an air-to-air antiradiation capability, unless such a capability has been secretly included in Air Force's latest missile, the Advanced Medium-Range Air-to-Air Missile.

Given the increasing difficulty of jamming advanced radars, it is likely there is a promising future for antiradiation missiles.

Electronic countermeasures can help a defender as much as an attacker. Thus defensive smoke screens — not included in the traditional definition of electronic warfare — ensured the survival for several years of the German battleship Tirpitz as it lay at anchor in a Norwegian fjord. The British and German use of false targets, especially when combined with jamming of navigational aids, often caused bombers to wildly miss their targets during World War II. Similar techniques could be used in modern war, augmented by new tricks. For example, if a ground war breaks out over the possession of Kuwait, will the Iraqis burn the oil fields to cut out light from the sun and stars? The loss of light would surely make it harder for U.S. soldiers and pilots to find targets, day or night.

It should be noted that 100 percent effectiveness in jamming or deceiving the enemy system is not always necessary. Often enough, only a crucial command or communications node needs to be overloaded or damaged for the overall enemy system to be disrupted enough for a particular tactic or even a large military operation to succeed. This is clearly a much simpler and more achievable task than trying to blind all enemy radars and deafen all enemy radios.

For instance, should the communications links between an attacking mechanized infantry battalion and its artillery support be jammed just at the moment when the infantry prepared to advance to the defenders' lines, the defenders would still have gained a major local advantage because the attackers' artillery would be unable to intervene during the climax of the battle. This localized electronic warfare success could then leave the damaged attacking force vulnerable to a subsequent counterattack.

Thus proper timing of electronic countermeasures is crucial to success. Clearly, there is little point in jamming artillery communications three minutes after it has completed its mission. But proper timing is very difficult to achieve because of the complexity and chaos of battle.

In the field of electronic warfare, dilemmas and trade-offs are legion. One of the more common dilemmas is the decision whether it is better to jam an enemy signal or to extract information from it. Although both operations can be carried out by using several signals intelligence units, a single operator must often quickly choose one or the other option. One of the earliest examples of this dilemma is related from a ship's brig by the unfortunate radio operator tasked with monitoring the "enemy" fleet in a 1903 U.S. Navy exercise during an era when the forces were codenamed Blue and Gold: "I was on watch and everything was working fine. I heard a message begin, and the first three letters were G, O, and L, so I knew it was going to be GOLD and that it was the other side. I reached for the [morse] key [to jam the message], but the Flag Lieutenant who was with me said, 'No, don't do that, I want the entire message.' When the message was ended, the Lieutenant said, 'make interference,' and I said, 'Sir, it is no use now. The message has gone with a speed of 186,000 miles a second and we can't catch up with it.' So here I am now on bread and water."[23]

Sometimes it is better to exploit rather than jam a new enemy system. Not only can military intelligence be gained, but enemy signals can be used to increase one's own effectiveness. An excellent

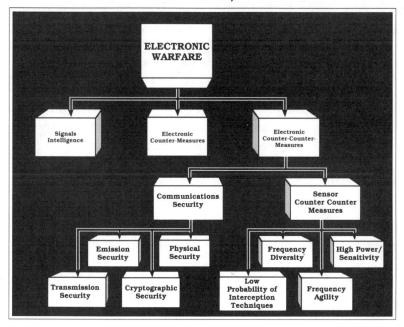

Fig. 5

example of friendly exploitation occurred during World War II antisubmarine campaign, when the British realized that German naval aircraft were using a new and very accurate radio navigation technique. On the suggestion of the brilliant British scientist R.V. Jones, it was decided not to jam this navigation system, but rather to train British crews to use it, so ensuring that the British antisubmarine patrols were considerably helped in their war against the U-boats.[24]

This trick is being replayed: many companies produce cheap navigation receivers that exploit signals from the U.S. Defense Department's network of Navstar navigation satellites. Once armed with the receivers, pilots and ship captains of all nations can accurately determine their location.

Because of the vast number of emitters and receivers in modern armies, perhaps the greatest problem faced by communicators and electronic warfare specialists is electronic fratricide.

This occurs when friendly electronic countermeasures hinder friendly systems. For example, airborne jamming intended to hide the approach of the Allied invasion fleet in 1944 caused a great deal of communications disruption in the fleet. However, this example is only the tip of a much greater potential fratricidal iceberg that has never been seen because no one has ever switched on the tens of thousands of emitters and receivers to be used in any future war. In all likelihood, the thousands of radios and radars will jam each other repeatedly and constantly, causing great confusion — which would be worsened by use of deliberate jamming — that could only be alleviated by skilled personnel and advanced antijamming techniques, so called electronic counter-countermeasures.

To deal with the problem, the U.S. military is developing computerized management systems to help soldiers quickly change radio networks, coordinate the use of frequencies, and distribute new scrambling codes.

ELECTRONIC COUNTER-COUNTERMEASURES

The third branch of electronic warfare tactics, electronic counter-countermeasures or ECCM, traditionally includes all efforts to foil signals intelligence and electronic countermeasures.

There are many electronic counter-countermeasures techniques designed to maximize the value of sensor and communications systems, including communications security (COMSEC), which is the effort to deny the enemy information from friendly communications signals. Like many other electronic counter-countermeasures techniques, communications security incorporates transmission security to prevent the enemy detecting friendly messages, emission security to prevent detection of accidental signals, cryptosecurity to make messages unreadable, and physical security to stop the enemy stealing what he could not get by electronic means.

Communications security is intended to frustrate enemy signals intelligence gathering activities. Poor communications security can lead to tactical failures and even operational disaster — as the Germans proved in 1914 when they smashed the Tsarist armies by penetrating gaps in the Russian lines discovered by listening to poorly encoded orders broadcast from the Russian headquarters.[25]

Even broader success was achieved by the British when they decrypted the 1916 German telegram offering Mexico a slice of the United States if Mexico joined Germany in war against the U.S. Publication of this intercepted Zimmerman telegram outraged American public opinion and helped push the country into joining the war against Germany.

But even these great successes were overshadowed by the Allies' amazing triumph in World War II when they were able to decrypt messages from the Enigma cipher machine used by the top officers of the Nazi military. This coup laid bare nearly every secret of the Nazi war machine, including day-to-day divisional strengths, U-boat locations, upcoming attack plans, unit deployments, and the intentions and worries of Hitler and his general staff — truly a war-winning triumph.

Although cryptosecurity is vital, transmission security is even more important, because it can prevent the enemy from even detecting friendly signals, let alone understanding them.

The most important part of transmission security is good operating practice. Good radio discipline — the ability to transmit no more information than is required at minimum power levels, using proper codes and procedures — is vital to hinder enemy communications intelligence and traffic analysis. One German officer noted how the excellent radio intelligence gathered by the Afrika Korps in the desert was greatly reduced following imposition by the British of good communications security measures, which was primarily the disciplined use of radio systems. But "the wireless intercept harvest improved again in Tunisia, thanks to American carelessness in wireless traffic."[26]

Similarly, if radio operators carelessly allow enemy detection by transmitting with too much power, or a pilot reveals his approach by turning on jamming devices too early, poor discipline will have nullified the effect of even the most sophisticated electronic counter-countermeasures systems.

In any future war, there will be little time and little likelihood of a second chance to learn radio discipline. Thus the better trained in peacetime the operators are, the more likely it is that they will survive and possibly contribute to victory.

But good operators must have good equipment, and modern technology has created many means of promoting transmission security, including frequency hopping and spread-spectrum radio systems.

Frequency hopping radios break messages into small packets and then quickly transmit them at normal power levels over a large number of different frequencies by hopping from one frequency to another in a prearranged but extremely complex fashion. Friendly radios are able to gather the signals because they know on what frequency each message packet will appear.

Although the enemy will usually be able to identify and record some of the individual information packets because they stand out clearly against the background noise, he will be unable to easily follow the signal across the frequencies rapidly enough to jam or intercept all the information packets. Most frequency hopping radios change frequency ten to 500 times a second, but some radios change tens of thousands of times per second. This makes it more difficult to intercept the entire message or to locate the transmitter, but cannot prevent the enemy detecting some part of the signals.

An even more advanced technology can hide a low-power radio signal in background electromagnetic static, in the hope of denying the enemy the ability to even recognize the weak radio signal. This technique is known as spread-spectrum transmission, and is done by dividing friendly digital signals into many low-power information packets, which are then transmitted by frequency hopping techniques across a wide range of frequencies. As long as the receiver knows the pattern by which the message is being broken up and transmitted throughout the bandwidth, it can reassemble the message by using sensitive electronic filters to strip away background noise and add up the information packets.

But since an enemy will not generally know the code by which the message is being broken up and transmitted, he will be unable to detect or recognize many of the information packets buried in the static. If the enemy is unable to even detect a signal, there is no way he can intercept the message, let alone decode, analyze, or decrypt it.

Another important technique with a low probability of interception is the use of highly directional antennas. For example, an ultrahigh or very high frequency radio or radar receiver can use a highly directional antenna that is deliberately designed to transmit and receive radiowaves very poorly in all directions except for signals within a narrow cone of coverage. This allows the radio to prevent signals getting near enemy listeners, and also prevent the radio picking up enemy jamming signals.

These frequency-hopping, spread-spectrum and directional-antenna techniques can be applied to radars just as easily as to radios. Thus a radar receiver might be made jam-resistant by giving it spread-spectrum ability, allowing it to strip out all the jammer's electromagnetic signals that do not match the particular signal being transmitted by the radar. With good spread-spectrum techniques, the radar may not even be detectable in the background noise, allowing the radar the normally rare gratification of surprising its target.

Another important set of security techniques is emission security. For example, many radios keep their generators operating even when they are not transmitting. Unless the generators are designed to minimize radiation leakage, sensitive enemy signals intelligence receivers will detect and classify the emissions. It would be a short step from associating the generator with its radio to destroying nontransmitting radios by targeting their generators. Effective electronic silencing of all military equipment — radios, radars, diesel motors, generators, computers, receivers — is not easy or cheap, yet is crucial for high-technology warfare.

For example — during World War II the German Metox radar-intercept system was developed to allow U-boats to detect submarine search radars on patrolling Allied antisubmarine aircraft. But had the Allies had adequate electronic intelligence, they could have sunk many Metox-equipped U-boats by homing in on the radiation accidentally emitted from the Metox receiver, which could be picked up at 115 km (70 mi), according to Gordon.[27]

Another important form of technical electronic counter-countermeasures is the encoding or encryption of friendly signals, known as cryptosecurity. Encoding messages means the one-for-one replacement of message phrases or words by prearranged words. For example, the codeword Barabrossa was intended to hide the meaning of references to the upcoming German surprise on the Soviet Union in 1941.

Encryption differs from encoding because it scrambles signal elements in a prearranged and often exceedingly complex — but ultimately consistent — pattern, theoretically allowing only friendly units to unscramble and understand the signal. For instance, the

German Enigma encryption machine had three rotating wheels each with twenty-six pins, as well as several sockets and levers. Using new positions daily for the wheels, pins and sockets, as well as sometimes a fourth wheel, users could encrypt signals by forcing signals to travel through the machine in complex but consistent paths. Given the extremely large number of possible paths — 150 million, million, million according to one source[28] — the Germans assumed that the Allies would never be able to decrypt the messages. Happily, the Germans were wrong and the Allies regularly decrypted German signals, using captured equipment, very smart people, pencils, and several primitive computers about as powerful as those in a modern microwave oven, so giving a major boost in the campaigns against the Nazis.

The development of digital communications and computer systems has increased the complexity of encryption schemes by millions of times. Although information about such topics is extremely secret, it seems certain the effort needed to break encryption schemes is much greater now than in World War II. Perhaps the only way to break computer-created encryption schemes is with a very fast computer (or a spy or extremely clever mathematicians). It is still perfectly possible that powerful number-crunching computer systems have kept pace with encryption machines. It would be a foolish mistake — on a par with the Nazis' misplaced faith in their Enigma machine — to think modern encryption schemes are unbreakable.

A critical question is the time needed to crack codes and ciphers. Modern encryption techniques may not prevent the enemy from eventually reading the message simply because he is free to mass many powerful computers to test billions and billions of possible answers. But in combat, even simple hand-written encryption systems can suffice to delay the enemy from reading the message before the information becomes obsolete.

The only encryption scheme claimed to be unbreakable is also extremely difficult to use. This is the one-time pad, which is simply a pair of matched pads containing identical strings of letters or numbers, so allowing sender and receiver to understand a short message. Since each page has a different encryption scheme and is used only once, it is practically impossible to decrypt the message because the schemes are so random and the message so short that no patterns should be detectable no matter how many messages are intercepted.

Nevertheless, Soviet electronic warfare expert A. I. Palii said no code is unbreakable.[29]

The price paid for such security is that the messages can only be sent between two people, and that new pads must be distributed once the old pads are used up. Clearly, this method is useless on the modern battlefield, but is quite useful for individual spies who want to talk with their headquarters.

In peace or war, codes and encryption schemes are usually broken by building on previous knowledge about enemy systems. If enough skill is applied and enough is known about the enemy encryption system and communications procedures, then mistakes such as repetitious message formats, simultaneous use of old and new schemes, common wording in broken and unbroken messages, and operator errors are used to lay bare the enemy's communications. Exploitation of such human errors lay behind the Allied Ultra success in World War II; they will likely be the basis of future decryption successes.

There are many other technical counter-countermeasures that are not included in communications security. Most concern radar because this is where the current technological contest is sharpest.

A basic electronic counter-countermeasure for active sensors is increased power on target. The higher the power and the greater the signal-to-noise ratio, then the quicker the jamming will be overpowered or "burned through." Of course, power cannot usually be increased without paying a price, such as reduced mobility or an increased chance of alerting distant enemies.

But there are various ways of increasing the power of echoes reflected from targets without emitting more watts. For example, a relatively new signal-processing technology is used in pulse-compression or chirp radars. They use complex software to squeeze the echo of a powerful long-duration radar pulse into a short- duration echo. This allows a long-duration radar pulse, which gives good range but poor target discrimination, to give good range and good target discrimination.

Another basic counter-countermeasure is frequency diversity. For example, if an antiaircraft gun's radar is jammed, the gunners can revert to a tried and trusted alternative: the Mark 1 eyeball and Model A brain. If it is dark, they can use infrared sensors. If it is cloudy, radio direction-finding. If there are no answers from passive sensors, then they can make an educated guess. If that does not work, they can just keep firing at random. In battle, anything is usually better than nothing.

Even within individual sensors, it is possible to build in diversity. For example, the Stinger antiaircraft missile uses both infrared and ultraviolet to look for the target. With radars, flexibility is gained by exploiting as many radar bands as possible.

Radars that are able to switch quickly between several frequencies are called frequency agile. The ability to rapidly change signal frequencies frustrates radar jammers in the same way frequency hopping frustrates communications jammers. A radar that is rapidly changing frequencies will force a jammer to waste its power across the entire bandwidth, allowing the radar to burn through the jamming quicker. Given these obvious advantages, radar designers build their radars to use as large a part of the spectrum as possible and to jump from frequency to frequency as quickly as possible.

Ideally, an air defense system should include many diverse types of search radars, tracking radars and other active and passive sensors exploiting the radio, optical and infrared frequencies. The diversity of frequencies and sensor types should ensure that at least one sensor can track the enemy at all times, despite jamming.

And if good communications systems are able to link all the sensors and weapons in this idealized integrated air defense network, then the attacking aircraft would have to jam or suppress all the sensors to prevent any weapons from being used against them. Clearly, knocking out all sensors would be very unlikely, unless the attacker committed an inordinate amount of resources to the task.

However, the problem with such a supposedly ideal collection of linked sensors is that the information can only be integrated with great difficulty. Without integration, the sensors are unable to help each other when jammed or attacked individually. Integration is sometimes extremely difficult because the data must be correctly and immediately transmitted without creating false targets or losing real targets. This requirement for real-time data has been the stumbling block of data-fusion systems so far, but the rapid fall in the price of computers has opened up many new possibilities.

Frequency diversity and sensor integration barely scratch the beginning of possible sensor electronic counter-countermeasures. There are still many more esoteric tricks in the designer's arsenal, including pulse jitter, coherent sidelobe cancellation, sidelobe blanking, constant false alarm rate, changing polarization, changing scan pattern, or simply tracking the jammer.[30] Moreover, many techniques can be combined; modern radars use spread-spectrum, monopulse tracking, and backup passive tracking. In addition, it would be very surprising if there were not many secret tricks waiting to surprise all participants in a future war.

Despite the importance of technical counter-countermeasures, they usually work best when used in conjunction with operational counter-countermeasures, active or passive. The simplest of many passive operational responses is radio silence, which is supposed to preclude the detection of friendly units by enemy receivers. The radars can then be turned on at the most opportune moment to inflict damage before the enemy jammers can respond. For example, when faced by the slow U.S. buildup in late 1990, the Iraqi military shut down its radar networks in an effort to foil American signals intelligence and traffic analysis. Such action revealed a disturbingly high level of expertise for a so-called developing nation.[31]

But silence has the obvious drawback that the sensors are not being used. And it should be noted that radio silence is not easily achieved because operators make mistakes and highly complex weapons and large military organizations both tend to leak electronic signals.

Human ingenuity will also throw up many interesting responses to jamming. One of the more amusing examples is R.V. Jones' story of how German jamming of radars based on the Mediterranean island of Malta was defeated. The Allies simply maintained regular operations as if the jamming was having no effect, so disheartening the Germans that they halted the entirely successful jamming.[32]

The combination of these numerous and clever technical and operational sensor counter-countermeasures suggest that they are very difficult to defeat.

According to Schleher, "there is little capability against pulse compression, continuous wave, or noiselike (spread-spectrum) waveforms."[33] Whether the signals are radio or radar, distinguishing between numerous spread-spectrum signals in a noisy environment is "practically impossible."[34]

Advanced counter-countermeasures techniques will change the communications intelligence arena. "The introduction of frequency hopping spread-spectrum communications systems is rapidly making the listening versus jamming debate academic because it is virtually impossible to listen to these types of transmissions."[35] Although this may be so during well-organized annual exercises, it may not be so during the confusion of battle.

CONCLUSION

By now, many readers might be convinced counter-countermeasures can resist all countermeasures. They might also be convinced that countermeasures can successfully defeat counter-countermeasures.

Who knows? Certainly not this author.

The technology is just too complex, there are too many secrets, war is too confusing, and soldiers in combat are too inventive at finding new ways to use technology for any but the roughest predictions.

However, on balance, in the war between electronic countermeasures and electronic counter-countermeasures, the advantage seems to be with the sensors and communicators rather than the jammers.

We can make this judgment using basic economics. The options available to the communicators and the sensor operators are often cheaper than those available to the jammer and hider.

A prime example is the tale of the United States' B-1b bomber. Although it is a $300 million dollar aircraft carrying 2,270 kg (5,000 pounds) of the largest and most expensive electronic warfare suite so far developed, it is unable to blind the latest Soviet radars. Undoubtedly, the extremely complex electronic countermeasures system of the B-1b is a failure — its jammers often jam the aircraft's own passive systems as well as its own terrain-following radar.

In response to this failure, critics charged that its rushed developed left no time for careful design. They are absolutely correct, but if the electronics had been developed at a slower and steadier pace, they would only have fallen even further behind radar technology.

The Air Force's only answer is to ask for billions of dollars to build the stealthy B-2 bomber — whose price is at least $500 million per aircraft, not counting roughly $20 billion spent on development.

The B1-b case is mirrored by the Air Force's very ambitious effort to develop airborne radar jamming pods capable of protecting each fighter aircraft against all radar threats, an effort that even currently active Air Force officers have described as a string of failures. The programs have nearly always fallen behind schedule, cost more than budgeted, and failed to do the job.

The real problem seems to be that it is extremely difficult to develop countermeasures that can defeat useful numbers of the wide variety of relatively cheap, relatively powerful sensors and communications systems linked to relatively powerful weapons.

But by no means is the fight over. Sensors and communications systems face new threats, such as stealth aircraft, antiradiation missiles, and destruction once they are radio-located. Sensors can be used to target other sensors. After all, the ultimate countermeasure is a 500 kg bomb landing on a radar crew.

Also very important is the critical role of time and communications in battle. A modern sensor can easily discriminate decoys from real targets on the battlefield, but can it transmit the information to its associated weapon in the chaos and confusion of war, before the attacker does damage and flees?

Measure and countermeasure rapidly pile up on each other, and there is no end in sight. Surely, no one can expect a magic bullet to decide the final issue. The real effect of any new countermeasure, or the response to it, is a temporary advantage, no matter how dramatic it may seem at first appearance. Each new step on the ladder of measure–countermeasure gives temporary relative superiority, which must be capitalized on with successful attacks and a subsequent peace treaty if there is to be a winner and a loser.

Although narrow technological countermeasures to the enemy's radar and communications are critical, the most important countermeasure is breadth. Like a three-legged stool, an army reliant on a few types of weapons can be toppled if only one leg is severed. However, an army that invests in a wide variety of technology, weapons, and tactics will be much harder to topple.

But such breadth requires high-quality soldiers with a good understanding of electronic warfare, extensive training, excellent leadership, and hopefully some combat experience. In the confusion of battle, these "soft" factors can have a much greater impact than a few superior weapons, and can even allow a technologically inferior but smarter army to soundly beat its opponent.

Vital to such breadth is a good electronic warfare doctrine, one that shows soldiers how to best use electronic warfare tactics to win campaign and theater victories.

To be useful, electronic warfare doctrines are much broader than the limited concept of electronic warfare with its threefold division into electronic support measures, countermeasures, and counter-countermeasures described in this chapter.

When broadened to include other ideas, such as surprise, deception, the importance of time, the destructive effect of firepower, as well as the central role of destructive attacks on command and control systems and radars, electronic warfare tactics become *electronic combat doctrines.*

This intellectual leap forward allows electronic warfare to power-fully affect the results of military campaigns and theater offensives, and to perhaps help determine the outcome of a war. The nature and impact of modern electronic combat doctrines are the subject of the rest of this book.

Notes

1. Lt. Col. Richard Fitts et al., eds., *The Strategy of Electromagnetic Conflict* (Los Altos, Ca: Peninsula Publishing, 1980), p. 1.
2. The narrowness of the official definition was caused by American and British disregard of their experiences during the bombing campaigns against Germany and Japan, and the naval campaign against the German U-Boats. The Allies were the victors, quick to disarm and quick to forget once the war was won, and so the lessons of World War II had to be quickly relearned in Korea and Vietnam. But those who relearned the lessons were individual designers building technologically ambitious bombing aircraft. Therefore the emphasis on integration of electronic and non-electronic techniques, the importance of time, the value of deception and surprise so recognized by the desperate British in 1940 and Germans from 1943 to 1945 have only recently begun to be reincorporated by the West into its military thinking - as chapter nine will show.
3. R.V. Jones, *The Wizard War*. (New York: Coward, McCann, Geoghehan, 1978), p. 368.

4. Of course, since Yurchenko's redefection to the USSR indicates he might have been a false defector, this claim could have been intended to cause trouble in the U.S. Navy and intelligence community.

5. David Kahn, *The Codebreakers* (New York: Macmillan, 1967), p. 208.

6. Anthony Cordesman and Abraham Wagner *The Lessons of Modern War* (Boulder and San Francisco: Westview, 1990), Vol. 1, *The Iran-Iraq War*, p. 419.

7. Ibid., p. 476.

8. Hans-Otto Behrendt, *Rommel's Intelligence in the Desert Campaign* (William Kimber & Co. Ltd, 1985), p. 83.

9. Fitts, *The Strategy of Electromagnetic Conflict*, p. 132.

10. David Kahn, *Hitler's Spies: German Military Intelligence in World War II*, (New York: Macmillan, 1978), p. 211.

11. Martin Streetly, *Airborne Electronic Warfare: History, Techniques and Tactics* (London: Jane's, 1988), p. 122.

12. Kahn, *Hitler's Spies*, p. 200.

13. In practice, the higher the ratio of jamming noise to peak signal noise (jammer/signal power ratio), the more likely the jamming will drown out enemy signals, all else being equal.

14. Don Gordon, *Electronic Warfare; Element of Strategy and Multiplier of Combat Power* (New York: Pergamon, 1981), p. 23.

15. *Defense Electronics*, October 1989, p. 75.

16. *Defense News*, 16 March, 1990.

17. *Defense News*, 15 June, 1990.

18. Cited in Fitts, *The Strategy of Electromagnetic Conflict*, p. 98.

19. One author claims it carries a payload of two tons. See Bill Sweetman, "B-2: The Shape of Things to Come," *Jane's Defense Weekly*, 19 November 1988, p. 126.

20. *Aviation Week and Space Technology*, 18 May, 1987, p. 22.

21. Streetly, *Airborne Electronic Warfare*, p. 83, 84.

22. Ibid., p. 115.

23. Alfred Price, *The History of U.S. Electronic Warfare* (Alexandria, Va: Association of Old Crows, 1984), Vol 1, p. 4.

24. Jones, *Wizard War*, p. 259.

25. It is not implausible to say this example of poor signal security cost the Tsar his head and gave the world the communist Soviet regime. It is to be hoped that no comparable error will occur again.

26. Behremdt, *Rommel's Intelligence*, p. 187.

27. Gordon, *Electronic Warfare*, p. 31.

28. Ralph Bennet, *Ultra in the West*, (New York: Scribners, 1980), p. 4.

29. A.I. Palii, *Radio Warfare*, (1963), trans. U.S. Army Foreign Service and Technology Center, FSTC-HT-23-470-69. See U.S. Department of Commerce, National Technical Information Service, Springfield, Va. Order No. 1384510.

30. D. Curtis Schleher, *Introduction to Electronic Warfare* (Norwood, Mass.: Artech, 1986).

31. *Washington Post*, 15 October, 1990, p. 1.

32. R.V. Jones, *Wizard War*, p. 256.

33. Schleher, *Introduction to Electronic Warfare*, p. 32.

34. Ibid., p. 331.

35. Ibid., p. 32.

Six

♦

SOVIET RADIOELECTRONIC STRUGGLE

Radio warfare is never declared and never ceases. It is not limited by time or space and acknowledges no political boundaries. The preparations for radio warfare and its "battles" are conducted incessantly and covertly both in the ether and in research laboratories, in construction offices, and at test ranges.

Gen. A. I. Palii, *Radio Warfare*

The Soviet military's doctrine for the use of the electromagnetic spectrum is called *radioelektronnaya bor'ba* (REB), which is translated as radioelectronic struggle.

The Soviet development of REB marks a great leap forward over the traditional Western idea of electronic warfare, because the Soviets combined the tactics of electronic warfare, surprise, deception and firepower to create a unique doctrine that shapes the operations of Soviet armies and of any other forces trained by Soviet advisers, such as the Iraqi army.

REB includes actions to disrupt enemy use of the spectrum and actions to protect friendly use of the spectrum. It incorporates *razvedka* (reconnaissance and intelligence) and *maskirovka*, a term without any satisfactory English translation, but one that combines concealment and deception.

In peacetime, REB is intended to help conceal Soviet military capabilities, deceive Western intelligence analysts, and best teach Soviet soldiers how to use the electromagnetic spectrum during high-intensity or low-intensity warfare.

In wartime, REB's two main missions are disrupting the enemy's use of the spectrum and protecting friendly use of the spectrum, so helping any Soviet assault blast and smash its way through the enemy's command structure. "In the Soviet armed forces, the essence of REB is the paralysis of enemy command, control and communications."[1]

To successfully execute its dual mission of protection and disruption, REB draws upon intelligence resources for information about enemy electronic systems and upon *maskirovka* resources for help in misleading the enemy about friendly activities.

According to Soviet soldiers, REB is becoming increasingly important for operational success on land, in the air and at sea because REB is of central importance for the new generation of long range ground weapons entering Soviet and NATO arsenals. Instead of merely using electronic warfare to help gain small, tactical successes, the Soviet military expects REB to help destroy armies, capture countries, sink fleets, and sweep entire theaters clear of enemy units. Indeed, it seems the Soviet military also expect REB to be of central importance in a nuclear war, if such a disaster should ever occur.

The Soviets recognize the growing importance of REB, and are putting corresponding effort into preparing for it. According to an oft-repeated quote from the father of the modern Soviet navy, Admiral Sergei Gorshkov, "The next war will be won by the side which best exploits the electromagnetic spectrum."[2]

Clearly, an understanding of REB is crucial to an understanding of Soviet military thought, and can teach Western soldiers much about electronic combat.

THE ORIGINS OF REB

Soviet REB gradually appeared in the early 1970s, partly stimulated by the airborne electronic struggles over Vietnam and Israel.[3] REB was born out of a 1974 book written by Gen. A. I. Palii called *Radioelectronic Struggle*, which laid out the basic structure of REB. Palii was one of the few Soviet experts on electronic warfare, and had published an earlier book called *Radio Warfare* in 1963.

Over the next few years, Palii's ideas were debated by the Soviet military. The success of those ideas was sealed in 1981 when the powerful Soviet general staff approved publication of 20,000 copies of a revised edition of *Radioelectronic Struggle*.[4] The book was reissued several times in the 1980s. Strengthened by endorsements from another Soviet electronic warfare expert, V. Grankin, Palii's ideas gradually came to be accepted throughout the Soviet military. However, despite Palii's Army background, the Soviet Navy has shown the most interest in REB, with the Air Force a long way behind, according to Chizum, an analyst for the secretive U.S. National Security Agency.[5]

REB quickly found a place in traditionalist Soviet military thought, which has always stressed early and aggressive offensives to seize the initiative and win a war. While Soviet political and military policy, enshrined in Soviet military doctrine, has always been defensive, Soviet military strategy has always been aggressively offensive. Thus, the traditional Soviet national security policy combined fire and water by being simultaneously defensive and offensive. The reasoning has been simple; the USSR does not seek a war, but if one were thrust on it, all means would be used to utterly destroy the enemy, not just to reach a peace.

The newest formulation of Soviet military doctrine, which calls for defensive sufficiency, does not mean the end of this offensive tradition. Public descriptions of defensive sufficiency say the USSR intends to reduce its military forces to the minimum required for reliable defense of the motherland. But Soviet officers reply that reliable defense of the motherland requires early and aggressive offensives to seize the initiative and win the war.

Perhaps part of the reason for the military's uncompromising attitude to war is that few if any civilians are involved in the formulation of military science. Thus the military has in the past controlled nearly all knowledge of things military in the Soviet Union. Although this dangerous monopoly of information is thankfully being changed by the extraordinary rule of the Gorbachev modernizers, changes in Soviet military strategy — the domain of Soviet military scientists, not politicians — will be slow in coming. Political strife, obsessive secrecy, Soviet history and bureaucratic conservatism will doubtless retard this hopeful progress. Military organizations are like gigantic supertankers; they take much strength, a great deal of patience, and a long time to change direction.

A comparison with the United States' experience is instructive; When Secretary of Defense Robert MacNamara decided to reform nuclear strategy in the 1960s, he declared national strategy was based on the politically defensive strategy of mutual assured destruction (MAD) in which war is deterred by the mutual vulnerability of both sides to nuclear weapons. Under MAD, MacNamara publicly foreswore any attempt to protect the U.S. by attacking Soviet weapons. But the U.S. Air Force simply ignored all these public declarations and carried on as before. Although by world standards the U.S. military is under tight civilian control, the Air Force never fundamentally altered its war plans, which aimed at aggressive and early destruction of Soviet nuclear forces.

Thus regardless of the potentially fundamental reforms of higher military doctrine and strategy in the USSR, in the short term the formulation and execution of REB, especially in wartime, will remain largely immune to Gorbachev's modernizers.

WHAT IS REB?

REB is the effort to ensure use of the electromagnetic spectrum while denying its use to the enemy.

According to the authoritative Soviet *Encyclopedia of Military Terms*, REB is "an integrated set of measures intended for *detection* ... and reconnoitering ... and subsequent *radioelectronic suppression* ... [including] neutralization or destruction ... of enemy radioelectronic resources and systems, used for command and control of forces and weapon systems. Radioelectronic combat also encompasses *radioelectronic protection* of one's own military radioelectronic resources and systems. ... In conjunction with REB measures, neutralization of enemy radioelectronic resources is conducted *mainly* with weapons [such as antiradiation missiles] that home in on emissions."

The official definition of REB says it is less important than intelligence and protection against nuclear weapons but more important than *maskirovka*, engineering, or chemical warfare.

According to Chizum, despite the emphasis on protection and suppression in the official definition, there is no doubt that radioelectronic intelligence belongs under the larger REB umbrella, with Palii calling radioelectronic intelligence the "principal element" of REB.[6]

Although REB is concerned with electronic means of combat, it clearly envisages use of physical destruction, as well as deceptive measures akin to the "Potemkin villages" named after the charming but fake villages constructed to give the Empress Catherine the Great a rosy view of serfs' living conditions.

RADIOELECTRONIC INTELLIGENCE

The Soviets believe the most important battle support measure is intelligence or *razvedka*, regarded as vital for the success of REB.

This Soviet emphasis on *razvedka* is quite reasonable, because successful implementation of REB depends critically on accurate intelligence of enemy activities and capabilities. It is important to note that the term *razvedka* combines the Western term of intelligence, which is collected by technical means, and of reconaissance, which is carried out by specially trained troops or pilots. Thus *razvedka* is gathered by all Soviet intelligence gathering assets, including spies.

In modern war, this intelligence is mainly acquired by *radioelektronnaya razvedka* which can be translated as "radioelectronic intelligence." Defined as "the gathering of information about an enemy with the aid of radioelectronic resources," it is subdivided into radio, radiotechnical, radar, electro-optical, radiothermal, laser, television, acoustic, and hydroacoustic intelligence.[7]

Of these terms, radio intelligence includes communications intelligence and direction finding; radiotechnical intelligence includes electronic, radar and radiation intelligence; while radiothermal intelligence refers to infrared sensors. It would appear that almost the only intelligence means excluded from this panoply of radiotechnical intelligence sources are the women and men of easy virtue under contract to the spymasters in the KGB.

According to Soviet authors, electronic intelligence has acquired an increasingly important role on the modern battlefield. Thus Lieutenant General F. Gredasov wrote in 1987 that "with the deployment of advanced technical means, the capabilities of reconnaissance subunits have significantly expanded. Now a large part of the information sought by them will rest with aerial, radio and radio-technical [means] as well as troop and artillery reconnaissance [units] equipped with new electro-optical means which are able to obtain information with great accuracy."[8]

The Arab–Israeli War of 1973 was a testing ground of REB for the Soviets and an introduction to REB for Americans. General Palii wrote that Israeli acquisition of electronic intelligence enabled them to disrupt Arab radio communications, including primary and reserve frequencies and both military and government radio nets.[9] Isby reports that Soviet artillery regiments of about 72 guns are equipped with radar, sound, flash and radio-direction finding equipment to locate Western artillery systems.[10] This was reflected in the 1973 Golan Heights campaign where Syrian radio-intelligence units on the Jabal al Harah hill provided direction-finding support for a 180 mm artillery batallion and a unit of 110 km (70 mi) range Frog-7 surface-to-surface missiles.[11]

Not surprisingly, the Soviets used radio intelligence systems to gather intelligence and track *mujaheddin* movements during the Afghan war. But war is a two-sided business; several Soviets died when some Afghans lured an attack helicopter into a Stinger ambush using deceptive radio transmissions.[12] Thus the Soviets do not place complete faith in electronic *razvedka,* according to Isby, and prefer visual detection because of the danger of electronic deception.

Radioelectronic intelligence is not an end: armed with knowledge of enemy capabilities and intentions gathered principally by electronic *razvedka,* Soviet REB units will implement radioelectronic suppression and protection — the central aspects of REB.

RADIOELECTRONIC SUPPRESSION

Radioelectronic suppression is defined as "an integrated set of measures and actions for *disrupting* the operations or reducing the effectiveness of enemy radioelectronic resources and systems. Targets for radio-electronic suppression include radars, radio communications, radio navigation aids, lasers, infrared devices, acoustic equipment, and other radioelectronic resources forming the basis for modern command, control, communications, and intelligence systems. Radioelectronic suppression includes active and passive jamming, the use of decoys and dummy targets, and other methods."[13]

The incorporation of destructive weaponry into REB gives it a much more violent flavor than the traditional Western view of electronic warfare, which includes only electromagnetic techniques such as jamming. This destructive core of REB is typical of the Soviet military, which believes that the best electronic countermeasure is a high-explosive bomb.

But jamming would also be used. Various types cited by Chizum include deceptive jamming, selective noise jamming, massive barrage noise jamming, antiradar aerosols, radar absorbent materials and several types of dummy radar reflectors.

Stealthy jamming is another option for the Soviets, made increasingly more plausible by modern technology; "They believe that there are no absolutes in weapons technologies. That any weapon can not only be countered but also warped so that it appears to be something it is not. In countering radar, for example, they would much rather make it appear to be functioning normally but cause it to yield inaccurate information than to jam it so that the operator knows it is not working properly."[14]

RADIO ELECTRONIC PROTECTION

Complementing the role of suppression in REB is radioelectronic protection. This is "an integrated set of measures for ensuring stable operations for (one's own) electronic resources. ... It includes protection from enemy radioelectronic suppression; protection from neutralization by. ... weapons, and provision of electromagnetic compatability with friendly radioelectronic resources."[15]

The German blitzkreig that rolled over the Red Army in the summer of 1941 used a combination of signals intelligence, radio direction-finding, artillery and dive bombers to severely disrupt the command systems of Soviet combat units. So successful were the Germans that "some Soviet commanders were gripped by 'radio fear' which sought to prevent any type of enemy radio intercepts. Radio fear promoted overreactions which forbade the use of any radio equipment, thus complicating command and control procedures."[16]

Throughout the 1970s and 1980s, the Soviets believed the U.S. might try to repeat the German's operational success; thus Grankin betrayed Soviet concerns by saying the enemy's most important mission would be the paralyzation of Soviet command and control of forces in the theater of war.

On the actual means of protection, Colonel Nazarenko said ground troops can protect themselves and their equipment from enemy direction finding, eavesdropping, jamming, and antiradiation missiles, which are considered by the Soviets to be one of the greatest threats, by "limiting radiated power, transmitting for short periods, using high-speed transmitting devices, strictly observing radio procedure rules, using encipherment devices, [and] working with directional antennas."[17]

Good signal security measures are as important today as during World War II. David Kahn, a prominent writer on electronic intelligence and codebreaking, noted that as Soviet discipline and code construction improved, so the fruits of German monitoring declined.[18]

Thus Palii wrote in 1963 that "in order to make it difficult for the enemy to intercept radio broadcasts, in addition to reduced power and directional antennas, radio stations may use high-sensitivity receivers, make a frequency change in call signs, operating wavelengths ... the strictest radio discipline and rules for radio interchange are observed in radio communications."[19]

Such writings help explain many assessments that Soviet communications security is "exceptionally strict."[20] In the February 1988 issue of *Life* magazine, a Soviet author told of a Soviet commando in Afghanistan who requested permission to break radio communications, excusing himself by saying that he had been killled by a *mujaheddin* bullet in the chest.

Such emphasis on signal security may not always rub off well on Soviet allies. For example, Iraq "had field radios that could use commercial-quality secure communications in some areas by the later years of the [Iran-Iraq] war but they generally had poor communications security and discipline. This is likely to be a major vulnerability in many Third World states."[21]

Good radio-discipline and communications security measures are not enough; sensors, radars and radios must have adequate internal electronic counter-countermeasures sophisticated enough to defeat deception and noise jamming. In 1987, French Air Force experts were unpleasantly impressed by the high level of counter-countermeasures built into a Soviet mechanically scanned Flatface radar, which had been captured by Chad forces from the Libyans. It would be well to note this radar was probably a simple version, built only for export and without the more secret Soviet counter-countermeasure techniques.[22]

Clearly, successful radioelectronic suppression also aids the protection of radioelectronic means. Palii linked these when he wrote that during the 1973 Arab–Israeli war, "Syrian commando detachments seized and destroyed [Israeli] radio-intelligence, radio-jamming, and command centers in the region of Mount Hermon ... As a result the Israelis were deprived of the capability to conduct observation of the Syrian forces and to create interference against the radar and radio communications of the armed forces of Syria."[23] Judging by the outcome of the war, it would seem this tactical defeat was not enough to stop the Israelis from soundly beating the Syrians.

Soviet emphasis on electromagnetic compatability indicates their awareness of the danger of electronic fratricide posed by the numerous electronic devices operating together at full power in battle. The Soviets are well aware of the fate of H.M.S. Sheffield, which was surprised and destroyed by an Argentinean Exocet missile during the Anglo-Argentinean Falklands war — the Sheffield could not see the missile coming because its early-warning radar could not operate when the satellite communications link was being used.

The Soviet military is conservative, and spends a great deal of money to keep many older and proven technologies in service to ensure wartime communications. Thus there are many pictures of Soviet troops using telephone wire, flags, loudspeakers or whistles in exercises. "On a battlefield in which electronic communications may be among the first casualties, the Soviets are better equipped than NATO to operate with alternative means," according to Isby.[24]

Soviet organizations are also shaped by the need to survive the collapse of radio communications. Whereas NATO armies use a radio-equipped forward observation officer to direct artillery fire, the Soviets keep artillery command posts well forward, even at some risk of destruction because "they believe [NATO's] almost total reliance on radio communications will cause its collapse in the face of Soviet electronic warfare, which includes the jamming and destruction of radio transmitters."[25]

RADIO *MASKIROVKA*

In action, REB operations will include large-scale electronic deception measures, called *maskirovka*. Although the West has no similar concept, roughly translated, *maskirovka* means camouflage, concealment and deception.

Intended "to conceal the activities and disposition of friendly troops and to mislead the enemy with regard to the grouping and intentions of such troops,"[26] electronic *maskirovka* is closely related to REB because REB's offensive and defensive measures are greatly aided by misleading the enemy's electronic reconnaissance systems. Technically, *maskirovka* is not part of REB, but is a closely related and complementary form of battle support.

Maskirovka includes electronic, acoustic and optical measures. For purposes of REB, the most important aspect of *maskirovka* is radioelectronic *maskirovka*, which is "an integrated set of coordinated technical and organizational measures directed toward reducing the effectiveness of enemy *radioelectronic intelligence (SIGINT)*. It is divided into radio, radiotechnical, radar, electro-optical, and hydroacoustic *maskirovka*."[27]

In turn, radio *maskirovka* is "an integrated set of technical and organizational measures for reducing the effectiveness of enemy radio intelligence [COMINT]. It is attained by limiting radio power and transmission times, using directional antennas and burst transmissions, radio silence, setting up dummy radio nets and links, and passing radio disinformation."[28] *Maskirovka* does not limit itself to electronic measures. Camouflage, double agents, provocation rumors and so on are all means that are recommended for use.

Maskirovka is also to be combined with political measures designed to reassure an enemy. For example, the Soviets promised American diplomats in 1962 that no missiles would be deployed to Cuba, even as Soviet soldiers were drawing camouflage nets over the newly installed launchers. Such lessons also rub off on Soviet clients; the Iraqi invasion of Kuwait in August 1990 was preceded by reassuring diplomatic hints, promises that no invasion was planned, and even invitations to Western diplomats to view the military buildup. Because of such measures — which effectively reinforced optimistic assessments of Iraqi intentions — U.S. intelligence agencies failed to predict the invasion until only hours before the attack, too late to deter the invasion.

The difference between radioelectronic *maskirovka* and radioelectronic protection is the difference between fooling the enemy and foiling his attacks. Although they share many of the same techniques, such as radio silence, radioelectronic protection is directed at ensuring continued use of the spectrum, while *maskirovka* is intended to deceive the enemy.

Unsurprisingly, they are also mutually supportive. Thus using directional antennas minimizes the chance that a *maskirovka* operation might be accidentally betrayed.

PEACETIME

Unlike the West's conceptions of electronic warfare, REB continues in peacetime. After all, properly translated, REB means radioelectronic struggle, not just warfare.

The word "struggle" carries the ideological connotation of constant back and forth battle against the enemy. The Soviets choose the term *bor'ba* or struggle because they recognize the fact that war springs from political conflict and that combat is an extension of a more fundamental political struggle. Moreover, when developed in the 1970s, the term *radioelektronnaya bor'ba* fitted well with the traditional conception of a beleaguered socialist USSR.

In peacetime, REB is intended to help the Soviets hide secrets and also gather information. Thus REB is used to conceal the technical characteristics of Soviet radars and radios, to help deceive Western intelligence organizations about the capabilities and intentions of the Soviet military, and also to gather electronic intelligence about NATO electronics systems.

Until the late 1980s, REB also was used to jam Western radio broadcasts, thought to be aimed at undermining the security of the Soviet Union. Soviet authors constantly railed against the "ideological sabotage" of the BBC World Service broadcasts or the Voice of America's "radio voices" in articles entitled "On the Fronts of the Ideological Struggle."[29] Even in 1989, after riots in the Soviet republic of Georgia, Soviet officials complained that "foreign radio voices" stirred up the unrest.

Although radioelectronic struggle continues through peacetime, it naturally becomes infinitely sharper in war because the stakes are infinitely greater.

CONCLUSION

The Soviet idea of REB much better reflects the nature of peace and war than does the traditionally narrow Western doctrine of electronic warfare. REB integrates what the West calls electronic warfare with intelligence gathering, deception, firepower, and command and control.

This chapter does not mean to suggest that Western militaries do not practice intelligence gathering, deception, firepower, or command and control in war and peace. It merely illustrates that the West's traditional view of electronic warfare was a shortsighted tactical concept that failed to combine these military operations with electronic warfare.

Despite being shackled with an outmoded view of electronic warfare, Western militaries have struggled to combine electronic warfare with intelligence, deception, firepower, and command and control. They have had some success, especially in the 1980s when the U.S. military began to understand the Soviet view of REB and to understand the war-winning potential of electronic combat. The next few chapters will show the impact of this gradual growth in understanding.

Notes

1. James Westwood, "Soviet Electronic Warfare; Theory and Practice," *Jane's Soviet Intelligence Review*, September 1989, p. 387.

2. Richard Bush, "Soviet Electronic Warfare: A Review," *The International Countermeasures Handbook*, 12th Ed., (Palo Alto, Ca: EW Communications, 1987) p. 66.

3. Floyd Kennedy, "The Evolution of Soviet Thought on Warfare in the Fourth Dimension," *Naval War College Review*, March-April 1984, p .42.

4. David Chizum, *Soviet Radioelectronic Combat*, (Boulder and London: Westview), p. 19-27.

5. Ibid., p 49.

6. Ibid., p. 36.

7. Soviet REB includes non-electromagnetic communications and sensor systems such as sonar, opening up a whole new field of underwater REB. This is not explored in this book, partly because the larger principles of REB are equally applicable.

8. F. Gredasov, article in *Voyenny Vestnik*, March 1987, quoted by Leon Goure, "The Soviet Strategic View," *Strategic Review*, Summer 1987.

9. Capt. Ronny Bragger, *Lessons Learned: The 1973 Middle East War, A Soviet Perspective*, (Garmisch, Germany: U.S. Army Russian Institute, 1981), p. 4.

10. David C. Isby, *Weapons and Tactics of the Soviet Army*, (London and New York: Jane's, 1981), p. 227.

11. Des Ball, "Soviet Signals Intelligence," *The International Countermeasures Handbook*, p. 86.

12. Isby, *Weapons and Tactics*, p. 372.

13. Chizum, *Soviet Radioelectronic Combat*, p. 96.

14. Richard E. Thomas, *Long Wave Infra-red Research in the Soviet Union*, (College Station, TX: Texas A&M, 1984).

15. Chizum, *Soviet Radioelectronic Combat*, p. 100.

16. Ibid., p. 3.

17. Ibid., p. 51.

18. David Kahn, *Hitler's Spies: German Military Intelligence in World War II*, (New York: Macmillan, 1978), p. 206.

19. A. I. Palii, *Radio Warfare* (1963), trans. U.S. Army Foreign Science and Technology Center, FSTC-HT-23-470-69.

20. W.J. Lewis, *The Warsaw Pact, Arms, Doctrine and Strategy* (New York: McGraw-Hill 1982), p. 249.

21. Anthony Cordesman and Abraham Wagner, *The Lessons of Modern War* (Boulder and San Francisco: Westview Press, 1990), Vol. 1, *The Iran-Iraq War*, p. 419.

22. *Aviation Week and Space Technology*, 9 February, 1988.

23. Bragger, *Lessons Learned: 1973 Middle East War*, p. 8.

24. Isby, *Weapons and Tactics*, p. 480.

25. Ibid., p. 244.

26. *Dictionary of Basic Military Terms* (1975), in Stephen Cimbala, *Soviet C^3I* (Fairfax: Armed Forces Communications and Electronics Association, 1987), p. 450.

27. Chizum, *Soviet Radioelectronic Combat*, p. 101.

28. Ibid.

29. Ibid., p. 16.

♦

Seven

PEACETIME ELECTRONIC WARFARE

When the fate of a nation and the lives of its soldiers are at stake, gentlemen do read each other's mail — if they can get their hands on it.

Allen Dulles, *The Craft of Intelligence*

In peace, political conflict is seen in economic disagreements, propaganda campaigns and diplomatic initiatives, as well as in saber rattling. Political conflict becomes bloody with the outbreak of war.

Even while nearly all states dread the uncertainty and ghastliness of war — especially nuclear war — all exploit the electromagnetic spectrum to strengthen their security, whether by keeping their eyes open or by eavesdropping on radio conversations. In peacetime political conflict, states use the electromagnetic spectrum to gather intelligence about the military strength of potential enemies, search for warnings of an impending attack, and monitor compliance with international treaties.

This melding of peacetime and wartime is seen well in Soviet radioelectronic combat doctrine. Unlike the West's conceptions of electronic warfare for which the only peacetime applications are signals intelligence and signals security, almost the entire panoply of Soviet *radioelektronnaya bor'ba* (REB) activities are carried out in peacetime. "Radioelectronic combat, like the ideological struggle from which its springs, continues as long as the enemy uses the electromagnetic spectrum to the Soviets' disadvantage. It would just increase in intensity and scope should war break out."[1]

Espionage, deception, diplomacy, propaganda, economic advantage, arms control monitoring, sabotage, and terrorism are the points where the self-interest of the competing nation-states and social systems come into the sharpest peacetime conflict. Skillful use of the electromagnetic spectrum can yield practical political benefits — and contribute greatly to military strength in time of war.[2]

Electronic warfare and combat helps shape these conflicts. For example, the role of electronic interception in the verification of arms control treaties has decreased because of Soviet REB, while the importance of electronic spying has increased because some countries try to improve their economic performance by stealing the financial and technological secrets of others.

INTELLIGENCE GATHERING

Espionage and electronic eavesdropping constitute one of the most important peacetime tasks of armies. Without an accurate appreciation of enemy capabilities and intentions, the scale and direction of friendly defensive preparations may be wastefully excessive or tragically inadequate.

Radio and optical intelligence are gathered by eavesdropping and photographic satellites, so called national technical means of collecting intelligence. For the United States and the Soviet Union, "technical collection systems represent the most significant and valuable source of intelligence, particularly with respect to accessing weapon performance, developing a target base for war plans and monitoring arms control agreements."[3]

Intelligence gathering is as old as war, and electromagnetic signals intelligence is as old as radios. The Nazi eavesdropper Flicke tells that during the 1920s the largely disarmed Wehrmacht placed signals intelligence units in the supposedly disarmed Rhineland disguised as German national public radio survey teams. Once deployed, the units were used to spy on French maneuvers and to calculate aircraft strengths.[4]

Currently, many countries — including the U.S., the Soviet Union, Germany, Britain, China, and Japan, maintain large or small electronic intelligence organizations.

For instance, the German *Amt Fur Fernmeldewessen Bundeswehr* (Defense Office for Signals Intelligence) eavesdropped on the Warsaw Pact with a large signals intelligence station at Hof, close to the East German border.

China shares with the U.S. any information collected by eavesdropping sites along the border with the USSR at Korla and Qitai in Xinjiang province of northwestern China,[5] while Britain shares many of its facilities and intercepts with the U.S., including the extensive installation in Cheltenham.

But by far the largest signals intelligence establishments are run by the U.S. and the Soviet Union.

The principal U.S. signals intelligence gathering organization is the National Security Agency (NSA), based in Fort George G. Meade, Maryland. The other main technical intelligence gathering organization is the National Reconnaissance Office (NRO) which operates most of the photographic spy satellites. The NRO is based in the Pentagon but is managed by the Central Intelligence Agency. Altogether, NSA and NRO employ roughly 70,000 people.

But the Soviets will not be outdone: their signals intelligence organizations have a combined staff of more than 350,000, according to Australian intelligence expert Desmond Ball.[6] The Soviets "maintain the largest signals intelligence establishment in the world... operating hundreds of intercept, processing and analysis facilities, with heavy exploitation of unsecured voice communications," according to testimony by the U.S. Assistant Secretary of Defense for Command, Control, Communications and Intelligence, Gerald P. Dineen.[7]

During the 1980s, the USSR had double NATO's number of signals intelligence stations, including more than roughly 300 land based collection sites in the USSR alone. It also had 150 sites in Warsaw Pact countries, many of which were divisional radioreconnaissance battalions tasked with peacetime collection and training.

Most Soviet signals intelligence sites are concentrated on border and coastal areas. Klimovsk, 32 km south of Moscow, is the largest station and the probable headquarters for the Soviet military intelligence organization, the GRU, which is chiefly responsible for Soviet signals intelligence. Apart from the central sites, the fifteen Soviet military districts, the four Groups of Soviet forces outside the USSR, and the four fleets all maintain signals intelligence units.[8]

The largest foreign station is the 28 square mile facility at Lourdes in Cuba, staffed by roughly 2,000 to 1,500 Soviets.[9] According to various sources, this station is used to monitor U.S. telecommunications satellites relaying civilian and military telephone calls, space flight operations from Cape Canaveral and various military operations in the Caribbean. Unhappily for Soviet intelligence, the existence of this base depends on Fidel Castro's continued rule, which given the recent examples of communist powers in Eastern Europe, does not look too solid.

While they lasted, the intelligence services of the East European allies also collected intelligence useful to Moscow. According to Hans Neusel, a West German intelligence official, the East German intelligence service, called *Stasi*, eavesdropped on West German political and administrative telephone conversations in Bonn and West Berlin. The East German computerized eavesdropping system was said to have used computers to recognize important telephone numbers, and was to have been upgraded to penetrate encryption and automatically recognize the voices of important callers.[10]

The Soviets also have about sixty ships dedicated to electronic intelligence gathering, several of which were designed from the keel up for the purpose of electronic spying. Some have been disguised as tramp steamers for covert collection.[11]

The Soviets have used undisclosed numbers of Aeroflot flights to collect information over important military bases such as the U.S. Trident submarine construction yards.[12] Soviet intelligence officers drive truck-borne cargo containers across Europe to covertly collect signals intelligence.[13] Drones and high-altitude aircraft were used for overflights of several Asian countries including China and Pakistan in the 1960s. Submarines are also used for secretive signals intelligence.[14]

The Soviets use their embassies and consulates for eavesdropping, including the embassy on Mount Alto in Washington, D.C., a location that allows easy monitoring of the Capitol, the Pentagon, and many microwave relay towers.[15]

They use large numbers of orbiting signals-interception satellites, including relatively heavy, low-flying, long-lived satellites, as well as short-lived "ferret" satellites. The impressive Soviet launch capability allowed them to quickly place several satellites to monitor the Falklands War, the Iran-Iraq War, and NATO exercises, especially naval exercises. For example, on June 1, 1987, the Soviets had eight signals intelligence satellites in orbit, ensuring that the important British naval base at Portsmouth was under observation for all but four hours of the day.[16]

With much effort and many redesigns, the Soviets continue to improve their space-based capability to monitor U.S. fleets using an Active Radar Ocean Surveillance Satellite (RORSAT) and a signals intelligence satellite called an Electronic Ocean Surveillance Satellite (EORSAT). Operating in pairs, the RORSAT looks for large aircraft carriers, while the EORSAT can passively listen for signals as well and back up the RORSAT in case of malfunction, destruction or jamming. Significantly, the satellites are reportedly directly linked to Soviet ships and submarines, greatly accelerating the ability of those vessels to target fast-moving U.S. Navy fleets.[17]

Ball judged that the electronic intercepts "provide the Soviet Union's principal means of surveillance and early warning; they provide the great bulk of Soviet intelligence with respect to Western military capabilities and activities; and they are a major source of commercial information," useful for improving international trade deals.[18]

Soviet industriousness is matched by that of the U.S. The National Security Agency and the Central Intelligence Agency use a wide variety of satellites, aircraft, submarines, land sites and warships, as well as covert systems. The National Security Agency uses signals intelligence satellites, and the CIA uses photographic satellites and radar satellites.

The main U.S. collection systems seem to be the several types of signals intelligence satellites parked in geosynchronous orbit above Singapore, Thailand, and India, where they can constantly monitor interesting areas of the globe, including the Persian Gulf.

These space-based systems are becoming increasingly important as U.S. interest in many developing countries increases, and as the Soviets draw their forces away from NATO borders and back into the Soviet Union. Such crises as the Iraqi invasion of Kuwait will only help redirect military intelligence systems away from the declining Soviet threat and towards various unstable areas in the world.

The U.S. has launched sixteen large SIGINT satellites from 1972 to January 1985, including four named Rhyolite, one Argus, three Aquacade, four Chalet and one Magnum.[19]

According to one source, the Argus satellite "could listen to any part of the [Soviet] microwave network and thus eavesdrop on conversations — for example — between members of the Politbureau or Soviet military commanders. It could also intercept shortwave radio conversations between, say, Soviet tank commanders on the Polish border. It could even penetrate the [data links between] Soviet military computer systems."[20] The Chalet satellites were able to intercept telemetry intelligence from Soviet ballistic missiles, but were primarily intended for eavesdropping on communications between people and between computers.

The most capable eavesdropping satellite series is said to be codenamed Magnum, and was first launched in January 1985. It is reportedly equipped with an antenna of up to 100 meters (328 ft) in diameter and is capable of monitoring a relatively large area and intercepting very faint signals.[21]

The U.S. also maintains a series of naval signals intelligence satellites systems codenamed Classic Wizard. These are intended for the wartime-oriented task of tracking Soviet naval vessels. This satellite reportedly consists of three subsatellites trailing behind a large mother satellite. The subsatellites transmit direction-finding data to the larger central satellite for analysis and transmission to earth. The Classic Wizard system was kept secret until it was revealed by a series of leaks, including a stamp designed by the National Astronautics and Space Administration that depicted the satellite.

The American geosynchronous satellites have been supplemented in the past by smaller, lower-orbiting and shorter-lived ferret satellites. It is not clear how many were launched by the U.S. in the 1980s, although it cannot be very many. Also, small eavesdropping satellites might be unneeded as recent U.S. photographic satellites are reported to also have a signals intelligence capability.[22]

Other U.S. signals intelligence gathering platforms include warships such as the U.S.S. Caron, and many ground sites in Western Europe and other parts of the world. The formerly isolated Western outpost of West Berlin was and probably still is, a well used lookout post deep in the heart of what was East Germany. Embassies are another useful listening post.

The Soviets gleefully revealed one unadvertised U.S. eavesdropping system: two covert nuclear-powered devices lowered by an American submarine onto an underwater cable off the Pacific Coast of the Soviet Union.[23] The bugging devices, built under the codename Ivy Bells, were betrayed by the spy Ronald Pelton for $35,000. It is unknown how long they were operating or whether the Soviets have tried to use them to eavesdrop on U.S. underwater cables. The Soviets have also claimed the discovery of signals intelligence devices hidden in simulated tree stumps placed in Moscow forests and at least one sealed railroad container intended to pick up whatever possible while journeying along the length of the Soviet Trans-Siberian railroad.

Sometime U.S. signals intelligence has been very aggressive. An RB-66C aircraft was shot down over East Germany in 1965, and Gary Powers' U-2 spy plane was carrying signals intelligence receivers when it was destroyed in 1960 over Sverdlovsk in the central USSR. After this loss, the U.S. continued to fly unmanned aircraft against North Vietnam and China in the early 1970s.[24]

U.S. signals intelligence operations continue all year round. Thus the U.S. Air Force runs eavesdropping flights, codenamed Rivet Joint, along the Pacific coast of the USSR, "We go in there every month or month and a half or so just to make sure that they aren't running exercises. A lot of times it's dead, but it's dead because of us. And sometimes we'd just walk into an exercise," one participant said.[25] If nothing else, this illustrates the value of surprise in intelligence gathering operations.

To supplement all these signals intelligence gathering efforts, the U.S. is launching a new series of photographic satellites supposedly codenamed KH-12 or KH-11+, and radar satellites codenamed Lacrosse. When deployed in space, these satellites should increase U.S. intelligence capabilities in war and peace, despite enemy countermeasures, such as massive smoke clouds caused by burning oil wells.

Clearly, the Soviet and U.S. intelligence operations are vast, and hugely expensive. But many other countries such as the United

Kingdom and Germany have similar, if smaller, capabilities. Improvements in technology will probably allow the intelligence gathering systems to vacuum up more and more intelligence, despite efforts to conceal and deceive. However, the technology of intelligence gathering is arguably less important than the use to which it is put by organizations in what is called the intelligence process.

THE INTELLIGENCE PROCESS

The surprise Iraqi invasion of Kuwait proved yet again that U.S. technical spying systems are not all-seeing eyes. Although they are technical marvels able to vacuum up a vast amount of technical or geographical information, the information they gather can only give a dim reflection of policy and plans. Despite their ability to produce vast quantities of pictures, electronic intercepts, and other raw data, they cannot reveal the intentions of foreign leaders, nor the war plans hidden in safes, nor the spies working for the other side, nor the technical capabilities of many weapons, nor what is being quietly developed in laboratories.

The trick for intelligence analysts is to distill important information from the combination of accumulated fragments of electronic and photographic data, from articles in newspapers, scientific magazines, and military journals, and from data secretly gathered by spies.

For instance, photographic satellites allow the U.S. to visually inspect the many large phased-array radars around the Soviet borders, while signals intelligence satellites allow the U.S. to analyze the signals produced by similar early warning radars at various other sites in the USSR. Yet it is only the reports of spies and the careful analysis of Soviet writings on military affairs that allows the U.S. to determine the radar sites' role in Soviet nuclear strategy. This vacuum cleaning, sifting and sorting approach is not easy.

Intelligence is not delivered on a golden platter. There is much room for many errors because intelligence gathering and analysis is a human activity — and humans misunderstand events, fall prey to deception, and are prone to inaction.

There are roughly five steps in the intelligence process: allocation, acquisition, analysis, acceptance, and action.

The first step is to direct the efforts of intelligence gathering assets such as satellites, spies and diplomats at the important targets, otherwise their efforts will be partially wasted.

The important intelligence must then actually be acquired by good sensors, alert spies, and other means. Obviously, this step must be completed before steps three and four — the study and drawing of conclusions — can begin. If the analysts err, they will draw incorrect conclusions, needlessly increasing the dangers or costs faced by their country.

And most important, the intelligence information must be acted upon if the entire process is to have any purpose or value.

All five steps in the intelligence process are vital, but perhaps the most glaring errors occur at the last step when politicians fail to take the proper action that is called for by the intelligence. In June 1941, Stalin was repeatedly told by his own intelligence services and by the British that the Nazis were about to invade the USSR. The evidence was clear, but Stalin was afraid that any defensive actions he took would only increase the chance of war breaking out. This fatal mistake in judgment and the consequent lack of action nearly resulted in the total destruction of the Soviet Union — an outcome only averted by the death of 20 million Soviet citizens. Similarly, Kuwaiti leaders in August 1990 seem to have ignored indications of Iraqi hostility. Instead of inviting U.S. troops to deter possible invasion, the Kuwaitis placed their faith in a diplomatic solution to Iraqi threats.

Understanding of the five steps allows us to better understand the strengths and weaknesses of intelligence organizations. But there are some additional problem areas in the gathering and use of signals intelligence.

For example, out of fear that they may miss some vital clue or important event, intelligence organizations like to collect as much information as possible. This leads to a situation in which the organizations are flooded with data, but are constantly seeking more.

Thus, "the trouble is that these sensors — especially satellite sensors in peacetime — produce so much data that analysts can evaluate only 1 percent to 10 percent of it, which is sufficient for most situations in peacetime, but inadequate in war," according to a Defense Department study.[26]

One solution to this dilemma is to better appreciate what to watch for and what is most important. Moreover, once analysts know what to do, they can use sophisticated computers to strip away useless data — such as photographs of empty fields or unchanged military bases — so helping them to sort through the mountains of data that they do want to collect.

Which brings us to another point. Because signals intelligence systems are not all-seeing unclosing eyes, they require constant guidance from other intelligence assets such as moles, agents, and diplomats, as well as aircraft and ships, photographic satellites, and allied intelligence organizations. Thus the U.S. intelligence agencies were surprised when the newly reformed Czechoslovakian and East German governments revealed that the Soviets had supplied their countries with ninety-six SS-23 land-mobile missiles, a type that had being banned by the 1987 Intermediate Nuclear Forces treaty.[27]

Also, neither signals intelligence nor other technical systems are good at gathering general political information, which is increasingly important in a world of many powerful nation-states. This shortcoming was glaringly obvious in late 1989 when the collapse of the East European communist states caught Western intelligence agencies and governments by complete surprise. Similarly, the spy satellites failed to help predict the collapse of the Shah of Iran, or the opposition's February 1990 electoral victory in Nicaragua, and the March 1990 Lithuanian independence crisis. Nor were they able to correct the Central Intelligence Agency's persistent overestimation of Soviet economic wealth and political stability during the 1980s.

Another important limitation of satellite signals intelligence is that both sides know what is going on and are therefore able to hide secrets and attempt deception. It is no surprise the most interesting information was obtained before the Soviets learned of the capabilities of the United States' first large signals intelligence satellite. Since then, even the open evidence strongly suggests the Soviets have made efforts to conceal activities from satellites and to mislead U.S. analysts. Unsurprisingly, U.S. efforts to mislead Soviet analysts are unpublicized.

Moreover, these signals intelligence devices are all operated by humans who are as vulnerable to mistaken assumptions, poor performance, complacency, and errors as men have always been. It does little good to intercept the signals from a secret radar if an analyst dismisses them as an irrelevant anomaly.

Armed with these caveats, let us examine the most important uses of signals intelligence; determining the enemy's electronic order of battle, warning of impending attack, and monitoring of arms control treaties.

DETERMINING THE ENEMY'S ELECTRONIC ORDER OF BATTLE

The electronic order of battle describes how many radars, radios, and other emitters the enemy has, what their strengths and weaknesses are, where they are deployed, how they are organized or their readiness for war. Determining this order of battle is a crucial peacetime task.

Accurate intelligence allows the creation of a baseline from which changes in enemy stance and capability can be judged. It also allows each side to develop electronic countermeasures against enemy radars, missiles and other technological and tactical threats.

For instance, because the U.S. relies upon manned bombers for a major part of its nuclear deterrent, it has made a great effort to map the peacetime deployment of Soviet antiaircraft missile defenses and estimate what their deployment would be in war. Clearly, knowledge of Soviet surface-to-air missile deployment would help U.S. bombers avoid defenses and destroy more targets in war. Also, close analysis of intercepted Soviet radar signals is needed to develop and field appropriate electronic countermeasures for the penetrating bombers. Although it is reasonable to assume that Soviet radars have secret capabilities they reserve only for wartime use, without this peacetime signals intelligence gathering NATO forces would be in a hopeless position at the outset of a short "come as you are" war.

However, even in this task, signals interception and photographic satellites cannot provide a firm answer because some technological features of enemy radars and radios can be hidden, other features can be changed very easily, and technology in general is changing very rapidly. So it is not surprising that the intended users of the information, the Pentagon engineers and managers who design electronic countermeasures, frequently complain they do not have accurate or reliable information to build up-to-date jammers.

Peacetime signals intelligence gathering is by no means a new development. Flicke reports that German radio intelligence units in the 1920s heavily monitored Polish Air Force communications. Once the Polish encryption scheme was cracked, "the results were so voluminous that the German intelligence service ... was able to obtain the very best kind of information. After a few months they knew every aeroplane with its number and engine number, every pilot, every officer, all details of equipment, organization, structure, tactical views, preparedness for commitment, etc., so completely as has perhaps never before or since."[28]

Gathering the voluminous intelligence needed for determining the enemy's order of battle requires years and countless manhours of patient effort by intelligence organizations.

Most such signals intelligence gathering is time-consuming, tedious and expensive work, and only rarely are listeners treated to bursts of dramatic and revealing activity.

One such intelligence bonanza occurred during and after the destruction of the South Korean airliner KAL 007 in September 1983, according to writer Seymour Hersh. An unidentified National Security Agency official said that during the hours and days following the shootdown the Soviets were "shocked and surprised. They did not know what was happening... Outfits we didn't know existed suddenly popped up [on the airwaves]. They went through their checklists and activated everything they had."[29]

One significant obstacle facing Western signals intelligence gathering is the Soviets' effort to foil and deceive the West, using *maskirovka*. Encompassing concealment, secrecy, and deception, the *maskirovka* effort is performed by a wide variety of means including severe civilian censorship on military matters, tight control of classified information, reservation of special frequencies for wartime use, tight peacetime signal security, as well as jamming Western signals intelligence devices. Of course, many of these tactics are also available to Western armed forces.

Soviet interest in what would eventually be called *radioelectronic maskirovka* dates from 1915, according to Wilhelm Flicke, who began his eavesdropping career with trench telephones in World War I and ended it in 1945 trying to track partisans' radios for the thousand-year Third Reich. After the war, Flicke told the American intelligence services that "the radio procedures used by the Russians were the best in all Europe as far as the camouflage factor was concerned... Of course, covering Russian maneuvers [before the outbreak of World War II] always gave a certain amount of information, but this was so slight that it scarcely repaid the time and effort expended."[30]

Maskirovka is not much less important in peacetime than it is in wartime. According to a book allegedly written by a reputed ex-Soviet officer called Victor Suvorov, the Soviets created a Chief Directorate of Strategic *Maskirovka* or *Glavnoe Upravleniye Strigicheskoy Maskirovki* (GUSM) in the 1960s. It answered the increasing need to integrate various peacetime and wartime deception measures to cope with spy satellites and other peacetime intelligence-gathering assets. GUSM is part of the powerful Soviet General Staff, and it is said to be charged with directing the various organs and services of the Soviet military to hide capabilities and deceive the enemy.

According to Suvorov,

Each chief directorate unit serving with a military district, a group of armies, or a fleet makes use of data provided by this same [imported] U.S. computer to carry out similar work for its own force and area. Each army, division, and regiment receives constantly updated schedules showing the precise times at which enemy reconnaissance satellites will overfly their areas, with details of the type of satellite concerned (photo-recce, signals intelligence, all-purpose, etc.) and the track it will follow. Neither the soldiers nor most of the officers know the precise reason for daily orders, like "from 12.20 to 12.55 all radio transmissions are to cease, and all radars are to be switched off," but they must obey them. At the same time, each division has several radio transmitters and radars which work only during this period and which are there solely to provide signals for the enemy's satellites.[31]

Although the Soviets naturally have not admitted the existence of this deception directorate, "the missions Suvorov ascribes to it make eminent sense in light of what is known about Soviet military practices," said one intelligence official.[32] In other words, if it did not exist today, the Soviet military would create it tomorrow. GUSM is important because while it exists, it reveals basic Soviet intentions, and because "of the bureaucratic imperative that organizations formed and trained for certain tasks will seek to perform them."[33]

Just as the Intermediate Nuclear Forces Treaty banning road-mobile SS-20 and SS-23 missiles was being signed in December 1987, a Soviet poem printed in *Pravda* extolled the virtues of *maskirovka*:

> A march of a missile division
> was occurring along
> a nocturnal, snowbound road,
> past sleeping villages,
> blizzard-smitten fields,
> through forests and clearings,
> over icy lakes, and rivers,
> shaking the earth,
> the column is rolling on...
> It is sinking into the wilderness,
> into nature,
> an itinerant military unit,
> changing its environment,
> unknown to the enemy...
> It is futile to seek it from space,
> to grope for it with radar rays.[34]

Passive *maskirovka* against Western espionage is combined with other active *maskirovka* measures. Examples are legion; such as the Soviet missile facility that has for years transmitted unexplained bogus weather reports[35] or the Soviets dropping a false sonar pinger into the sea to lure American searchers away from the destroyed KAL-007's black box.[36]

More active *maskirovka* measures were recounted by the *Philadelphia Inquirer*, which carried a front page article on January 24, 1988, reporting that administration sources said optical sensors on board U.S. photographic satellites were temporarily blinded by lasers when trying to check the Soviet missile testing base of Tyuratam. Indeed, the story went on to say that "several U.S. intelligence specialists said they believed that some of America's most sophisticated spy satellites, the KH-11 photographic reconnaissance models, had malfunctioned after being focused on by Soviet ground based lasers." Defense Department space officials also told this author that U.S. space satellites had been hit by lasers and "tickled" by unexplained signals.

Unsurprisingly, officials say there is no hard proof that the Soviets had disrupted the satellites. However, the U.S. will soon install laser warning receivers on its newest generation of low altitude satellites, enabling detection of laser attacks and subsequent defensive maneuvering.

Perhaps more interesting, the *Philadelphia Inquirer* story also said the sources acknowledged that the Pentagon has blinded Soviet satellites with lasers and has jammed Soviet transmissions from eavesdropping trawlers as they monitored U.S. missile tests. Clearly, the Soviets are not alone in the practice of peacetime concealment and deception. The U.S. special forces troops being held ready for the ill-fated attempt to rescue hostages held by the Iranians were ushered inside hangers whenever Soviet satellites passed overhead, and training facilities were constructed far from normal training areas to maximize secrecy. Also, the F-117A Stealth fighter was only flown at night up to 1989 to prevent Soviet cameras from getting a good view, and every B-2 Stealth bomber will be kept inside its own hangar, partly to protect its antiradar coating from needless erosion by the weather and partly to minimize Soviet spying.

Other countries also use deception. Iraqi disguised preparations for several offensives against Iran, and for its invasion of Kuwait, while Libya has apparently painted burn marks on its chemical weapon factory at Rabta to deceive Western intelligence analysts into thinking that fire had destroyed the factory. But such a simple deception unaccompanied by a diversion was quickly uncovered.[37]

The security and *maskirovka* techniques used to defeat enemy intelligence gathering are complemented by other security measures, such as secrecy or the physical security of jamming devices. Good spies have also helped, such as when the English spy Geoffrey Prime betrayed the U.S. ability to monitor Soviet microwave links with the Argus electronic intelligence satellite.

Mistakes have been made by all sides. For example, after the North Koreans seized the U.S. signals intelligence gathering ship, the *Pueblo*, the National Security Agency listened as the North Koreans transmitted to the Soviets copies of extremely secret documents, which had been kept on board the *Pueblo* despite regulations. Prior to this security setback, the U.S. was able to predict when the Soviets would change fleet call signs and what the new call signs would be: "We were way ahead. We knew where they were and when. The *Pueblo* gave away this enormous advantage," one source said.[38] Unsurprisingly, Western intelligence agencies are reluctant to reveal Soviet errors from which they have benefited.

It is very important to note that intelligence information — however skillfully gathered — is useless without an appropriate response. According to one signals intelligence expert who witnessed the start of the Korean war; "The fact that we were caught without satisfactory jammers in the early stages of conflict was no fault of electronic intelligence .... [U.S. intelligence agencies] had been reporting Soviet bloc preoccupation with low-frequency radars ever since 1947. In fact, it can be argued with good support that the intelligence was far superior to the ability of our planners to use it."[39]

Clearly, few if any observers are in a position to judge how well the U.S. or the USSR have protected their intelligence systems or how well each side has estimated the enemy's electronic order of battle during the long Cold War. After all, no one has ever discovered something that was successfully hidden.

WARNING OF IMPENDING ATTACK

Another vital role of peacetime signals intelligence is to give warning of impending war. Using traffic analysis and codebreaking — as well as spies and other intelligence assets — it is frequently possible to detect hostile enemy intentions even if only by recognizing unusual departures from peacetime practice.

Thus the author of a ground-breaking book on nuclear war and C^3I vulnerability, Bruce Blair, told a congressional committee that the primary communications links used by U.S. nuclear forces "can be eavesdropped upon by the Soviet Union in realtime and it is not inconceivable that Moscow could know about our [nuclear] retaliatory decisions and orders before our own forces received the order."[40]

Although this statement was rejected by Donald Latham, then the Assistant Secretary of Defense for C^3I, the evidence is in Blair's favor. For example, Soviet eavesdroppers could monitor the U.S. bomber bases to see if many on-board radar and radio sets were being tested, so giving several hours advance warning of a possible mass takeoff.

This technique is no different from that used by the Nazis to get early warning of Allied bomber raids, although the modern eavesdroppers can use satellites.

According to the Soviet defector Viktor Suvorov:

> In addition, the activity of the radio stations was compared with the activity of the enemy's forces. We obtained priceless information from the men who drove Soviet trucks abroad, from the stewards on Soviet trains, from Aeroflot crews, from our sportsmen, and of course from our network of agents. This sort of information was very scrappy and disconnected... Our computer compared these scraps with what was going on in the ether. Any apparent regularity was noted and special cases and exceptions to the rule studied. And as a result of many years spent analyzing such things, it became perfectly possible to say: "If RB-7665-1 went on the air, its means that in four days' time there will take place a mass takeoff at Ramstein [a large U.S. Air Force base]."[41]

But placing reliance on such electromagnetic alarms is very unwise. There are so many opportunities and means of deceiving the enemy that a successful surprise attack is the rule, not the exception — despite the advent of modern technology.

One central problem for the intelligence analyst is that the destructiveness and mobility of modern weaponry reduce the time available for acquisition, analysis and action. Thus the Panamanian military learned of the impending U.S. invasion in early 1990 several hours before the troops landed, but were unable to respond adequately. Despite warning from Cuban electronic eavesdroppers, from U.S commercial television stations and from government leaks, the speed and destructiveness of the U.S. attack decapitated Panama's command structure in the first hour of the attack.

And sometimes the attacker can achieve complete surprise, despite years of tension, crises and near-war. This was certainly demonstrated by the Israeli destruction of Arab airbases on the first morning of the 1967 Six-Day War, which also showed that the initial attacker often has the luxury of choosing the best day for the attack and has the additional luxury of being able to spend years preparing complex and integrated deception schemes.

When trying to detect preparations for an attack, analysts face a very difficult time separating the wheat from the chaff. In her work on the surprise attack on Pearl Harbor, Roberta Wohlstetter suggested that the warning signals that could have revealed Japanese intentions to attack Pearl Harbor were buried in the noise of other information, such as routine activities, faulty assumptions, ambiguous statements, and economic indicators. Limited intelligence assets and Japanese secrecy reduced the U.S. signal-to-noise ratio, despite the decryption of the most secret Japanese diplomatic traffic. It was only well after the event that U.S. analysts were able to filter the noise from the signals with the perspective granted by hindsight, and learn the errors of their ways.[42]

So it is with modern signals intelligence and other warning systems. Although they are capable of sucking up vastly more information much more efficiently than in the past, they also collect vast amounts of extraneous noise or nonvital information. Of course, like Rommel's eavesdroppers in the desert, analysts may find a single critical warning indicator of an attack. Thus activation of Soviet tactical radio networks "is seen as a key indicator of offensive action. A division will have not only to test its radio but also get them all 'on net' before moving out, a process that can take 24 hours."[43]

But it would be well to remember that the Soviet invasion of Afghanistan was a stunning surprise, despite the mobilization of six low-readiness mechanized divisions in full view of any orbiting photographic satellites. These divisions had practiced for several weeks, leaving behind dummy radio networks before they invaded Afghanistan, according to Isby.[44]

This raises the important role of deception. While camouflage and secrecy hide signals, deception creates misleading signals, greatly complicating the analysts' tasks. Modern vacuum-cleaner intelligence gathering systems can collect and reinforce deceptive information just as easily as true information. Thus Soviet Major General M. Iononov said, "the group of techniques for shaping the opponent's decision making requires substantial expenditure of effort, particularly the technique of regular conduct of strategic-scale exercises on one plan with the aim of decisive actions on another plan which sharply differ from the training exercise."[45]

Faced with deceptive signals of intention, intelligence organizations must argue whether the signals are true or false, whether they are just noise or real signals. The analysts must then convince their political masters to act on their recommendations in the increasingly short time available.

Clearly, proper secrecy by the aggressor will help hide real signals and bias analysts toward the deceptive signals. Thus good deception is dependent on good security.

Crucially, there is no reason to presume that faulty assumptions and poor intelligence analysis are less likely today than just before Pearl Harbor. Signals intelligence is not a science, but an art. As one source told Seymour Hersh, understanding enemy conversations is "like the problem in translating the New Testament scriptures into any language. There is more than one rendering of what Mark said."[46]

Numerous factors influence the interpretation of signals or the assessment of an intercept's importance. These complicating factors include ingrained assumptions, language problems, enemy deception, and the suppression of information that could help interpret signals. And unless expert management is able to keep the intelligence organization from falling into an intellectual rut, there is every danger the organization will fail to understand innovative technologies, original strategies, or unfamiliar patterns of behavior. As one expert wrote, "The necessity of [intelligence assumptions] gives analysts an opportunity to indulge their own prejudices. With continued indulgence, these prejudices may harden into axioms."[47] If they do harden, the opportunities for deception by an alert enemy will greatly increase.

Another factor working for deception is misplaced trust. The more trusted the intelligence gathering system, the more likely it is that the deception will succeed. Apart from a visibly self-sacrificing spy, signals intelligence is the most trusted of intelligence gathering means — especially because it is one of the speediest. Thus Peter Wright, former technical adviser to the British counterspy organization, suggested that the Soviets used already-detected British bugs hidden in the Egyptian embassy to deceive the British government during the 1956 Suez Canal crisis. Precisely because the British believed they were directly eavesdropping on secret conversations between the Soviets and the Egyptians, they were much more intimidated by the overheard Soviet threats to intervene in the crisis.[48]

And complete deception or total secrecy is not at all necessary for military surprise — especially because intelligence analysts must successfully convince their political leaders that the indicators actually point to an enemy intention to attack, not just an enemy capability to attack. Thus the German invasion of the USSR — the most destructive surprise attack ever — was correctly predicted by British and Soviet intelligence services well in advance of the day, but Stalin refused to act. Part of the reason for inaction was that Stalin's fear of attack was abated by German deceptive measures, which included radio silence and deceptive radio broadcasts such as "Hans of the 21st Panzer division says hello to Helga from his camp near Paris." In fact, Hans was loading ammunition into his tank only a few miles from the Soviet border.

One perfectly valid reason for Stalin's refusal to act was fear of precipitating a German attack, thereby causing what he wanted to avoid. The lesson here is drawn from the start of World War I when Russian mobilization tipped the world over the abyss. Although the Russian mobilization was only meant to illustrate support for Russia's ally of Serbia, which was threatened by German's ally of Austria-Hungary, it caused the Germans to mobilize and activate their only war plan, which called for aggressive offensives into France. Thus an apparently defensive move by Russia can be said to have precipitated World War I, a mistake no Soviet, European, or American politician wants to repeat. Thus politicians may well do their very best to avoid antagonizing their potential enemy by mobilizing their defenses, despite clear warnings from intelligence analysts.

Intelligence information is not only rejected because of this perfectly reasonable fear of escalating a conflict, but also because the top leaders simply ignore unpleasant information. General Douglas MacArthur's unwillingness to study intelligence indicators enabled the Chinese army to achieve complete surprise when it moved into North Korea to attack United Nations troops. As one American observer wrote, "It was not the absence of intelligence which led us into trouble, but our unwillingness to draw unpleasant conclusions from it."[49]

Deception can be used to greatly reinforce these human and political tendencies to reject intelligence information. In the face of nuclear danger, even simple deceptive measures could combine with other factors to justify a decision to do nothing. So it can be argued that the greater the danger, the greater the chance of surprise. Many observers predicted that the undisciplined multinational NATO organization would do nothing in the face of attack warnings for fear of precipitating the attack whose consequences might well be apocalyptic. Even the simplest deceptive measures used by the Soviets — such as predictable calls for negotiations — might have been seized upon by NATO leaders to justify continued inaction and a refusal to mobilize for fear of upsetting negotiations.

In addition to this list of factors that prevent signals intelligence from being converted into political action, there are several related factors that reduce the chance for successful achievement of surprise. These include the very large number and wide distribution in modern armies of radios, radars, generators and other devices that would probably create many signals for detection by the many intelligence gathering platforms — despite the tightest radio silence. Moreover, mistakes are likely to be made by the deceivers as well as the deceived, such as errors in signal security, camouflage or deception. One example is the Soviets' construction in Cuba of standard pattern nuclear missile bases, which allowed the U.S. to rapidly recognize the bases as intended for nuclear-tipped missiles rather than antiaircraft missiles.

Has the advance of signals intelligence technology reduced the opportunity for surprise? The answer is yes, despite increased opportunities for deception and confusion. But technology remains less important than the skilled analyst, the wise intelligence chief, and the courageous politician, all three of whom are decisive factors in detection of a surprise attack.

ARMS CONTROL VERIFICATION

One of the sharpest areas of electronic conflict between East and West is the monitoring of enemy nuclear capabilities. Revealed in great detail by the related public debate on arms control, this endless battle between the nuke hiders and intelligence finders continues to be fought over the entire electromagnetic spectrum.

We can hope that Gorbachev's modernizers will end this competition, but only time will tell whether increased openness of the Soviet Union will reduce the need for technological monitoring of arms control treaty compliance.

From the early 1960s on, the most important means of counting Soviet missiles was the photographic spy satellites, which could see the Soviet missile silos, and sometimes their reload missiles.

But the chief means of monitoring the capabilities of these missiles was interception of Soviet missile test telemetry by signals intelligence satellites and ground stations. Telemetry signals are sent by test missiles to show ground observers how the missile is performing. Without these signals, developers would be unable to tell why some missile tests were successes and others failures.

In the early 1970s, the U.S. relied on telemetry signals gathered by Rhyolite signals intelligence satellites to assess the capabilities of the Soviet missiles, unknown to the Soviets. It is from these satellite intercepts that the U.S. was able to release quite detailed information about such Soviet missiles as the SS-17, -18, -19, and -20, including the number of warheads as well as the missile's range, accuracy and carrying potential or throw-weight. Ground stations in Iran also provided crucial telemetry data, until they were closed down by the Ayatollah Khomeni's revolution.

Yet despite past successes, there are many obstacles facing U.S. signal intelligence gathering. One of these obstacles is Soviet encryption of communications. From about 1975, shortly after the secrets of the Rhyolite had been betrayed, the Soviets began to encrypt significant portions of their missile telemetry, reduce the strength of the telemetry signals and to use more directional antennas.

According to Desmond Ball, Soviet telemetry signals were typically transmitted at the low power of ten watts until 1978. Although transmitting power was further reduced again in 1984, the increasing size of antennas on U.S. satellites allowed continued interception of the signals.[50] The *Washington Times* reported in July 1984 that telemetry signals were reduced to such an extent that only Soviet aircraft flying near the missile could intercept the signals.

The Soviets also continued to increase encryption of telemetry. The U.S. was warned of this trend by a 1978 test of the ten-warhead SS-18 missile, which was encrypted to "an unprecedented extent."[51] The encryption included the messages showing the number of warheads carried by the missile, but powerful cameras mounted on modified Boeing 707 jets codenamed Cobra Ball were able to count the warheads as they splashed down in the Pacific.

Through the late 1970s and early 1980s, the Soviets gradually increased the levels of encryption of missile tests. After a test of a Soviet naval SS-N-20 nuclear-tipped missile in January 1980, during which about 70 percent of the channels were encrypted, the Defense Intelligence Agency reported that "the unreadable data appear to include all of the guidance computer information and at least some of the propulsion and altitude measurements.... If the Soviets continue to encrypt data at this level, the United States' ability to determine the missile's launch weight, throw-weight and accuracy will be significantly lessened."[52]

By the time the new generation SS-24 missile was tested, encryption had reached 95 percent, and some tests of the new SS-25 were totally encrypted.[53] To foil photographic satellites, the Soviets also tested the road-mobile SS-25 at night, ensuring that the high-quality visible light cameras mounted on satellites could not see the launcher.

Other *maskirovka* measures further reduced U.S. monitoring capabilities. According to Seymour Hersh, the Cobra Ball aircraft that photographed Soviet warheads as they plummeted toward their aim points relied on signals intelligence for warning of impending tests. Without the warning given by signals intelligence, the aircraft would not be positioned to take pictures when the warheads reentered. But in the early 1980s, the Soviets changed radio traffic patterns to reduce the U.S. warning time. One intelligence official said, "Now, we see a communications pattern that looks good and we go — and then they don't launch [a test missile]. It's expensive to launch these birds [aircraft], and our hit rate is not that great."[54]

The Soviets were not content with just good signal security. Richard Perle, assistant secretary of defense for international security policy, told a congressional committee that signals intelligence satellites had been jammed, saying "It is very worrisome... There is a pattern, and a growing pattern, unhappily, of the Soviets resorting to a variety of devices that have the effect of denying us information that is critical to judging their performance under existing [arms control treaty] obligations. And interfering with satellites... is one of the devices that they have been resorting to."[55]

The U.S. responded to Soviet *maskirovka* by introducing ever more advanced signals intelligence satellites such as the Magnum and the Vortex. Also, the National Security Agency was able to decrypt Soviet telemetry by applying large numbers of powerful computers to perform immense number-crunching tasks. In turn, this decryption revealed other Soviet deception measures. In 1978, ex-Secretary of Defense Melvin Laird said that in 1976 the U.S. had decrypted telemetry of an SS-20 missile, which was then believed to be an intermediate range missile unable to threaten the U.S. "When we finally deciphered SS-20 telemetry, military analysts concluded that the missile had been tested with some 900 kilos (1,980 lbs.) of ballast. Were this ballast to be replaced by fuel, the SS-20 could become an intercontinental missile capable of menacing North America," he said.[56]

Interception and decryption of the signals only gets the listeners halfway, because they must interpret the decrypted signals correctly. Typically, telemetry appears as continuous traces on a roll of paper or a computer screen. To interpret the readouts correctly, the scale of the signals must be assessed accurately. If mistakes are made in reading the scale, the analyst will misjudge the missile's size and accuracy.

In the 1960s, the Soviets did manage to deceive U.S. analysts by installing biased versions of critical components called gyroscopes in their test missiles, according to William R. Harris, an expert on intelligence issues and a former adviser to the Senate Intelligence Committee.

Gyroscopes can be used to measures movement, so three gyroscopes can measure the movements of an object in three dimensions. Accurate gyroscopes are vital if the missile is to control its rocket motor and direction to maximize accuracy. According to Harris, the Soviets installed three sets of three gyroscopes in their SS-7 missiles. This was an early Soviet missile design, and transmitted the unencrypted telemetry signals from the gyroscopes to ground stations. When the U.S. picked up the telemetry signals, it found that the gyroscopes were giving very different readings. To the analysts, these different figures indicated that Soviet gyros were of poor quality, which meant that Soviet missiles would only be very inaccurate. And inaccurate missiles would pose no threat to U.S. nuclear forces. This meant the U.S could rest secure.

It was only when the accuracy of the next generation of missiles, the SS-17, -18 and -19, was observed in the early 1970s, that the U.S. decided the Soviet missiles were a threat to the American retaliatory forces. Intelligence analysts then reviewed the earlier telemetry readings and concluded that only some of the gyroscopes had reported accurate information. The others reported deceptively inaccurate information.

But why would the Soviets wish to mislead American analysts? Because the Soviet military regarded peacetime radioelectronic combat as only a precursor to wartime radioelectronic combat. Clearly, Soviet planners responsible for *radiomaskirovka* and radioelectronic protection would have been derelict in their duty if they failed to try to influence U.S. analysts by planting subtly misleading indicators that gently lead analysts away from the truth. Moreover, U.S. confidence in their missile superiority helped overcome conservative opposition to the 1972 Strategic Arms Limitation Treaty, which allowed the Soviets more missiles than the U.S.

A long-standing problem with good intelligence is that it is sometimes too valuable to be openly discussed for fear of betraying how it was acquired. Thus Desmond Ball wrote, "as Soviet practice has confirmed, the more the Soviets learned about U.S. telemetry intelligence collection and decryption abilities, the more they were able to obstruct those abilities."[57]

This leads to a more important point. Even if U.S. systems can detect possible Soviet cheating, can the intelligence agencies collect enough evidence to convince the U.S. administration and Congress that the Soviets are cheating? For politicians and pressure groups of every stripe, conclusions frequently come before facts. Thus a signals intercept of an illegal missile test can be dismissed as ambiguous or as contradicted by other data. And any violation can also be viewed as military insignificant. Or a clear picture of a illegal missile might be rejected as an isolated violation caused by a bureaucratic error in the Soviet military. For example, the Soviet large phased array radar at Krasnoyarsk was revealed to be several hundred miles from a legal location and also pointing in an illegal direction. Yet some politicians and pressure groups said it was not a blatant Soviet violation of the 1972 ABM radar, but was built in the wrong place to save money or actually as part of the civilian space-tracking effort.

The basic point is that intelligence gathering is carried out by intelligence agencies, while only politicians can decide to ignore or accept the information, decide how important it is, and what should be done about it.

Because of all these technical, intelligence and political issues, U.S. faith in telemetry to verify Soviet violations has been greatly reduced. President Reagan explained the intelligence establishment's view to Congress in March 1988 when he said that "in the future, reliance on telemetry for verification purposes must be minimized since it is under the complete control of the other party and so can easily be denied."[58]

Instead, the U.S. is pinning its faith for the 1990s on a combination of techniques, including on-site inspection and the new generation of space-based radar satellites codenamed Lacrosse, which are harder to foil than passive eavesdropping devices. Good intelligence analysts and the combination of these new intelligence gathering systems should greatly help overcome obstacles to nuclear weapon counting laid by Soviet REB and *maskirovka*. Also, Gorbachev's modernizers may curtail the use of deception, and promote *Glasnost* in Soviet military matters. Better still, the communist system in the USSR might well be replaced by a democratic system where the military is firmly under the control of the government.

NON-MILITARY PEACETIME ELECTRONIC WARFARE

There are clearly many opportunities in peacetime electronic warfare beyond gathering military signals intelligence. Consequently, the organizations practicing diplomatic spying, international trade, propaganda, guerrilla warfare, and terrorism have not hesitated to exploit the spectrum for their various purposes.

Few observers would doubt that nations monitor each other's communications to further their own foreign policy - especially when involved in international negotiations. During the 1921 naval disarmament negotiations, the U.S. gained a powerful advantage by decrypting Japanese messages. In trying to agree on a ratio of naval forces between the five main naval powers, the U.S. favored a 10:6 force ratio between the U.S. and Japan. However, the Japanese were determined to hold out for a better ratio of 10:7. But the U.S. Black Chamber, a secret team led by Herbert Yardley, was able to decrypt

Japanese diplomatic codes. In November, after the negotiations had gone on for several months, the team decrypted a message which stated that because it was necessary to avoid a clash with Great Britain and America, the Japanese delegation was permitted if all else failed to accept a 10:6 force ratio, instead of the previously demanded ratio of 10:7. As the chief codebreaker Herbert Yardley wrote: "With this information in its hands, the American government, if it cared to take advantage of it, could not lose. All it need do was mark time. Stud poker is not a very difficult game after you see your opponent's hole card."[59]

Gradually, decrypted telegrams showed Japanese resistance steadily wilting under international pressure, demonstrating the success of U.S. intransigence. Eventually, the Japanese capitulated and accepted the U.S.'s 10:6 position in December 1921.[60]

With the increased use of radio, opportunities for communications eavesdropping and decryption have increased manyfold. In contemporary conditions, when nuclear arms control treaties could have an extremely important impact upon the fate of nations, knowledge of an opponent's bargaining positions would yield proportionately important advantages.

For example, assistant Secretary of Defense Richard Perle told a Senate hearing that in 1972 U.S. eavesdroppers were able to intercept a conversation between Soviet chief Brezhnev and Chief of the General Staff Dimitri Ustinov in which Ustinov promised that the new generation of highly secret Soviet SS-19 missiles would be unaffected by the SALT 1 arms control negotiations. If the U.S. had wished to restrict the SS-19, this information would have alerted its negotiators to tighten their demands.

Signals intelligence can also be used profitably in seemingly nonpolitical negotiations. Thus former intelligence official Jeffrey Richelson writes of Soviet eavesdropping: "Also of great value may be the intercepts of phone conversations passing through the phone lines of the Departments of Commerce, Agriculture, and Treasury. In the early 1970s the Soviets monitored all telephone calls to the Department of Agriculture so as to be as well informed as possible of the state of the U.S. grain market. They used this information to negotiate a grain deal in 1974 that is referred to by many U.S. farmers as the 'great grain robbery.'"[61]

The Soviets also take advantage of their facilities in Glen Cove, New York, to monitor the nearby stock markets in Manhattan. "Some intelligence sources believe the Soviets are the biggest inside traders in the various U.S. stock and commodity markets," according to television reporter Bob Franken.[62] Desmond Ball wrote that signals intelligence was a "major source of commercial information," to the Soviets, adding that "the targets of the Soviet signals intelligence establishment and the capabilities of the Soviet signals intelligence systems go far beyond official government signals."[63]

Spying by electronic eavesdropping has become easier and more fruitful since the 1970s because of the exploding number of computers in use by the West, all of which leak signals that can easily be intercepted.

For example, the Dutch scientist Wilem Van Eck demonstrated how a simple homemade monitoring device costing barely $150 was capable of reading computer screens at a range of 2 km (1.2 mi). This machine intercepted the signal emitted by any computer display screen and replicated the signal on a second-hand TV. To prove the vulnerability of modern computers, he publicly demonstrated his device at a conference on computer security by using the nearby computers as victims. He subsequently demonstrated his device on British television by eavesdropping on computers at what was suggested to be Scotland Yard, headquarters of the British police.

With the computer explosion in U.S. society, and the increasing use of computers for everyday writing of classified memos and reports, for the design of complex weaponry, for the processing of secret data and for the control of classified phone conversations, devices similar to the Van Eck type promise an intelligence bonanza.

Needless to say, it is very unlikely that the intelligence services did not develop the technique many years before Van Eck demonstrated his homemade device to a prime-time television audience.

Radiation leaking from electric or electronic systems has compromised security efforts in the past. For example, Peter Wright revealed that the British successfully bugged the French embassy in 1960 by tapping a low-grade cipher machine's power cable and using electrical feedback to read the clear text of messages as they were being punched in. Even worse for the French, the British were able to analyze electrical interference created in the cable by an adjacent but separate high-grade cipher machine. This enabled them to read much higher grade secret messages as they were being punched into the second machine. Although this success over England's traditional enemy was seen in London as a "worthy successor to Agincourt, the burning of Calais, and other ancient blows against the perfidious French," it had no long-run benefit because the British lost their diplomatic battle with the French: De Gaulle's adamant opposition prevented Britain from joining the Common Market.[64]

To help prevent similar electronic eavesdropping on computer emissions, the U.S. National Security Agency has created the classified TEMPEST program. Using electrical shielding, special circuits, sealed containers, and metalclad rooms, the agency has sought to prevent eavesdropping of the radiation emitted by the rapidly increasing number of computers in the US security establishment. Although TEMPEST protection can reduce emissions by more than 10,000 times, it can never suppress them enough to guarantee secrecy. the reduction in emissions has greatly increased the cost and risk of electronic spying.

Signals intelligence is also used to detect and capture spies. Thus Nazi intercept expert Flicke spent the last few months of World War II tracking down Polish and Russian partisans by their radio transmissions. But spy-hunters can also use other emissions from radios. British spycatcher Peter Wright revealed how he helped develop a device that detected signals leaked from radio components, so allowing discovery of supposedly passive radio receivers.

Also, traffic analysis of transmissions to and from spies can be of crucial help to counterspy organizations. The monitoring of the Soviet embassy in 1960 helped convince Wright there was a Soviet mole in the British counterspy organization. The crucial clue was the radio that did not transmit: signals intelligence specialists failed to detect any messages from the Soviet embassy when the British arrested several Soviets working undercover in London. Moreover, the signals to and from one of the spies were unusually sparse for such an experienced agent and indicated he was only handling one British agent. When combined with other indicators, such as the calm reaction of recognized KGB agents to the news of the arrests, this evidence strongly suggested the Soviets already knew their spies were going to be arrested. Thus, Wright suggests, there was a Soviet mole buried deep in British intelligence, whom the Soviets were willing to protect by sacrificing two other spies. The arrest of the spies also showed they were equipped with very advanced burst transmitters. Presumably Soviet spies now use more covert spread-spectrum satellite-relayed signals.[65]

Peacetime political struggles are also reflected in radio wars — known as propaganda to one side and as truth to another. Unsurprisingly, the Soviets were early practitioners of this radio propaganda technique during World War I: "The German and Austrian soldiers, weary of war, filled with questions of a new order, were eager to hear and to absorb what was coming out of this land of consistent socialism.... [and] the troops which had been left there began to drop out of the picture as a dependable military force for the central powers. At that time Russia was the first country to recognize and make use of the value and power of modern radio propaganda."[66]

What goes around, comes around. Up until 1989, the Soviets fiercely criticized Western radio broadcasts to the Soviet audiences who were denied accurate news. Although in recent years the Soviets have ceased jamming the Western news stations, and have even let them open bureaus in Moscow, they are still used by the Soviets as scapegoats for internal problems. For example, blame for the 1989 riots in Georgia, Armenia and Azerbaijan was placed on "foreign radio voices" by Soviet internal security officials.

With the benefit of hindsight, it appears that these broadcasts steadily helped undermine communism in East Europe, sowing the seeds that led to the popular uprisings of 1989. Of course, radio and television broadcasts into Eastern Europe cannot claim all the credit for the eventual appearance of mass resistance to communism, but they helped greatly by continually supplying information that gave the lie to the claims of communist governments. The news they carried helped destroy any misplaced public faith in communism and also helped rot the morale of the apparatchiks who controlled the communist governments, until they collapsed with hardly a whimper.

Worldwide, Western radio stations seem to be regarded by many listeners as authoritative sources. They continue to serve the Western world well by disseminating near-truths generated by Western journalists. They undermine the Soviet, South African, Chinese, North Korean, and Islamic versions of reality, so strengthening pressure for internal political reform and bolstering the struggles of many to free themselves from the dominance of the state. More than one observer has noted how well the BBC was, and is, listened to in war-torn Afghanistan, where sixteen clandestine radio stations operated intermittently at one period, including one using commentaries recorded by Soviet emmigrants intended to sow dissension among Soviet soldiers.[67]

Meanwhile, the 1989 revolt in Rumania seemed to center around the national television station, which was used by the anti-Ceaucescu forces to demonstrate their success and rally public support, despite some apparent attacks by the much-feared *Securitate* secret police that were fended off with the help of radio intercepts gathered by friendly Hungarian military.

As any coup-plotter knows, seizure of government-controlled radio and television stations is critical to convincing the public and resisters that the plotters have won.

But radio propaganda is also used for many other, less noble purposes. Radio propaganda experts Lawrence Soley and John Nichols cited a 1960s CIA radio station which masqueraded as a mainland China radio station criticizing Mao's Red Guards. Its purpose was to foment further chaos during the Cultural Revolution. This station, operated from Taiwan, apparently duped many listeners in China and in the U.S., where academics and officials in the State Department cited its rantings as evidence for one argument or another.[68]

In Iran during the 1980s, American and Soviet propaganda stations purported to broadcast from inside Iran and sought to mobilize Iranians in favor of U.S. or Soviet interests. Sometimes, U.S. and Soviet radio stations tried to discredit each other by masquerading as one another while spouting outrageous statements and lies. The propaganda struggle reached new peacetime heights when the American station called the Free Voice of Iran was "extensively jammed" from inside the borders of the USSR.[69]

This radio war for the hearts and minds of embattled populations continues apace in the Caribbean, where Castro is trying to fend off the U.S. government-sponsored news and pictures broadcast by the first television propaganda station, TV Marti. Only time will tell whether TV Marti or the Cuban government will win the battle of the airwaves.

The Kuwaiti crisis of 1990 escalated the international war of words and images to unprecedented levels. As the U.S. sought to muster support for an anti-Iraq coalition, Iraqi leaders aggressively used the

CNN international television network to weaken the coalition. Thus CNN broadcast Saddam Hussein's speeches, "popular" demonstrations against the economic blockade, defiant Iraqi declarations of determination, and blustering threats by Iraqi spokesmen. One top Iraqi diplomat told a visiting journalist that "your presence here and the reporting you do means that Baghdad ceases to be an abstraction in the minds of people in the West. It becomes for you a real place, with real people. If the Americans bomb us, everyone knows that ordinary people like themselves will be killed. In a way, you are a form of national defense for us."[70]

CONCLUSION

Even in the absence of war, the peacetime practice of electronic struggle will remain a vital prop of national security and military strength. And through the years of peacetime, radio and television broadcasts — called propaganda if performed by the enemy — can accumulate to cause great impact, as the public rejection in 1989 of communism by East Europe showed.

Notes

1. David C,. Chizum, *Soviet Radioelectronic Combat* (Boulder and London: Westview), p. 17.
2. Most of the information on peacetime activities used by the author largely originates from Western intelligence sources, and chiefly concerns Soviet spying and radioelectronic combat activities. Western intelligence organizations do not like to advertise their failures or successes, and Soviet organizations have no wish to publicize anything about their activities.
3. Jeffrey Richelson, *Sword and Shield: The Soviet Intelligence and Security Apparatus* (Cambridge, MA: Ballinger, 1986), p. 89.
4. Wilhelm Flicke, *War Secrets in the Ether* (Fort Meade, MD: National Security Agency, 1945), p. 99.

5. Desmond Ball, "Soviet Signals Intelligence," in *The International Countermeasures Handbook*, 12th ed. (Palo Alto, CA: EW Communications, 1987), p. 6.

6. Ibid., p. 73.

7. Testimony to Congress, march 1977. Department of Defense Appropriations for 1978, part 3, p. 639. See Ball "Soviet Signals Intelligence," *International Countermeasures Handbook*, p. 73.

8. Ball, "Soviet Signals Intelligence," in *International Countermeasures Handbook* (1987), p. 74.

9. Ibid., p. 78.

10. *Defense Electronics*, March 1990, p. 16.

11. Richelson, *Sword and Shield*, p. 99.

12. Ibid., p. 96, 98.

13. For one glaring example that occurred in Australia, see Desmond Ball, in *Pacific Defense Reporter*, 1 October, 1987, p. 16.

14. Ball, "Soviet Signals Intelligence," in *International Countermeasures Handbook* (1987), p. 73, 83.

15. Richelson in *Sword and Shield*, pp. 101-103, but also see Desmond Ball, *Pacific Defense Reporter*, 1 October 1987 and June 1989.

16. *Jane's Defense Weekly*, 11 July 1987, p. 45.

17. See Richelson, *Sword and Shield*, pp. 87-98 for information about Soviet signals intelligence, pp. 97-98 on ships, and pp. 103-105 on satellites.

18. Desmond Ball, "Soviet Signals Intelligence," *The International Countermeasures Handbook*, (1987), p. 88.

19. Desmond Ball, *Pine Gap* (Winchester, MA: Allen and Unwin, 1988), p. 14-15. The U.S. also tried to launch a Vortex satellite in September 1988, but it reportedly failed to get into its planned orbit; See *Washington Post*, 6 September, 1990.

20. Ray S. Cline, *The CIA under Reagan and Casey; The Evolution of the Agency from Roosevelt to Reagan* (Washington DC: Acropolis, 1981)

21. Ball, *Pine Gap*, p. 27.

22. *Aviation Week and Space Technology*, 5 March, 1989. p. 22.

23. *Washington Post*, 3 September, 1988. p. 1.

24. Martin Streetly, *Airborne Electronic Warfare; History, Techniques and Tactics*, (London: Jane's, 1988), p. 171.

25. Seymour Hersh, *"The Target Is Destroyed": What Really Happened to Flight 007 and What America Knew About It* (New York: Random House, 1986), p. 220.

26. *The DARPA Neural Network Study* (Cambridge, MA: Lincoln Laboratory, Massachusetts Institute of Technology, July 1988).

27. *Los Angeles Times*, 23 March, 1990, p. 8.

28. Flicke, *War Secrets in the Ether*, p. 91.

29. Hersh, *"The Target is Destroyed"*, p. 237.

30. Flicke, *War Secrets in the Ether*, p. 94. Flicke's complaint about Russian secrecy was not new; Around 1800, Austrian foreign minister Metternich complained during the Napoleonic wars of the "difficulty of obtaining any true information from Russia and thus the uncertainty of any reciprocity of confidence."

31. Viktor Suvorov, *Inside the Soviet Army* (New York: Macmillan, 1982), p. 106.

32. John Dziak, "Soviet Deception: The Organization and Doctrine for Strategic Deception," in Brian Dailey and Patrick Parker, eds., *Soviet Strategic Deception*, (Palo Alto, CA: Hoover Institution, 1987), p. 16.

33. Richard Heur, "Soviet Organization and Doctrine for Strategic Deception," in Dailey and Parker, *Soviet Strategic Deception*, p. 47.

34. *Washington Times*, 6 April 1988, p. 6.

35. Hersh, *"The Target is Destroyed"*, p. 257.

36. Ibid., p. 244.

37. *Washington Post*, 7 March, 1990.

38. Hersh, *"The Target is Destroyed"*, p. 260.

39. Richard Fitts, eds., *The Strategy of Electromagnetic Conflict*, (Los Altos, CA: Peninsula Publishing, 1980), p. 60.

40. U.S. House of Representatives, Legislation and National Security Subcommittee of the House Government Operations Committee, *Our Nations Nuclear Warning System: Will It Work If We Need It?* (Washington DC: Government Printing Office, September, 1985), p. 34.

41. Viktor Suvorov, *Inside the Aquarium: The Making of a Top Soviet Spy*, (New York: Macmillan, 1986).

42. Roberta Wohlstetter, *Pearl Harbor: Warning and Decision* (Stanford, CA: Stanford University, 1962).

43. David C. Isby, *Weapons and Tactics of the Soviet Army* (London and New York: Jane's, 1981), p. 480.

44. Ibid., p. 484.

45. M. Ionov, *On the Methods of Influencing an Opponents's Decision*. Quoted by Notra Trulock, "The Role of Deception in Soviet Military Planning," in Dailey and Parker, *Soviet Strategic Deception*, p. 283.

46. Hersh, *"The Target is Destroyed"*, p. 154.

47. Angelo Codevilla, "Space, Intelligence and Deception," in Dailey and Parker, *Soviet Strategic Deception*, p. 470.

48. Peter Wright, *Spycatcher* (New York: Viking, 1987), p. 86.

49. Harvey De Weerd, "Strategic Surprise in the Korean War," *Orbis*, Fall 1962.

50. Ball, *Pine Gap*, p. 34.

51. Ibid., p. 37.

52. Ibid., p. 40.

53. Ibid., p. 40.

54. Hersh, *"The Target is Destroyed"*, p. 41.

55. 20 June 1984.

56. Ball, *Pine Gap*, p. 43. See also Melvin Laird, "The Soviets are Cheating," *Readers Digest*, January 1978, p. 85.

57. Ball, *Pine Gap*, p. 42.

58. Ibid., p. 43.

59. Herbert Yardley, *The Black Chamber* (Indianapolis: Bobbs-Merrill, 1931), p. 313.

60. Yardley was very shabbily treated in 1928 by President Herbert Hoover's secretary of state, Henry Stimson, who supposedly pronounced piously that "gentlemen do not read each other's mail" as he fired Yardley and closed down the United States' only codebreaking organization: see Lt. Col. Richard Fitts, *The Strategy of Electromagnetic Conflict*, p. 131.

    Yardley later betrayed his successes to the world in his book, *The American Black Chamber* (n. 59, above). His self promotion produced this hyperbolic passage: "The Black Chamber, bolted, guarded, sees all, hears all. Though the blinds are drawn and the windows heavily curtained, its far seeing-eye penetrates the secret conference chambers at Washington, Tokio, London, Paris, Geneva, Rome."

    But in an article by Rear Admiral Kemp Tolley in *Proceedings of the U.S. Naval Institute*, September 1988, p. 74, said that the information might have been gained after the U.S. burgled the Japanese consulate's safe to get the codebooks.

61. Richelson, *Sword and Shield*, p. 102.

62. *CNN* broadcast, 24 August, 1987.

63. Ball, *International Countermeasures Handbook* (1987), p. 88.

64. Wright, *Spycatcher*, p. 111,

65. Ibid., p. 139-144.

66. Flicke, *War Secrets in the Ether*, p. 77.

67. Lawrence Soley and John Nichols, *Clandestine Radio Broadcasting,*
     (New York: Praeger, 1987), p. 130.
68. Ibid., p. 2.
69. Ibid., p. 127.
70. *Washington Post*, 13 November, 1990, p. 23.

Eight

◆

SOVIET REB IN CONVENTIONAL WARFARE

The fight to win time is the primary problem in the process of command and control. The saying by Suvorov "One minute decides the success of the battle, one hour the success of the campaign, and one day the fate of the war" has now acquired literal meaning. Victory in modern warfare will be on the side of the commander who best organizes control, who is more energetic in his actions, and who is more perspicacious in his plans and decisions.

Marshal A.A. Grechko,
The Armed Forces of the Soviet State

If it becomes embroiled in a war, the Soviet military plans to use its doctrine of radioelectronic struggle (*radio-elektronnaya bor'ba* or REB) to support war aims, military strategy, and combat operations.

Naturally, the Soviet politicians will try to control their military instrument for political purposes. But at lower level of command, REB will be combined with *razvedka* and *maskirovka* to protect Soviet command and control and to wreck enemy command and control.

Indeed, "The system of command and control is now considered to be a primary target of reconnaissance and destruction," according to Colonel General P.K. Altukhov.[1] This emphasis on command and control reflects the Soviet military's concentration on land warfare, and shows Soviet determination to use REB to help win battles, campaigns, and even wars.

The Soviet military's vision of REB is unabashedly aggressive, stressing heavily the annihilation of enemy command and control. Two of the primary means of such annihilation will be the reconnaissance–strike complex, and its shorter range brother, the reconnaissance–fire complex, which directly link powerful weapons to long-range sensors. Thus Soviet radio-direction finders might act as target spotters for artillery batteries, or spy satellites might be used to seek worthwhile targets for long range SU-24 Fencer bombers.

The Soviets expect reconnaissance-strike complexes to accelerate the pace of battle, and so help reduce the role of massed columns of heavy tanks and to increase the role of long-range battles fought with sensors and rockets. According to Soviet generals, they may also allow the Soviets to bypass the colossus of nuclear weapons, allowing them to win political crises without suffering nuclear devastation.

Little or no information is available on whether the Soviet Army, Air Force, or Navy have different approaches to the use of REB. However, it can be said that the Air Force and Navy emphasize the blinding of enemy radars and other sensors over the wrecking of enemy command and control. But whatever approach the services might have or whatever type of war may occur, Soviet REB will rely on surprise, and integrated and massive use of intelligence, jamming, and weaponry.

The extent to which Soviet politicians can control the Soviet war machine in wartime is unclear. The political conflict, fears, uncertainty, and chaos of war allows the violence to acquire enormous momentum, making control very difficult. No doubt, aggressive practice of electronic combat will make control even more difficult, even as failure to practice aggressive REB will give the enemy the upper hand.

However Soviet civil-military relations change in the coming years — hopefully towards ever-greater infusion of Western ideas — close examination of how the Soviet military plans to use REB for its war aims will help the West influence Soviet military activity, and also better exploit electronic combat for its own purposes.

SOVIET COMMAND AND CONTROL

The Soviet wartime use of REB is inextricably bound up with their idea of command and control because the main emphasis of REB is the disruption of the enemy's command and control.

The Soviet military's theory of command and control or, more properly, *upravleniye voiskami*, is defined as "the purposeful activities of commanders, staffs, and other agencies to maintain combat readiness, their preparation for combat actions, and their guidance during accomplishment of assigned missions. The purpose of control is to assure maximum effectiveness in employment of available resources under specific situational conditions and with the fewest losses."[2]

According to the Soviets, *upravleniye* is critical to the offensive and to wartime success. The importance of *upravleniye* became even more important after the post-war revolution in military affairs caused by nuclear weapons, ballistic missiles, and modern command and control systems. Thus, in 1975, Soviet Minister of Defense Marshal Grechko said, *"High combat readiness of all directing elements and of the entire systems of command and control as a whole has now assumed exceptional importance."*[3]

But as troop control has grown in importance, so has the difficulty of exercising it. The greater mobility of combat units, and the longer range of weapons connected by data links to sensors, have increased the need for prompt and reliable information for the commander. "The volume of information that the staffs must process has increased manyfold since World War II, and the time allowed for decisionmaking has decreased manyfold. ...As a result the only escape from this incompatible situation lies in the extensive application of automation, primarily computers," according to General Shtemenko.[4]

But the new computers, practices and techniques needed to make maximum use of available time, such as the simultaneous planning of all aspects of an attacks were — and are — difficult to learn. Mere computerization is not sufficient; new planning and management techniques as well as better junior officers and staffs are needed, according to Soviet authors.

Y.E. Savkin's 1972 primer *The Basic Principles of Operational Art and Tactics*, elaborated the concept of "critical time." According to Savkin, critical time is the period within which the mission can be executed successfully. After the critical time is exceeded, the enemy will be able to defeat the Soviet attack.[5]

Thus time spent on troop control must be minimized to spare time for implementing the order. Any waste of planning time or time spent on troop control only gives the enemy more time to defeat the assault. Crucially, this concept also forcefully underlines the value of disrupting the enemy's use of time.

The Soviet ground forces chief of the General Staff, Colonel General D. Grinkevich wrote in 1986 that "The importance of the time factor in battle is constantly increasing. ... Whereas in past wars, the belligerents had weapons with which they could attack each other and inflict only partial losses, the modern means of destruction, with their enormous destructive forces (including nuclear weapons), allow entire subunits, units and elements of a force's combat formation to be almost instantly put out of action...battle is somehow being condensed in time. ...Time has taken on a material quality and has been transformed into one of the decisive factors of combat force. One can say without exaggeration that to forestall the enemy in contemporary battle is to beat him, and to delay is to suffer defeat."[6]

The battle for time also continues in nuclear war. Major General I. Anureyev wrote in the late 1960s that "the introduction of automated systems of control in troop units, and primarily in the strategic nuclear forces, makes it possible to reduce the time of the control cycle, and consequently, to increase the correlation of forces after the nuclear strike to our advantage."[7]

But one unfortunate result of using computers and modern communications to minimize time is, according to Y. E. Savkin, that "stress has begun to be placed not on personal contact with subordinates, but on leadership from a distance, from control points and through a staff. The military commander has begun to resemble more a scientist at the control panels and radio station consoles than a general ... who drew the reserve cavalry regiment into the attack behind himself at minutes of crisis in combat."[8] Brigadier Hemsley, author of a book on *upravleniye*, blasts this as "boardroom management with a vengeance," and Simpkin suggests this "forward leadership from the rear" could be especially vulnerable to disruption by attacks on the relatively rigid Soviet command system.

To avoid this danger, Savkin recommends that battalions and regiments or divisions have their autonomy and independence increased while high-level control is centralized within "strictly requisite limits." However, "there must always be assurance of the possibility of establishing a rigidly centralized troop control in the hands of the senior commander at critical moments of battle."[9] Savkin does not explore the possibility that rigid control would expand and stiffen as the battle progressed, greatly reducing the regiments' and battalions' relative independence and their flexibility to deal with crises or opportunities.

Such techniques and expertise require a great effort to develop, even with well-trained and educated troops. Unsurprisingly, these capabilities have been even more difficult to instill in foreign armed forces trained by Soviet advisors, which were frequently in politically unstable developing countries. For example, at the start of the Iran-Iraq War, Iraqi C^3I systems which were established using Soviet equipment by Soviet advisors were crippled by the need to suppress potential military coups. "Iraq's key C^3I problems were political; Iraq had put its prewar emphasis on political control to prevent coups and simply was unready to use C^3I technology effectively. Like Iran, Iraq's C^3I capabilities also improved after the beginning of the war [in 1980]. By 1988, the Iraqi C^3I system had far better radio and landline [wire] links and more flexibility at the major and mid-level command levels. However, the fighting in 1986 and 1987 showed that Iraq's C^3I system could still be a system of lies [where officers frequently lied to each other]. Iraq's command structure also often still proved that it remains too inflexible for effective counterattacks, combined arms and combined operations."[10]

To protect friendly C^3I systems against enemy electronic combat operations, the Soviets prefer hard-to-intercept radios, disciplined radio operators, good camouflage, and other traditional radio protection techniques — with good reason. During the Great Patriotic War against the Nazis, the Soviets used camouflage and radio silence to hide the Fifth Guards Tank Army as it moved southward almost 500 miles from its basing area near Moscow to the jumping-off position for the Stalingrad counteroffensive. Even as the tank army was marching southward at night and hiding up during the day, German radio intelligence swallowed Soviet radio deception efforts and mistakenly reported that intercepts "clearly indicated the army was in the Sukhinchi area and receiving reinforcements there."[11]

Although some German listeners identified the army on its way south by the characteristic "fist" or style of one of its Morse code operators,[12] and while other intelligence units concluded that several infantry units of the Fifth Guards had moved near Stalingrad, higher level German intelligence officers failed to comprehend the situation. Thus, only one week later, the Fifth Guards burst into the rear of the 250,000 man German Sixth Army and destroyed it in the Stalingrad pocket.

In any future war, the Soviets will "make much use of messengers and employ reliable wire communications systems whenever possible, [but] they realize that any modern army must rely on radio communications in modern war," according to Isby.[13] By minimizing the number of radio networks, and using hand signals and flares whenever possible — which are aided by compact Soviet vehicle formations — the Soviets hope to reduce vulnerability to radio direction-finding and jamming, while increasing secrecy. Another author concluded that "the Soviets are better accustomed than most Western armies to working in conditions of radio or even electronic silence, at least when out of contact with the enemy."[14] However, limited use of radios reduces battlefield flexibility — a price the Soviets seem willing to pay.

To ensure their C^3I survives, the Soviets "have deployed an array of field mobile and airborne command posts and communications units for theater forces. At higher levels of command, field mobile command posts would be used primarily to supplement the system of large bunkers from which staffs would direct operations. ... at lower levels, command functions would be exercised from field-mobile command posts once mobilization was completed. These command posts would be relocated regularly with the forces themselves. Small airborne battle staffs add an additional layer of redundancy at each echelon, although they are inherently less capable than the large, ground based command posts."[15]

But clearly, REB will be most important for disrupting enemy command and control.

In a 1971 article in the secret general staff journal *Voyennaya Mysl*, one author argued, "Neutralization of the opponent's deduction, increasing the uncertainty of our intentions, on the one hand makes it more difficult for the opponent to shape the objectives of his actions, and on the other hand disrupts the algorithm [sequence] of his decisionmaking, requiring additional effort and more time to reach a well-founded decision."[16]

In the interest of training their troops, the Soviets have not tried to hide the destructive elements of REB. Colonel M. Belov indicates the central place of such means in REB when he writes that electronic suppression of enemy systems "is also considered an important requisite for the normal functioning of friendly radioelectronic means and, consequently, for successful employment of various weapons and uninterrupted troop control. The best method of its realization is, of course, destruction of enemy electronic countermeasures means."[17]

The Soviets will also make heavy use of antiradiation missiles to attack enemy communications sites and headquarters. During the 1973 Arab–Israeli War the Egyptians used about twenty-five modified AS-5 Kelt antiship air-to-surface missiles as antiradiation missiles,[18] reportedly hitting a supply depot and two radar sites.

Despite the attraction of antiradiation missiles, electronic jamming is also a primary means of radioelectronic suppression. Thus Palii wrote that during the 1973 Arab–Israeli war; "Egyptian and Syrian radio jamming subunits disrupted command and control radio communications to aircraft and ground forces, and suppressed the working of the guidance and control systems of Hawk missiles. As an example, on October 6, 1973, 79 Syrian planes under cover of active and passive radio interference, which was created by aircraft and ground stations, struck a massive blow on the Israeli forces in the region of the Golan Heights, while losing only one plane. According to the foreign press, the radio interference that was created was so effective that Israeli air defense units and fighters were not able to act against the Syrians."[19]

Electronic jamming of enemy sensors also can be complemented by electronic *maskirovka*.

Maskirovka tactics can be used offensively. Soviet advisors constructed dummy targets in North Vietnam to lure U.S. bombers into antiaircraft traps. According to Soviet Sergeant Kolesnik, several U.S.

A-4 fighter bombers were destroyed by the trap. "This had the (desired) effect on the Americans ... Within two weeks they stopped all flights over the region," Kolesnik claimed.[20]

But *maskirovka* is most useful for disruption of enemy command and control efforts. In the battle for time, *maskirovka* is valued for the "potential it affords for the introduction of uncertainty into enemy decisionmaking and the accompanying delay in decision cycles."[21]

Soviet interest in *maskirovka* has only increased since Palii's writings in 1963. After studying the Israeli victory over the Soviet-backed Arabs in 1973, Soviet General Matsulenko cited the use of deceptive broadcasts that the Israelis made to the Arabs as a form of military disinformation. Matsuylenko also said the experiences of World War II are of "urgent significance" for current operations.[22] For obvious security reasons, the Israelis have not yet published an account of their deceptive actions in combat, so there is no way to corroborate the general's views. "The Soviets will make extensive use of dummy and deceptive radio nets to confuse enemy electronic support measures, as was done in the 1968 invasion of Czechoslovakia," according to Isby, who added that specially trained personnel will use Soviet radio networks to spoof and deceive Western listeners.[23]

In 1987, the Commander in Chief of the Soviet Navy, Admiral Chernavin, wrote that "an important factor of success in combat is the skillful use of military cunning. ... The experience of past world and local wars shows the most effective method of achieving this is to deceive the enemy, in the course of combat actions, with the aid of *maskirovka*, disinformation, [and] misleading demonstrations of action."[24]

SURPRISE

Soviet writings on command and control and on the importance of time are closely intertwined with the great importance they ascribe to surprise.

Surprise has been a "most important principle of military art since olden times," said Savkin.[25] Surprise makes it possible to achieve operational successes and "to inflict heavy losses on the enemy, crush the morale of the troops and disorganize them, sow confusion, disrupt control and thus successfully accomplish one's mission," he continued. The lesson was brutally rubbed in on June 22, 1941, when the Red Army was caught asleep by Hitler's Panzer divisions and was smashed into pieces.

The existence of nuclear-tipped intercontinental missiles capable of swiftly hitting their targets in only thirty minutes has only increased the impact of sudden and overwhelming attack.

Technological surprise and operational surprise work hand in hand. According to a 1970 *Morskoy Sbornik* article, "In the radioelectronic struggle, the one will win who is able to secretly develop and suddenly employ more effective means and methods of neutralizing the enemy's electronic means."[26]

A critical term in Soviet thinking is the "initial period of the war," which describes the time before the defending side can mobilize its industrial and economic resources. Given Soviet economic and population inferiority compared to the West — and their fear of war's destructiveness — Soviet military writers constantly stress the importance of winning a war during that initial period.

If a war with a superior industrial power can be won, it will be won in the initial period. Citing the increasing deadliness of weaponry, the longer range, and the reduced time available in wartime, Kir'yan wrote in 1985 that "from the experience of earlier wars, it is clear that up to this time no one has fully achieved victory over the enemy in the initial period. However, the presence of nuclear weapons and large groupings of armed forces located in a high state of readiness, *in the case of their surprise use in the present time,* as in no other time, permits one to achieve in the very beginning of war those results which have a *decisive* effect." Soviet soldiers are careful about their words; decisive means decisive victory over the enemy's military and government.[27]

Soviet writers often recommend tactics and operations by saying Western armies are already using them. Thus Kir'yan urged Soviet officers to prepare surprise nuclear strikes by writing: "The aggressor will try to unleash a war by surprise. In this regard the development of means for achieving *strategic* surprise is allotted exceptionally great attention."[28]

Kir'yan's literary sleight of hand complements Savkin's writings from almost twenty years before. Citing Lenin and recommending "new, nonstereotyped methods of employing weapons and equipment" as aids to surprise, Savkin wrote, "A deciding condition for assuring the achievement of surprise has begun to be the ability to hide from an enemy ... weapons and equipment, the concept and plan of an operation or battle....*All* commanders, staffs, and troops are obliged to *always* take *all* steps to deprive the enemy of an opportunity to collect data relative to the actual location and conditions of our troops, especially nuclear missiles, aviation, tank groupings, and control points."[29]

But even as the importance of secrecy and camouflage for successful surprise has increased, it has become more difficult to defeat advanced sensors that can see great distances, despite camouflage. Thus the importance of *maskirovka* and *radioelectronic maskirovka* to distract the enemy's attention has further increased in importance.

MASS

If successful, a surprise assault can inflict a decision-numbing shock to enemy command and control systems, so helping the attacker win his victory, much as the Panzer divisions destroyed France in 1940.

Thus Soviet writers frequently urge massive use of firepower. This principle extends to REB. Ivanov writes in *Fundamentals of Tactical Command and Control* that "certain principles have been developed in implementing [REB]. The most important of these are the following: massed employment of resources in the sector of the main thrust to support accomplishment by the troops of the most important tactical missions; continuous pressure on enemy electronic devices and systems; surprise in the employment of weapons."[30]

Failure to make massive use of REB deserves censure. Using the standard trick to elude Soviet censors, Palii quotes "foreign experts," to criticize Israeli practice: "The reasons for the low effectiveness of the neutralization of the radioelectronic stations at the beginning of the [1973 Arab–Israeli] war were the small number of electronic warfare units."[31] But later "mass use" of REB allowed the Israelis to reduce their losses threefold, according to Palii's never-identified foreign experts.[32]

Soviet procurement of REB equipment reflects this concern for mass. A 1978 report by the London-based International Institute of Strategic Studies said the Soviets had 1,000 ground-based radar jammers, 1,200 ground-based communications jammers, 180 communications jamming helicopters, and 250 electronic warfare aircraft. The fact that these figures are not repeated in later editions indicate some concern about their correctness. But since then, the Soviets have fielded more modern direction-finding and radio-interception systems, frontline radio jammers in armored vehicles, modernized Mi-8 jamming helicopters (used by the Cubans to jam the U.S. TV Marti propaganda television station), as well as specialized versions of the MiG-31 interceptor and the Su-24 bomber intended to support Soviet air strikes with jamming and antiradiation missiles.

While U.S. forces emphasize timely jamming of a few critical radios or radars, the Soviets have a more blunt — and more conservative — approach. According to an oft-quoted 1978 U.S. Army report, *Soviet Army Operations*, "An estimated goal of the [Soviet REB] system is to destroy or disrupt at least 50 percent of the enemy's command, control, and weapons systems communications, either by jamming or by destructive fires."[33]

The Soviet affinity for mass should not suggest they would line up their ground-based jamming vehicles wheel to wheel as they massed artillery against the Nazis. Rather, modern long-range communications and centralized control allow the armies to concentrate widely dispersed but very mobile jammers, eavesdroppers, and weapons on a small area to provide maximum benefits for an attacking force.

It will be interesting to see how this Soviet liking for mass survives a very likely radical reduction in the size of the Soviet military. Probably, the Soviets will further emphasize the use of centralized control, long-range communications and powerful computers to mass firepower from fewer — but more dispersed and more powerful — weapons onto the targets. In effect, mass is no longer envisioned as a concentration of hundreds of heavy tanks preparing to steamroll their way through enemy lines. Instead, massive firepower is envisioned as massive barrages from long-range firepower, guided by modern sensors and directed by a central commander onto suitable targets at appropriate times.

REB INTEGRATION

The close relationship of REB with *upravleniye,* surprise and mass underlines the central importance of integration, "the essence of the [REB] concept."[34]

According to Chizum, integration signifies that REB is an integral part of overall Soviet military doctrine. Integration denotes the integrated, massive, and combined use of all methods of manipulating signals and indicates that several components of the REB are to be used simultaneously for maximum effectiveness.

The close relationship between radioelectronic intelligence, suppression, protection, and *maskirovka* ensures that all support one other. According to Chizum, "Clearly, the new REB gospel proclaims as its number one message that integration is central to any hope of crippling the West's electronic juggernaut in the event of any future conflict between NATO and the Warsaw Pact."[35]

Integration has long been a central theme of Soviet military thought, and has resulted in a strong emphasis on combined arms operations and tactics. Thus Palii emphasized that "deception by radio is usually carried out in combination with other measures ... false paratroop drops and demonstrations of the occupation of a initial position, dissemination of provocation rumors, building of false fortifications, store houses, and imitation of loading of a road network, aviation activity, and other means ... as well as false espionage data."[36]

This integration can be seen in Soviet organization of their frontline units, which combine intelligence, direction-finding, jamming, and firepower to maximize combat power.

Thus each Soviet division is supposed to have a reconnaissance company with eight communications-intercept, three communications direction-finding and three radar direction-finding vehicles.

Each Soviet Army of four to five divisions should have an attached communications intelligence and direction-finding battalion with 650 men and 171 trucks, equipped with two radio-interception companies, one radio direction-finding company, and one radar direction-finding company plus an intelligence analysis and distribution company.

Each Front of several Armies should have an attached communications intelligence and direction-finding regiment of 1,550 men and 406 trucks, with a radio-interception battalion, a radio direction-finding battalion, a radar direction-finding company, and an intelligence analysis and distribution company. Each Front should also have a jamming regiment intended to be used alongside the air defense forces to jam and deceive enemy pilots.

Each Front is meant to have two jamming regiments, one to wreck enemy ground force communications and another to jam the communications and radars of the enemy air force. Similarly, each Army would have two jamming battalions directed against the enemy army and air force. These ground-jamming battalion of about 400 men and 137 trucks include two radio jamming companies each with fifteen jammers and a radar jamming company of eleven radar jammers plus ten radar direction-finding systems needed to aim the jammers at their victims. Front and Army units can also use helicopter-borne jammers to help blind enemy radars and sever enemy communications.

Each Army also has an attached intelligence battalion and each Front have an intelligence regiment, both of which combine information collected from the radio intelligence units, but also from Ilyushin 14 Crate communications intercept aircraft, as well as Ilyushin 18 Coot A aircraft capable of intercepting radar and radio signals.

Information from Soviet signals interception satellites, photographic satellites, reconnaissance aircraft, *Spetsnaz* commandos operating deep behind enemy lines, as well as the many static signals interception sites scattered across the Warsaw Pact, can be combined by these specialized intelligence units to help give Soviet commanders a clear view of the battle.

In war, the Soviet signals intelligence and REB battalions are intended to cooperate closely with each other and with the special artillery, missile, aircraft and commando units controlled by the Army and Front headquarters. This close cooperation is intended to enable Army and Front radio intelligence units to quickly identify targets for artillery, missiles, and bombers, and also allows the jamming units to better direct their jamming to support the Army and Front tank divisions as they advance toward the enemy.[37]

The Army- and Front-level intelligence units would probably also control *maskirovka* battalions and regiments, intended to deceive Western observers by setting up false radio nets, dummy missile sites, and hiding important targets.

The Soviet Air Force has its own series of air- and ground-based REB equipment intended to collect, process, and communicate the intelligence needed for massive air attacks on critical enemy targets. These most obvious Air Force REB assets include the MiG-25R, Ilyushin 18 Coot A, Antonov 12 Cub B electronic intelligence aircraft, the HIP J and HIP K helicopter jammers, An-12 Cub C and Yak 28 E jamming aircraft, plus the specially configured MiG-31 and Sukhoi 24 aircraft designed to hunt and attack enemy antiaircraft missile sites.

Soviet space systems are also well integrated into Soviet war plans for *upravelniye, razvedka,* and REB. In early 1990, the Soviets had about 100 satellites in orbit, including 2 photo reconnaissance, 11 SIGINT, 3 naval reconnaissance, and 50 communications satellites, plus 10 satellites used to help navigation and 9 satellites used to give early warning of missile attacks.

To protect these satellites, and to attack U.S. communications and reconnaissance satellites, the Soviets will use antisatellite weapons and REB systems, according to the DoD. The antisatellite effort is probably managed by the Soviet PRO antispace organization, which runs a Moscow-based antiballistic missile system with 100 new missiles and a large network of phased-array radars.

The importance of wrecking enemy space systems was revealed by General Moiseyev, who said space satellites can increase the effectiveness of air, ground and naval combat units by 150 to 200 percent.[38]

Expectations of such enormous increases in combat effectiveness can help explain the very large Soviet investment in space and space technology — and the Soviets' bitter opposition to the U.S. development of space technology under Reagan's controversial Strategic Defense Initiative effort.

But the most important means by which Soviet satellite, airborne, and ground based intelligence and communications systems are integrated with weaponry are reconnaissance–strike complexes (*razvedyvatel'nyy udarnyy kompleka*).

RECONNAISSANCE-FIRE/STRIKE COMPLEXES

For many years, the Soviet military has sought to find ways to simultaneously attack the enemy throughout his deployment area — a task being increasingly given to reconnaissance–strike complexes.

These complexes exemplify the tight coordination of intelligence, REB, and firepower. In battle, they would use high-speed communications and number-crunching computers to speedily connect new electronic sensors with long-range, highly accurate weapons to allow speedy destruction of enemy targets within minutes of their detection.

These two complexes differ only in the ambition of their purposes. Reconnaissance–fire complexes have short-range tactical roles, while reconnaissance–strike complexes have longer range operational roles. Reconnaissance-fire complexes will primarily use artillery, Russia's God of War.[39] Army- and Front-level reconnaissance–strike will use aircraft, helicopters and especially surface-to-surface missiles with ranges of up to 300 km (240 mi).

According to U.S. Army analysts, the Soviet complexes would "provide field commanders with the capability to annihilate [American and NATO] high-precision deep-strike assets, semimobile command and control bases, forward Army refueling points, autobahn and other contingency airfields, logistic installations, electronic warfare units, and reserves rapidly."[40]

But the idea of an integrated complex of weapons and detection systems is valid even at the short-range tactical level. Thus, crude reconnaissance–fire complexes were used in Afghanistan when the Soviets co-located small infantry-detection surveillance radars with rapid-firing AGS-17 grenade launchers to allow them to ambush small bands of *mujaheddin* guerrillas.[41]

According to the Soviets, these automated complexes will be extremely important in future war, and can help decide the outcome of campaigns or theater offensives. The 1985 Soviet textbook, Taktika, written by a group headed by General V. G. Reznichenko, said they will be "one of the most important elements in securing real-time reconnaissance information and destroying, with high accuracy, enemy targets."[42]

Such expectations have prompted the Soviet military to invest heavily in new forms of extremely destructive explosives, long-range sensors, artillery computers, and new artillery weapons such as the Smerch multiple rocket launcher, capable of throwing twelve 300 mm diameter (12 in) rockets out to 70 km (45 mi) range.[43]

But unhappily for the Soviets, the U.S. is following this trend also. The U.S. version of a reconnaissance–strike complex will be formed of an airborne radar aircraft called the Joint Surveillance and Target Attack Radar System (Joint STARS), the All-Source Analysis System, and various weapons, including the F-15E fighter bomber, the Multiple Launch Rocket System, and the long-range Army Tactical Missile.

On a peaceful day, the Joint STARS radar aircraft can quickly find and track many armored units at a range of hundreds of kilometers. Information from the radar is automatically fed to a truck-mounted computer, which can be used to help allocate targets for missiles and aircraft.

The general threat posed by this computerized American network of sensors, communications and weapons — for which the West has no name — led one Soviet author to write that "the introduction of superaccurate self-guiding weapons combining reconnaissance and strike functions allows for very short times to acquire the target, prepare, and fire the weapon. ... allow engagement times to be reduced by a factor of 10-15."

Such an extreme compression of battlefield violence means that "the general speeding up of the battlefield has sharply curtailed the time available to commanders and staff for making and implementing decisions. This has made it most important to speed up the collection of intelligence, its analysis, making a decision, giving orders, organizing cooperation, and so on. The guidelines of the past are not longer appropriate. In the Great Patriotic War, a regiment and a battalion often had up to 3–4 days to prepare for an offensive – now it is much less."[44]

The same Soviet author also argued that the entire detection–destruction cycle is only six to ten minutes long, ensuring a speedy death for incompetent or unlucky soldiers.[45]

Naturally, the widespread use of such reconnaissance–fire and reconnaissance–strike complexes would place great stress on command and control systems, and would only increase the importance of battlefield REB and *maskirovka*. Soviet authors say improved technical command and control systems, better leadership, and new tactics and offensive operations to destroy enemy complexes are needed to minimize the danger to Soviet operations.

Developing these computerized complexes is neither easy nor cheap, as technical delays and continually rising costs in the U.S. have shown. As far as is publicly known, the closest the Soviets have come to fielding a fully automated complex is at sea, where the information gathered by radio direction-finding and radar satellites is apparently directly downlinked to central Navy headquarters and to ships at sea. If sufficient computer automation is used, then the satellite-gathered data could be very quickly transferred to Soviet SS-N-19 antiship missiles for rapid launch toward their targets.

Soviet military writers say deployment of land-based complexes by NATO would pose a grave threat to Soviet military strength, and especially to Soviet troop control. "If the enemy has guided or homing weapons, reconnaissance-and-strike and firing complexes, as well as other highly accurate means of destruction, it is necessary to do everything possible to reduce the time for carrying out fire missions. At the present, time calculations are not made in hours, but in minutes or even seconds. The side that can count on victory is the side that first detects a target and attacks, is first able to make an aimed shot or volley, that is faster at completing its maneuver and overcoming obstacles, and that uses the results of weapons strikes without delay."[46] Thus the Soviets recognize that modern weaponry is increasing the value of surprise attacks.

No less an authority than ex-chief of the Soviet General Staff Marshal Nikolai Ogarkov indicated how important the complexes might be for Soviet doctrine: "Rapid changes in the development of conventional means of destruction and the emergence in the developed countries of automated search and destroy complexes, long-range, high-accuracy terminally guided combat systems, unmanned flying machines, and qualitatively new electronic control systems make many types of weapons global and make it possible to sharply increase (by at least one order of magnitude) the destructive potential of conventional weapons, bringing them closer, so to speak, *to weapons of mass destruction* [nuclear and chemical weapons] in terms of effectiveness."

This development of these conventional versions of nuclear weapons means, according to Ogarkov, that "the sharply increased range of conventional weapons makes it possible *immediately* to extend active combat operations ... to the *whole country's territory,* which was not possible in past wars. This qualitative leap in the development of conventional means of destruction will inevitably entail a change in the nature of the preparation and conduct of operations. This, in turn, predetermines the possibility of conducting *military operations* in qualitatively new, incomparably more destructive forms than before. This means a sharp expansion in the zone of possible combat operations [and] the role and significance of the initial period of the war."[47]

Using the usual unidentified Western sources, Ogarkov warned that "work on these new types of weapons is going on in a number of countries, for example in the USA. Not to take into account the creation of these weapons — a reality in the near future — would be a serious mistake. There cannot fail to be a change in the established ideas about the methods and forms of armed combat and even about the military power of the state."[48]

The hawkish Ogarkov was eventually removed from the top post by his civilian bosses — but only to be made commander of the Soviet Western theater of operations. From that high office, Ogarkov successfully spread his vision of ROKs through the Soviet military, so that whatever the level of funding the Soviet military extracts from future leaders of the Kremlin, the military will give development of ROKs a very high priority.

While sounding the alarm that the Soviet military was falling behind in development of automated reconnaissance strike complexes, Ogarkov also strongly emphasized the growing importance of integrated theaterwide operations, controlled by a central staff.

Thus the reconnaissance–strike systems and REB are not only seen as vital by the Soviet military at tactical levels, but are increasingly seen as vital in theater wide levels of war.

This shift of focus from front-level to theater-level operations is partly caused by the increasing range, speed, and destructiveness of modern weapons, but also by the ability of a central commander to use modern communications to concentrate theaterwide firepower on critical breakthrough areas.

Thus Soviet war plans, no matter how unlikely to be used, incorporate REB into theater-level operations for the seizure of an entire region, such as Europe from Norway to Portugal to Greece. If ever called upon by Moscow, the Soviet military will use REB to find targets throughout NATO — and also targets in Poland and Czechoslovakia — and to jam communications between top commanders, while the complexes are used to attack enemy radio-intelligence systems in England, Spain, or France.

Using World War II to illustrate the current issues, Palii wrote that during the final assault against the German armies defending Berlin, because of Soviet jamming, the German HQ was "not able to establish communications ... did not know the situation, was not able to lead its subordinate formations and coordinate its actions with actions of its forces attempting to help the surrounded groups. As a result, enemy divisions were thrown in various directions, were not able to organizationally conduct combat operations in order to pull out of the encirclement and were liquidated by Soviet forces."[49]

Soviet REB would be applied across entire theaters of war, as well as against individual divisions and corps. According to the DOD; "Soviet attempts to counter enemy strategic command and control in wartime would involve disrupting the entire range of communications media available for strategic command, control, and communications. Using their concept of *radioblokada* (radio blockade), the Soviets would attempt to isolate entire geographic regions and prevent deployed forces from communicating with their higher headquarters ... The large number of high-power transmitters and long-range directional antennas under the Soviet Ministry of Communications constitutes an additional pool of strategic jamming assets. Used for worldwide broadcasts of programs such as Radio Moscow, these facilities could be employed effectively against U.S. and NATO strategic high-frequency communications."[50]

Space systems help elevate the importance of REB beyond tactical, operational, or theater campaigns to worldwide campaigns. For example, the U.S. Navstar satellites provide extremely accurate guidance signals to many smart missiles, aircraft, ships, tanks, helicopters and soldiers. If such guidance can be severed, or better still, secretly distorted, all these advanced U.S. systems would be crippled and the missile, aircraft, ships and helicopters would miss their targets.

Importantly, disruption of Navstar signals would also severely effect the U.S nuclear force. In Soviet military writings, enormous issues are sometimes buried in small phrases, such as the 1975 statement by Grankin that "not one operation by any type of armed forces does not begin with or is not conducted without the wide use of forces and means of REB."[51] In Soviet argot, the phrase "not one operation" means that REB will be used in nuclear warfare as well as conventional war — with enormous implications that will be explored in a later chapter.

Sooner or later, space satellites could be used to direct conventional attacks on the enemy homeland. This might allow the Soviets to gradually attack nuclear missiles, nuclear command centers, industrial targets, and military facilities even thousands of miles distant. Naturally, the increased importance of satellites as target-finders for conventional weapons is only increasing the importance of destroying enemy satellites.

The integration of sensors, computers and weapons is also creating a new form of military power, according to Edward Luttwak, a military analyst based in Washington, D.C.

Luttwak argues that the Soviets expect reconnaissance–strike complexes to be improved until they can replace the armored divisions used since World War II. In his view, the Soviets believe reconnaissance–strike complexes will eventually allow them to exercise military and political power with only minimal "conventional" military forces. This would allow the Soviets to discard the massed tank armies they have placed their faith in since the Stalingrad campaign in the summer of 1942 — and which have proved very expensive in people and money.

Instead, the complexes will allow the Soviets to wield political influence by the threat of accurate conventional destruction of targets such as parliaments, factories, and military facilities. Moreover, the complexes will greatly reduce the need to actually invade other countries in any crisis, such as the Soviets felt they had to do in Afghanistan in 1978. Thus the complexes would exert political power without the price of physical occupation by troops, Luttwak said.

In theory, this would allow the Soviets to continue their strategically defensive military policy by using a purely offensive weapon to help end political conflicts on terms satisfactory to the Soviets. However, the Soviets will need to maintain defensive armored units to help fend off attacks by enemy tank armies, and will need a significant number of expeditionary forces, such as paratroops and helicopter assault troops, when they want to occupy someplace, Luttwak said. Whenever such defensive and expeditionary forces need fire support, they would call on the complexes for direct support.

Because the complexes would depend on long range missiles and spaceborne sensors, the main American threat is the politically controversial Strategic Defense Initiative. "Even the lousiest SDI is quite good enough to knock out the satellites," Luttwak said.[52]

The combination of a strategic defense that could destroy the complexes' satellites and the persistent threat of nuclear weapons would ensure that the Soviets will continue to seek good relations with the United States — so that it will be more likely to stand aside if the Soviets use their complexes to influence political struggles.

But the scheme might make the world a more dangerous place because it does not deal with the threat of nuclear war that makes American or Soviet use of force dangerous — especially as the Soviets build a global satellite network that will orbit alongside an American satellite network. The close proximity of the two nations' satellites, and the crucial importance of such satellite for conventional and nuclear war, will make wartime control even more difficult — and could mean that conventional war between the U.S. and the Soviets would be more likely to escalate to nuclear war.

If Luttwak is correct, despite the chaos in the Soviet Union, then the Soviet military can claim credit for the earliest understanding of the importance of the complexes — just as the 1930s Soviet army was the first to appreciate the impact of tanks, years ahead of the American, British, or French armies.

But Luttwak's vision of Soviet ROKs is not widely supported. For example, using ROKs to project political power without occupation troops is the equivalent of trying to control Lebanon by lobbing 16-inch shells into the hills outside Beirut as the U.S. Navy tried in the early 1980s, according to Michael McGwire, an expert on the Soviet military now working at Cambridge University in England. And while the technology trends are helping the creation of ROKs,

Soviet ROKs are irrelevant, simply because the Soviet state has abandoned any ambition to use military forces as a political tool, McGwire argues.[53]

The Soviet miltary's desire for the complexes could also reflect what the Soviets fear the West is aiming for. According to John Hines, an expert on ROKs working for the RAND Corp. in Washington, D.C., the Soviet military imposes its own intellectual framework upon its interpretation of Western technological developments. Thus the West's advanced technology has convinced the Soviet military that the West seeks to develop ROKs, when in fact Western research is somewhat disorganized, and military study is less well developed, so that the U.S. seems to view the systems as a improved means of slowing enemy movement rather than a new form of fighting power.

Whatever the case, the future development of Soviet military technology, strategy, and doctrine — as well as wartime plans for ROKs and REB — are utterly entangled with the continuing political upheavals in the Soviet Union. The ongoing revolution in the Soviet Union will determine whether the Soviet military ever gets the money and technology it wants and whether the Soviet Union becomes a democracy, a reactionary right-wing state or simply breaks apart into a series of separate national states.

SOVIET TECHNOLOGY AND SOCIETY

Clearly, the Soviet military's conception of REB, *upravleniye*, and high-technology warfare depends on stable political support for military investment and on the ready availability of modern electronics — which are the greatest weaknesses of the conflict-racked, technology-poor, centrally planned Soviet state.

Predicting the Soviet Union's political future is a very hazardous practice for an author's reputation - that lesson was learned in late 1989 when the Soviet empire in Eastern Europe collapsed without a whimper from the Kremlin. Yet decision makers must make some estimate of the future, hopefully striking a wise balance between worst case analysis and wild optimism.

It is reasonable to predict that the Soviet military will continue to place more emphasis on REB and reconnaissance–strike complexes. Even as Soviet military spending falls (precipitously, one hopes), the new technology and style of warfare will receive increasing shares of investment.

But political changes may place even great limits on the Soviet military than spending cutbacks. For example, the end of conscription is no longer impossible to imagine. Such a change would happily shatter the militarization of Soviet society that occurred in the 1970s, and in the long term divorce the Soviet military from the Soviet people. But it would also lead to a better and more professional Soviet army, freer to invest more of its resources and skilled troops in the new technology and style of warfare.

Of course, such a leaner, meaner Soviet army would be much less of a threat because the ideological conflict between East and West would have ended. Providing nationalism or territorial disputes in Europe were satisfied or controlled, then a strong Soviet military would not be a great reason to worry.

If Kremlin reformers or revolutionaries like Boris Yeltsin succeed in jump-starting the wrecked Soviet society, then the Soviet military will be in a good position to modernize its technology. After all, the Soviets have more scientists and engineers than any other country in the world. They lead the world in some technologies — working with metals, building high-power electromagnetic wave generators, tanks, and artillery. Moreover, the quality of Soviet antiaircraft and antiship missiles, communications systems, radars, fighters, warships, and space program is very impressive.

But the Soviets have only acquired high-quality weaponry by storming the problem with their best scientists. The Soviets have expended on their military truly inordinate research, development, and production efforts that annually consume from 15 to 30 percent of their national wealth. Such disgusting overexpenditure on weaponry has impoverished Soviet civilians, consumer industries, civilian science, manufacturing technology, and the basic research needed for the next generation of technology.

This underinvestment in the future is already hurting the Soviet military. Apart from shrinking national wealth, which actually reduces available funding, the Soviets are facing lengthened research and development cycles because of the increasing difficulty of combining advanced sensors, computers, and missiles into modern weapons, such as the long-range Su-27 Flanker fighter or the mobile ZSU-30-2 antiaircraft tank. The Soviet difficulties will surely worsen as future weapons require increasing use of powerful computer systems and incredibly complex software.

Meanwhile, outside the Soviet Union, improved computer technology will continue to expand American, Japanese, and European economies much faster than the Soviet economy, so allowing the capitalist countries to fend off Soviet military power with an ever smaller share of their own economic wealth.

The American advantage in this technological and economic competition lies not with its slow and woefully inefficient military research and procurement system, but with its dynamic, innovative, and extremely powerful civilian software and computer industries. Although initially created by military investment in the 1950s and 1960s, the industry has since wildly outgrown its parent, and is now forcing the Pentagon to adopt civilian computer technologies because they are so much better than the military's. Only by buying and strengthening civilian computers for service on the battlefield can the military prevent the technology from being obsolete — and so very expensive to maintain — from the moment it first enters service.

The Soviets lack this inventive and dynamic civilian computer industry and a civilian marketplace able to buy its products, and must instead rely on the clumsy instrument of military-controlled research programs for technology advances.

Gorbachev's modernizers and his supporters within the military seem to recognize that this massive failure is hurting Soviet economic and military strength, and can only be corrected by radical revitalization of Soviet political and economic life. Thus the policies of *glasnost* (openness or publicity) and *perestroika* (restructuring) are at least partly stimulated by the Soviet military's inability to build the modern technology it wants. Moreover, visions of high-technology trade with the advanced countries of Western Europe appear to have helped the Soviets take the risk of dismantling the Warsaw Pact and allowing the two Germanies to reunite.

Apparently, the Soviet reformers have recognized that modernization thrives best within the integrated combination of a partially capitalistic industrial base and a partially democratic, free-thinking society. So Karl Marx was at least halfway right: technology really does help shape the development of society, although in a very different direction than he expected.

Initially, the Soviet military supported this wrenching reform of the Soviet Union's economic and political system, largely because they recognized that high-technology weapons can only be built by high-technology societies. Thus, while supporting a relaxation of tensions with the West, and even reduced spending on military weaponry, the Soviet General Staff has looked forward to an army equipped with more modern weapons. General Mikhail Moiseyev, first deputy minister of defense, said, "We cannot allow the [planned] reduction of troops and armaments to bring down the combat and defense capabilities of the country, or to disrupt the military/strategic parity. Hence the budget spotlights the development of military science and research and design work."

"It is clear that only better tactical and technical characteristics of weapons, automation, and computerization of military hardware will enable us to more or less painlessly reduce the number of personnel and weapons systems without affecting combat readiness."[54]

But there is a vast gulf between the ramshackle Soviet present and the bright new semisocialist future, a gulf that will be overcome only after years of political upheaval, great effort and careful management of the numerous problems that beset Soviet society.

And will Soviet visions of high-technology war be changed by this change in Soviet society?

Current Soviet military thought reflects the 1980s focus on a NATO–Warsaw Pact war as a continuous, relentless, destructive struggle, unparalleled in ferocity and unequaled in historical importance.

During the 1980s, Soviet military thought would have likely helped escalate any political conflict, not have restrained it. Although the aggressive Soviet military strategy is subservient to the defensive doctrine, Soviet generals would be telling their political masters that surprise is necessary to avoid defeat, that attack is needed to carry the war from Soviet borders, and that a violent offensive is needed to prevent the conventional war from escalating to nuclear war. Remember Kaiser Wilhelm on the eve of World War I: Appalled by his realization of the impending disaster of war, he asked his leading commander, von Molkte the Younger, if the war plans could be changed to reduce the chance of world war. But Molkte simply replied that it was too late; if plans were changed now, chaos would result and Germany's enemies would turn upon her. Unhappily for the world, the Kaiser did not have the courage to take the risk of not waging war.

Hopefully, in any future crisis, both Soviet and Western leaders will have the courage and skill to arrest the momentum of their military machines, which might be marching in lockstep to higher levels of alert until war broke out.

There are some very encouraging signs. Top-level Soviet military policy now says war prevention is the primary goal of military preparations. Also, the civilian reformers in the Supreme Soviet and in the communist party's central committee are moving to better control development of military strategy and doctrine. Moreover, the Soviets say they are moving to a defensive strategy under which they would stay on the defensive for some period of time.

These changes are to be heartily welcomed, and the withdrawal of many Soviet forces from Central Europe as well as the collapse of the European communist states gives them a great deal of credence.

But the Soviet's defensive proclamations do not go all the way to the heart of the matter. The basic problems for the U.S. and Europe are twofold: the instability of the Soviet Union, and the offensive prescriptions of Soviet military thought.

The Soviet Union is being rent by internal schisms, caused by any number of ethnic group nationalisms, or by religion, the ideological attraction of the West, economic difficulty, geopolitical decline, bad luck and bad management.

And the outbreak of war is not always a rational or even a deliberate decision. Sometimes, as in World War I, war is created by the uncontrolled snowballing accumulation of many small events. Thus Western political leaders would be unwise if they refused to recognize that war might again appear — as happened in late 1990 — so they must choose policies that deter war, while creating new conditions that eliminate the political circumstances that might create war. The painful democratization of the East European states and their decoupling from vital Soviet security interests are surely the greatest advance so far, and are far more important than military results of the various arms control treaties.

The other basic problem is the Soviet military's preference — largely justified by the destructiveness of modern technology — for offensive over defensive operations. Thus the great importance of the news that Gorbachev's modernizers seem to have seized control of Soviet military doctrine, and perhaps someday, will seize control of Soviet military planning.

The subservience of the Soviet military and Soviet military planning to the modernizers, although good in the long run, will mean little in any severe crisis or war that occurs in the next few years. This is simply because, once unleashed, the violence and velocity of modern war would make it very difficult indeed to control the bloody and aggressive execution of Soviet military plans, even if the war remained conventional.

For long-term stability, the world must endure years of instability until the defensive-minded children of Gorbachev's political reform eat their offensive-minded military parents.

But until this happens, given the appalling consequences of any conventional or nuclear war in this overarmed world, every effort must be made to smother the causes of war much as every attempt is made to prevent and smother a spark in a gunpowder mill.

Notes

1. *Strategic Review* (Summer 1986), trans. Daniel Goure.
2. John Hemsley, "Upravlenie and the Battlefield," in Stephen Cimbala, ed., *Soviet C^3I*, (Fairfax, VA: Armed Forces Communications and Electronics Association, 1987), p. 100.
3. A. A. Grechko, *The Armed Forces of the Soviet State* (Moscow, 1975), trans. auspices U.S. Air Force (Washington, DC: Government Printing Office, 1977), p. 210.
4. Quoted in Cimbala, *Soviet C^3I*, p. 94.
5. Savkin expressed the problem in a mathematical calculation in which Tcon is the time used up in the control cycle from the receipt of the attack order until the attack begins, Tcrit is the critical time, and To is the time used for the execution of the received order. His

resulting formula of efficiency is: Tcon< Tcrit - To. Any wasted time in the control cycle, or in the time spent carrying out the order could only increase the chance of failure.

6. *Strategic Review* (Spring 1987), p. 90, trans. Daniel Goure; my parentheses.

7. Cimbala, *Soviet C³I*, p. 131.

8. Hemsley, "Upravlenie," in Cimbala, *Soviet C³I*, p. 96.

9. Cimbala, Soviet C31, p. 184.

10. Anthony Cordesman and Abraham Wagner, *The Lessons of Modern War* (Boulder and San Francisco: Westview, 1990), Vol. 1, *The Iran-Iraq War*, p. 421.

11. See Earl Ziemke, "Stalingrad and Belorussia; Soviet Deception in World War II" in Donald C. Daniel and Katherine L. Herbig, eds., *Strategic Military Deception*, (New York: Pergamon, 1982), p. 253.

12. David Kahn, *Hitler's Spies: German Military Intelligence in World War II* (New York: Macmillan, 1978), p. 203.

13. David C. Isby, *Weapons and Tactics of the Soviet Army* (London and New York: Jane's, 1981), p. 480.

14. Charles Dick, "Soviet C³I Philosophy: The Challenge of Contemporary Warfare," in Cimbala, *Soviet C³I*, p. 225.

15. U.S. Department of Defense, *Soviet Military Power* (Washington DC: Government Printing Office, 1989), p. 63.

16. Notra Trulock, in Brian Dailey and Patrick Parker, eds., *Soviet Strategic Deception* (Palo Alto, CA: Hoover Institution, 1987), p. 201.

17. Barney Slayton, "War in the Ether: Soviet Radioelectronic Countermeasures," *Military Review*, January 1980, p. 58.

18. Richard Bush, "Soviet Electronic Warfare: A Review," in *The International Countermeasures Handbook*, 12th Ed. (Palo Alto, CA: EW Communications, 1987), p. 65.

19. Capt. Ronny Bragger, *Lessons Learned: 1973 Middle East War; a Soviet Perspective* (Garmisch, Germany: U.S. Army Russian Institute, 1981), p. 8. Here again Palii uses never-identified "foreign sources" to sidestep the ever-ready blue pencil of the Soviet military censors, always eager to erase any possible hints of Soviet policy.

20. *New York Times*, 14 April, 1989, p. A13.

21. Notra Trulock, in Parket and Dailey, *Soviet Strategic Deception*, p. 281.

22. Notra Trulock, in Dailey and Parker, p. 277.

23. Isby, *Weapons and Tactics*, p. 480, 483.

24. *Strategic Review* (Summer 1987), p. 96, trans. Daniel Goure.

25. Savkin, in Cimbala, *Soviet C³I*, p. 186.

26. Capt. Floyd Kennedy in Cimbala, *Soviet C³I*, p. 293.
27. M. M. Kir'yan, "The Problems of Military Theory in Soviet Scientific Reference Publications," Moscow 1985. quoted in David Glantz, "Maskirovka," *Miltary Review*, December 1988, p. 51.
28. Ibid., p. 52.
29. Cimbala, *Soviet C³I*, p. 187.
30. D.A. Ivanonv, *Fundamentals of Tactical Command and Control: A Soviet View*, trans. auspices U.S. Air Force (Washington, DC: Government Printing Office, 1977), p. 269.
31. Palii, in Bragger, *Lessons Learned*, p. 9.
32. Ibid., p. 11.
33. U.S. Army Intelligence and Security Command, *Soviet Army Operations* (Washington DC: Department of the Army, 1978), p. 5-81.
34. David Chizum, *Soviet Radioelectronic Combat* (Boulder and London: Westview), p. 44.
35. Ibid., p. 46.
36. A. I. Palii, *Radio Warfare* (1963), trans., U.S. Army Foreign Science and Technology Center, FSTC-HT-23-470-69, p. 127.
37. Isby, *Weapons and Tactics*, pp. 184-185. Also, Headquarters, Department of the Army, *The Soviet Army: Operations and Tactics* (Washington, DC: Government Printing Office, 1984), pp. 15-1 - 15-6.
38. From testimony by Gen. John Piotrowski, Chief, U.S. Space Command, to Senate Armed Services Committee, 7 March, 1990.
39. Artillery has always been a primary weapon of the Russian military. According to a nineteenth century Irish folk song:
    Remember, me lad, though the Irish fight well,
    the Rooshian artillery's hotter'n hell.
"The Kerry Recruit," c. 1855, quoted in Isby, *Weapons and Tactics*, p. 160.
40. *Army Times*, 19 June, 1989. p. 6.
41. Isby, *Weapons and Tactics*, p. 484.
42. D.L. Smith, A.L. Meier, "Ogarkov's Revolution," *International Defence Review*, No 7, (1987).
43. *Jane's Defense Weekly*, 7 April, 1990, p. 623.
44. Maj. Gen. I. Vorob'yev, "Time in Battle," *Krasnaia Zvezda*, 9 November, 1985. Quoted in Congress of the United States, Office of Technology Assessment, *New Technologies for NATO: Implementing Follow-on Forces Attack* (Washington, DC: Government Printing Office, June 1987), p. 107
45. Ibid., p. 187.

46. Chief of Ground Forces, Soviet General Staff, Col. Gen. Grinkevich, in *Strategic Review*, Spring 1987, p. 92, trans. David Goure.
47. *Krasnaya Zvezda*, May 1984, my emphasis.
48. Phillip Petersen and Notra Trulock, "A 'New' Soviet Military Doctrine: Origins and Implicatins," in Clarence McKnight, ed., *Control of Joint Forces* (Fairfax, VA: Armed Forces Communications and Electronics Association, 1989), p. 43.
49. A. I. Palii, *Military History Journal*, no 5, 1977, cited by David R. Beachley, "Soviet Radioelectronic Combat in World War II," *Military Review*, March 1981.
50. U.S. Department of Defense, *Soviet Military Power* (Washington, DC: Government Printing Office, 1989), p. 53.
51. Beachley, "Soviet Radioelectronic Combat," *Military Review*.
52. Conversation with the author, 25 April, 1990.
53. Luttwak, McGwire and Hines in conversation with the author, June and July 1990.
54. *Flight International*, 11-17 April, 1990, p. 11.

Nine

◆

THE MATURING OF U.S. ELECTRONIC COMBAT

As in a building, which, however fair and beautiful the superstructure, is radically marred and imperfect if the foundation be insecure — so, if the strategy be wrong, the skill of the general on the battlefield, the valor of the soldier, the brilliancy of victory, however otherwise decisive, fail of their effect.

Alfred Thayer Mahan,
Naval Administration and Warfare

The Soviets were the first to develop a well-rounded understanding of electronic combat. Several years later, the U.S. military began its effort to combine the tactics of electronic warfare with intelligence, deception, surprise, command and control, electronic suppression, and electronic protection.

The result of the U.S. analysis is a new, somewhat wider definition, and a new set of electronic combat doctrines. These are still in a state of flux, partly because of the rapidly changing state of technology. Yet if learned well, these doctrines will help the U.S. military use the tactics of electronic warfare to win operational and theater successes in a war.

The Army doctrine is geared towards gathering signals intelligence, and also towards wrecking the enemy's command, control, communications, and intelligence systems. But little of the equipment demanded by the new doctrine is ready for fielding.

The Air Force doctrine is called Electronic Combat and is intended to disrupt the enemy's air defense systems of radars, fighters, and missiles. However, the great implications of the electronic combat are ignored by the service's bureaucracy in favor of funding traditional bombers and fighters.

The Navy doctrine is focused on allowing the Navy to get off the first effective shots in any engagement. It emphasizes protecting U.S. sensors and communications while wrecking enemy sensors and communications. However, the Navy still focuses too much on the Soviet Navy and relies too heavily on independently operated surface ships, which are increasingly vulnerable to massed attacks by anti-ship missiles. As in the Air Force and Army, electronic combat is low on the Navy's funding priority.

The development of these doctrines by the armed services prompted a significant change of the DoD's traditional definition of electronic warfare, which has severely stunted Western understanding of how electronic combat can be used to help win battles, campaigns, and wars.

Reflecting a formula suggested by a few Air Force officers as far back as 1978, the new 1990 definition says "electronic warfare is military action involving the use of electromagnetic energy to determine, exploit, reduce, or prevent hostile use of the electromagnetic spectrum through damage, destruction and disruption while retaining friendly use of the electromagnetic spectrum."

This somewhat confused definition simultaneously restricts electronic warfare to use of electromagnetic energy while endorsing physical destruction — presumably with bombs and other high explosives.

Also, reflecting increased concern with electronic warfare, the DoD has released a new electronic counter-countermeasures (ECCM) testing policy in 1990. According to the new DoD directive, all electronic systems must be tested to ensure they have adequate electronic counter-countermeasures. For purposes of the testing policy, ECCM was redefined as "that division of Electronic Warfare involving actions taken to ensure friendly effective use of the electromagnetic, optical and acoustic spectra despite the enemy's use of electronic warfare, to include high power microwave techniques."[1]

By recognizing how electronic counter-countermeasures extend into the optical regions and by including acoustic measures, the DoD has taken a significant step towards the Soviet's integrated concept of electronic combat. Also, the new testing policy recognizes the increasing importance of directed energy weapons because it includes directed energy weapons under the rubric of electronic warfare. However, the new policy does not change the more important DoD definition of electronic counter-countermeasures.

The DoD's many bureaucracies make progress in small steps, so presumably the contradictions and restrictions in the new definition of electronic warfare will eventually be removed. However, the new definition of electronic warfare and the new policy on electronic counter-countermeasure testing show how the DoD is trying to move into the present, and has belatedly recognized how electronic combat has made obsolete the older definition of electronic warfare.

But it remains true that the three services have failed to fully appreciate the impact of electronic combat. Many U.S. weapons are too vulnerable to enemy antiradiation missiles, there is too little investment in C^3I systems, deception, space systems, or unmanned aircraft, and there is too little intellectual or financial investment in electronic combat.

But perhaps the greatest problem is that the three services are not ready to coordinate their electronic combat operations in a theater-wide or global strategy to win campaigns or wars.

Making the situation even worse is the incredibly clogged and cumbersome U.S. procurement process that prevents new technologies from appearing on the battlefield for decades. According to U.S. Navy officials, it takes twenty-three peacetime years to get a major weapons system through the Navy's bureaucratic hoops before it can be sent out to sea. The Air Force began development of the Airborne Self-Protection jammer in the mid-1970s and only began to test it in

1990. The U.S. Army began developing its first frequency-hopping radio in the mid-1970s, and only began deployment of the radios in the late 1980s, while full scale production was delayed until 1991. The tri-service Joint Tactical Information Distribution System was conceived in the early 1970s but only entered low-rate production in 1990. The endless and expensive delays prevent soldiers receiving the technology in time for war. U.S. forces going into the Persian Gulf were armed with very few — if any — of the systems named above. According to one report citing Israeli intelligence sources, the Iraqi military was equipped in August 1990 with some equipment superior in quality to that of the U.S. troops.[2]

The bureaucratic hoops and extensive regulations hemming in these programs seem to be primarily intended to ensure that no one — from the President to Congress down to a low-level contracting officer — is publicly blamed for any waste, fraud, and abuse in the spending of $280 billion every year. Moreover, it is not at all clear that such buck-passing increases the quality of the equipment or saves money. Because of the excessive regulation and bureaucracy, "we waste more than we could steal," according to one irate manager at an electronics company. But the greatest cost could be paid in soldiers' lives, when they enter battle without equipment that is still stuck in the procurement process.

One note of caution here; the Department of Defense spends an enormous amount of money every year on highly classified "Black" programs, such as the research into the B-2 Stealth bomber or the KH-11 satellites. It is highly likely that there are several, if not many, electronic combat programs in the black budget which will have significant effects on the outcome of any combat. For example, Navy ships might be protected from antiship missiles by making the air around a ship impenetrable to radar beams, or perhaps the Air Force's aircraft might become effectively invisible to radar by using Schiff Base salts to absorb radar echoes.

However, this book does not analyse the approaches taken by the services toward electronic combat on the quality of their technology — which is just too complex and classified to be judged except by combat. The services' approaches to electronic combat can be reasonably subjected to review by examining their statements and combat records, as well as their unclassified research and production programs.

ARMY DOCTRINE

The Army doctrine for electromagnetic combat leapt forward in the 1980s partly because of lessons learned from the study of Soviet REB doctrine and the 1973 Yom Kippur Arab–Israeli War.

Most effort has gone into developing doctrine for high-intensity armored combat, as could be expected in Europe. But this intellectual effort will apply well to many other conflicts, such as in Korea or in the Persian Gulf. This chapter discusses the doctrine for high-intensity combat, before dealing with lower intensity conflicts, including guerrilla wars.

The Army doctrine for electronic combat is buried in its Intelligence and Electronic Warfare (IEW) effort.

In high-intensity combat, according to one Army manual, the highest priorities of the intelligence and electronic warfare effort are to gather information about the enemy's most probable course of action; find targets for armored units, artillery, airpower, and electronic jamming; practice electronic warfare tactics, and frustrate enemy intelligence gathering.[3] To perform these missions, the Army uses four general tactics.

These include signals intelligence to gather information, operational security to conceal friendly activities, electronic jamming to disrupt communications, and counterintelligence to deceive and blind enemy sensors.

The Army's concept of command, control and communications countermeasures (C^3CM) unites electronic warfare and counter-intelligence, and is directed at wrecking enemy command systems and protecting friendly command systems.

In war, the Army's ability to carry out the C^3CM, intelligence, and electronic warfare efforts largely rests with the corps-level military intelligence brigades, and the division-level military intelligence battalions.

A corps headquarters has its own intelligence, artillery, and logistics units, and is normally used to control the operations of two or more divisions. The corps-level military intelligence brigade is intended to provide intelligence and targeting information to the corps commanders, the divisions, and the various weapons controlled by the Corps headquarters.

Under the TENCAP or Tactical Exploitation of National Capabilities Program, the corps brigade is the main receiver of intelligence collected by the highly classified national photographic, radar, and electronic-eavesdropping spy satellites. Using computer systems linked to the satellites and to the satellite control centers, the troops are able to quickly get copies of highly detailed satellite photographs, information about electronic intercepts, or the location of far distant targets detected by radar-equipped satellites.

The brigade can also receive information from Air Force radar-equipped aircraft and photoreconnaissance aircraft as well as the ground-based signals intelligence facilities run by the National Security Agency. The brigade also has its own medium range sensors, including Army signals intelligence aircraft, OV-1D Mohawk radar aircraft, and truck-mounted high-frequency radio interception systems.

As the range of sensors and weapons increase, the corps becomes more important because of its ability to directly and quickly influence the battle. For example, if it convinces Congress to spend the money, the Army plans to buy about 2,800, 280 mi range Army Tactical Missiles to enable the Corps commander to rapidly support his divisions by switching firepower up and down the frontline as he wishes, or deep into the enemy rear, without having to wait several hours for Air Force bombers to appear. Thus the corps-level intelligence capability becomes increasingly important.

However, most ground electronic combat is short-range and tactical in nature. Thus great reliance in the U.S. Army is placed on the divisions' CEWI battalion.

The CEWI battalion, whose official title is the Military Intelligence (Combat Electronic Warfare and Intelligence) battalion, collects electronic intelligence and performs electronic jamming for the divisional staff.

In addition to the CEWI battalion, the divisional staff also has the invaluable benefit of intelligence gathered by frontline troops, by armored reconnaissance units, by the long-range radars used by the artillery troops to track enemy artillery shells in flight, so revealing the location of enemy artillery guns, and by the corps-level military intelligence brigade.

But for purposes of the IEW effort, the CEWI battalion is critical. At the divisional level, it integrates electronic warfare and military intelligence roles, providing valuable signals intelligence to the maneuver commander. The battalion also helps oversee C^{3}CM operations, manages deception efforts, watches enemy sensors and manages electronic warfare attacks.

Although the organization of CEWI battalions is constantly changing and is never identical from division to division, the CEWI battalions are supposed to include a headquarters company, a collection and jamming company with six jammers, an intelligence and surveillance company, and an electronic warfare company, as well as three electronic warfare helicopters.

Information from the CEWI battalion and all other sources of intelligence are fed to the divisional staff's All-Source Production Section. This section combines the intelligence reports and data to advise the top staff officers and divisional commander on enemy activities, high value targets, and possible opportunities for deception. The All-Source Production Section also includes an artillery officer who is tasked to quickly funnel targeting information to the division's 25 km (16 mi) range artillery guns and 40 km (25 mi) range rockets.

The divisional staff also includes an electronic warfare section that coordinates use of electronic jamming and artillery fire against enemy targets, so that the artillery do not waste their time destroying something that is being effectively jammed. Another staff group is responsible for implementation of the Army's Suppression of Enemy Air Defense doctrine, which is intended to disrupt air defenses that might hinder an Army helicopter strike or an Air Force bombing raid. Suppression of air defenses is performed by artillery and jamming.

An estimate of the effectiveness of the CEWI unit's ability to perform its intelligence gathering role might be drawn from the experience of one corps-level intelligence officer who tracked other NATO combat units during the large 1987 REFORGER field exercise in West Germany: "From the beginning to the end of the REFORGER FTX [field exercise], III Corps knew with deadly precision where enemy maneuver formations, support elements and headquarters were located. The sole intelligence lapse over a period of several weeks was due to human error — one national component was 'lost' for approximately three hours. The key point is that the sort of decisions that had to be made involved *when* to shoot at which target. For instance, the battlefield was so consistently transparent to IEW personnel that a key headquarters might be patiently tracked for days and exploited for information and indications, until, at a critical moment, the decision was made to destroy it to disorganize a critical enemy operation, such as a counterattack about to cross its start line. Had real munitions been employed, not a single enemy formation could have survived the first day of the war."[4]

Naturally, the intelligence effort was very greatly aided by the absence of actual war: No one was killing U.S. intelligence analysts, blinding their sensors or destroying their computer systems. In a March 1990 letter to the author, the officer said, "That was the best I've ever seen us do. We had the right people with the right priorities under the right commander. I have also seen MI [military intelligence] units flounder uselessly, but, when we're good, the taxpayers really do get their money's worth."

Although perhaps unique, this success indicates strongly the growing ability of armies to combine signals intelligence, airborne radars, and other systems to detect and destroy their targets at ever-increasing range.

After supplying intelligence to the division staff, the CEWI battalion must implement a command, control and communications countermeasures (C^3CM) effort.

"The objective of C^3CM is to inhibit the enemy's command, control and communications ability while at the same time protecting friendly command, control and communications capability," according to Army manuals. If done successfully, it "allows the friendly commander to act faster than his enemy."[5]

Similar to the Soviet idea of radioelectronic struggle, C^3CM is defined by the DoD as "the integrated use of operations security, military deception, jamming, and physical destruction, supported by intelligence, to deny information to, influence, degrade, or destroy adversary command, control, and communications capabilities and to protect friendly command, control and communications against such actions."[6]

In Army doctrine, the C^3CM effort combines electronic warfare, counterintelligence and operational security. The purpose of C^3CM is to destroy, deceive, disrupt, and defend.[7]

The electronic warfare portion of C^3CM is based on the traditional narrow definition, with electronic support measures, electronic jamming and electronic counter-countermeasures.

But the jamming is focused on radios rather than radars. According to an Army manual, "electronic countermeasures assets jam command and control and fire support [radio] nets at critical times during the battle, preferably as the enemy attempts to deploy his forces and assault friendly troops in the defense."[8]

But jamming is often less preferable than direct destruction of enemy weapons. "As [enemy] fire support systems are located, they are suppressed by indirect fire systems or Air Force assets. Those systems which cannot be or need not be physically suppressed may be attacked by electronic countermeasures assets."[9]

Jamming is especially effective when the enemy is thrown off balance by a failed attack or a friendly offensive: "When the enemy offense is impeded and he is forced to change his battle plans, his communications and electronics become increasingly vulnerable to intercept, direction finding and targeting. At this point, the use of electronic countermeasures against enemy command and control nets becomes increasingly effective."[10]

Besides electronic warfare, C^3CM includes counterintelligence, which is intended to frustrate enemy intelligence gathering by destroying enemy commando teams, and by frustrating enemy intelligence gathering efforts.

But counterintelligence must be complemented by operational security, which is the duty of every combat unit to carry out. Operational security consists of keeping secret friendly locations, movement, plans, and intentions. Typical operational security techniques include radio silence, camouflage, careful distribution of plans, and speedy maneuver.

Although the Army is still arguing about whether divisions or corps should direct deception schemes, the deception operations are carried out by a nineteen-soldier team at division level and a twelve-soldier team at corps level. Based on the commander's plan, deception units are supposed to create electronic diversions, help mask friendly movements, blind any enemy sensors that might uncover the deception, and otherwise help convince enemy commanders that U.S. units are doing what the enemy wants — even while American combat troops might be massing elsewhere for a surprise attack.

The Army conception of C³CM operations is closely tied with its idea of command and control, which is defined as the exercise of authority and direction by a commander over his forces in the pursuit of his mission.

Throughout its literature, the Army emphasizes that units must be synchronized properly so they can combine their strengths. If synchronization is disrupted by leadership failures or enemy electronic combat, then U.S. forces will find themselves fighting piecemeal against a presumably more numerous enemy.

Moreover, synchronization of many types of complex combat units must be performed faster than the enemy can respond. For the U.S. Army, as for the Soviet army, time is crucial in command and control. "Decision making is increasingly time-critical — in the collection of information, the generation of meaningful intelligence, the formulation of viable courses of action and the implementation of maneuver and firepower actions."[11]

The requirement is that the commander and his staff think and act quicker than the enemy. As General George Patton, Jr. said, "The best is the enemy of the good. A good plan violently executed now is better than a perfect plan next week."[12]

Clearly, acting faster than the enemy is considered vital. Whereas the Soviets have the concept of critical time (the time after which the enemy can frustrate the friendly attack), the U.S. has a concept of a decision cycle that consists of a continuous process of detection, decision, action, detection, decision, action. If U.S. forces can complete their decision cycle faster than the enemy, then the U.S. forces can move faster, shoot faster, and react faster, giving them a major advantage in wartime.

The C³CM strategy has a central role in slowing the enemy's decision cycle: "Communications jammers are weapons which serve to reduce an opponent's combat power by injecting delay and confusion into his control mechanism," so slowing his decision cycle.[13]

But there are significant problems for the Army in implementing its signals intelligence effort and its C³CM effort.

Problems

Electronic combat does not get the funding, attention or priority it deserves.

Although the Army has indicated willingness to end production of tanks and cut back on delivery of attack helicopters to preserve funding for C^3I and tactical missiles, the electronic combat effort simply does not have the urgency needed. Even if a war is not expected for years, electronic combat needs more money, more urgency and more top-level attention.

The Army does not have adequate jammers, sensors, electronic eavesdropping systems, nor enough data links to transfer information, computers to process information, or long-range weapons to destroy any targets that are found.

For example, the Army — like the other services — has failed to exploit the opportunities offered by cheap unmanned, radio-controlled aircraft that could help detect enemy sensors, headquarters, and other targets. The Army's Aquila drone cost $1 million per aircraft, a price that caused the cancellation of the Aquila program. Better unmanned aircraft could carry Army cameras, infrared sensors and electronic eavesdropping systems — as well as jamming and communications relay equipment — far behind the enemy's lines at little cost. However, the Army's slow exploitation of unmanned aircraft is no slower than that of the U.S. Navy or the Air Force.

Army intelligence is still suffering from a surplus of soldiers trained by the Army Security Agency, which is the predecessor to the existing Military Intelligence branch of the Army. Until its dissolution in the 1970s, the agency devoted itself to collecting intelligence for top Army planners in Washington, D.C., despite the needs of frontline soldiers in Korea and Vietnam. This history is reflected in the continued conflict between older, agency-trained soldiers and younger troops over the value of jamming or the importance of quickly sending intelligence to frontline troops. As a result, many frontline soldiers distrust the intelligence troops, reducing the chances for good cooperation.

Army troops must train as they will fight, and so they need to be exposed to realistic effects of electronic combat. During field training exercises, CEWI troops lack training equipment, and are not allowed to show their stuff, for fear of wrecking the exercises' value for the infantry and tanks, who need to practice their tactics without the chaos engendered by jamming, spoofing, and electronic intelligence. But only when an exercise is wrecked by electronic combat will the army's troops and commanders sit up and pay attention.

Other problems are the need to minimize dependence on radios — despite their growing importance — and to train better for electronic combat. This problem is worsened by the Army's lack of modern frequency-hopping radios. In the worst case, "some NATO officers believe that Soviet jamming would reduce any future battlefield communications to the level of 1916, and that the U.S. Army, heavily dependent upon radio communications ... would suffer heavily. U.S. Army exercises conducted under electronic warfare conditions tend to confirm this view."[14] In more likely clashes with non-Soviet troops such as the Syrians, Iraqis or North Koreans, this dependance could be very damaging.

Another major problem is the limited conception of counterintelligence, deception and operational security — an error underlined by the Soviets' enthusiastic adoption of reconnaissance–strike complexes. "This is an age of fatal visibility ... Warriors speak confidently of hiding amid the battlefield clutter, or of OPSEC [operations security] and deception measures. When we pause to seriously consider contemporary and impending capabilities, however, it is unnervingly clear that our concepts of OPSEC, of deception, and even of the role of counterintelligence elements are antiques," according to Ralph Peters, an Army intelligence officer.[15]

Because of this visibility to enemy intelligence sensors, the U.S. must concentrate its efforts immediately on finding and destroying enemy intelligence systems, argues Peters. This is especially true if the Soviets or Soviet-trained troops were the enemy: "Given the hunger for intelligence implicit in the Soviet way of war, it is essential to warfighting that we blind the [enemy] decision makers as swiftly and as thoroughly as possible."[16]

The Army's failure to recognize the electronic combat threat extends to other areas. For example, the Army's premier antiaircraft system, the Patriot radar-guided missile system, is needlessly vulnerable to antiradiation missiles, despite its advanced radar that makes enemy electronic interception difficult. Once located, the Patriot radar is vulnerable because the Army has not felt it worthwhile to buy decoy radars to divert antiradiation missiles, nor to make the radar easily movable to avoid enemy artillery or air strikes. Moreover, nearby explosions could wreak heavy damage because the radar system is completely unarmored.

At the tactical level, a critical Achilles heel is the vulnerability of overcentralized U.S headquarters. "We now have the ability to find, track, and destroy even the smallest tactical command posts. Locating the huge electronic orgies that constitute our divisional and corps command posts is terrifyingly simple. It is unlikely that a single division or corps command post in a priority sector will survive the first 24–48 hours of war unless we immediately focus our efforts on wrecking the enemy's IEW [intelligence and electronic warfare] system."[17]

Thus the Army needs headquarters vehicles that are better armored, smaller, and more mobile. To hide from enemy sensors, they must disperse, requiring better communications systems that are very hard to intercept, locate, or identify.

The Army's desire for a supersophisticated communications network able to funnel intelligence information to anyone who claims to need it creates the expectation that such communications will be available. The communications systems and computers described in earlier chapters are the foundations of the Army's preparations for future warfare, yet only one communications system and one computer system have been fielded in significant numbers. Declining budget levels may prompt Army planners to cut several of the other communications and computer systems, such as the computerized data distribution system which is not slated for a production decision until 1994. Current budget cuts are stretching the programs out and will probably kill some of them, raising the possibility that the Army's current preparations for electronic combat might be built on the sands of unrealistic fiscal planning.

Continuing conflict between the various communities of the Army is also retarding progress in electronic combat. However, the Army has done better in this than the Navy or the Air Force, as we shall see.

Internal disputes slow the development of Army electronic combat capabilities. For example, the Army intelligence community and artillery community bicker over the design and operation of the All-Source Analysis System, intended to combine information useful to both artillery and intelligence officers. *Their* calling each other "spooks" and "the gun club," is evidence of the poor relations that stem from each community's priorities. While the artillery wants to destroy enemy firepower or targets such as headquarters, the intelligence community wants to maximize the flow of useful information. Moreover, while artillery troops prefer to attack at enemy artillery (which is presumed to be already attacking U.S. artillery), intelligence officers prefer the artillery to shoot at enemy headquarters and the enemy command and control network. "Why chop off the fingers one at a time when you can whack off the hand?" asks one intelligence officer.

But similar internal disputes take place inside the intelligence community; for several years in the 1980s, the Army intelligence community opposed deployment of tactical radio jammers, fearing they would disrupt the collection of radio intelligence.

Cooperation has increased greatly since the Vietnam War, when Army intelligence officers would refuse to tell battlefield commanders anything about enemy activities until intelligence headquarters in Washington, D.C., gave clearance several weeks or months later. But full cooperation inside the Army will be unlikely in peacetime, especially because without war there is no great pressure on the bureaucracies to resolve their differences.

There was no great error in the fact that the U.S. Army's intelligence and electronic warfare effort has been directed largely against the Soviet Army. Now that the threat from the Soviet Army is minimal for the foreseeable future, the intellectual investment in electronic combat must be applied to mid- and low-intensity wars.

Additional thought is required on how signals intelligence and C^3CM can be used in wars against poorly armed and unsophisticated opponents. For example, for such "low-intensity" wars where infantry rather than armored units are dominant, the intelligence and electronic warfare equipment purchased by the Army must be made lighter and more transportable. According to Army officials, the command, control, and communications systems used by infantry in such wars do not need the range, redundancy or antielectronic warfare capabilities needed by armored troops in battle against the USSR. This issue is tied up with the Air Force's approach to electronic combat, and is dealt with below.

Despite the problems in the Army's intelligence and electronic warfare effort, the overall outlook appears good. The fat years of the 1980s allowed Army thinkers time to understand the role of the intelligence and electronic warfare effort in high-intensity war, and the lean years of the 1990s may prompt the Army to use its knowledge by preparing its soldiers to best use intelligence and electronic warfare systems.

The Army is making efforts to deal with its problems. For example, the Army offered to end production of tanks in the early 1990s, and instead spend the money on helicopters, long range missiles, and C^3I systems. An equivalent move by the Air Force or Navy — for example, slashing production of fighter aircraft or destroyers — is impossible to imagine, because their budgets are so tightly controlled by conservative supporters of fighter and destroyer production.

To deal with the problem of fatal visibility, the Army has increased the importance of the counterintelligence effort. "Winning the reconnaissance/counter-reconnaissance battle is absolutely imperative," according to the Army's chief training and doctrine official, General John Foss.[18] Perhaps this increased emphasis will cause the Army to concentrate more of its firepower on the enemy's intelligence gathering system.

The Army plans to bolster corps-level fire and intelligence units by drawing helicopters, artillery, and logistics units from the division. This increased emphasis on corps-level units will increase the mobility and endurance of the frontline combat battalions, better allowing them to avoid enemy sensors and weapons.

These changes in Army organization reflect continued Army thinking about the nature of future high-technology warfare. Rising above technological and tactical problems, Army planners now envisage a very fluid battlefield without distinct front lines, where rear areas would be monitored by long-range sensors, and continually attacked by fast-moving stealthy helicopters, armored vehicles, or long-range missiles. To survive in such a rapidly changing and destructive battle, battalions will use advanced sensors to see over the next hill, use modern communications to stay organized even when dispersed over large areas, and use computer systems to exchange information or to signal supply troops for new truckloads of ammunition and fuel.

But however well the Army prepares itself for its own wartime intelligence and electronic warfare effort, its battlefield success will be critically dependent on the Air Force's ability to provide airborne firepower and surveillance — which largely depends on how the Air Force understands and uses electronic combat.

AIR FORCE ELECTRONIC COMBAT DOCTRINE

The U.S. Air Force's doctrine is called Electronic Combat. Offensively oriented, it combines command, control, and communications countermeasures with a set of tactics called Suppression of Enemy Air Defenses (SEAD) as well as with the traditional set of electronic warfare tactics.

The doctrine is largely a child of the Vietnam War. Since then, the Air Force has concentrated on electronic combat against the high-intensity threat from the Soviet Union. However, like the Army, the Air Force must prepare itself for low-intensity conflict, perhaps recalling the Vietnam experience from its dusty memory.

Air Force electronic combat doctrine is a major improvement over the traditional narrow definition of electronic warfare.

The official Air Force definition says electronic combat is "action taken in support of military operations against the enemy's electromagnetic capabilities. It includes electronic warfare, suppression of enemy air defenses, and elements of command, control and communications countermeasures."[19]

Electronic combat builds on the narrow definition of electronic warfare and includes direct attacks to disrupt or destroy enemy antiaircraft systems. According to one expert, "The functions of disruption are to reduce engagement time and to create confusion in an opponent's [air] raid handling capability ... destruction is the ultimate electronic combat tool."[20]

The crystalizing event in the creation of the U.S. Air Force electronic combat doctrine was American experience in the Vietnam war, where the Air Force continually sought to destroy what industry North

Vietnam possessed, interdict and wreck the transport of war supplies to the armies fighting in the south, and also provide immediate close air support to troops locked in combat.

The close air support mission of the Air Force was never seriously contested in South Vietnam by the communist armies, which were only armed with light weaponry. The missions were carried out much more effectively as the Air Force relearned the use of forward air controllers — skilled pilots in light aircraft able to direct the fast-moving bombers onto the targets well hidden under jungle foliage.[21]

But the American bombing raids aimed at industrial, military, and transportation targets in North Vietnam were met by a strong defensive screen. To defeat the defenses, the Air Force developed a series of tactics that included the use of jamming aircraft, specialized hunter-killer teams intended to track down and destroy missile sites, as well as clever tactics to confuse and disrupt Vietnamese air defenses. But the use of these tactics greatly restricted tactical Air Force raids, and made them very similar to the massive strategic bomber raids on Nazi Germany, ultimately failing to win a victory for the United States.

When the Air Force first began raiding targets in North Vietnam, it was only somewhat restricted by relatively simple defenses composed of simple Soviet-built Firecan radars guiding many types of 37, 57, 85, and 100 mm antiaircraft guns. In turn, the Vietnamese defense was largely frustrated when the pilots began to fly too high for the guns to hit (and too high for the bombs to be aimed accurately).

In the Spring of 1965, U.S. pilots were forced back down into the fire of the antiaircraft guns when the Vietnamese introduced Soviet-built SAM-2 antiaircraft missiles and their Fansong radars.

These Vietnamese guns and missiles were bolstered by an effective electronic intelligence system that warned of incoming U.S. bombing raids. For example, because of lax secrecy and inadequate use of deceptive tactics, Soviet radio-intelligence trawlers in the South China Sea and North Vietnamese ground-based eavesdroppers were able to warn the communist units of incoming strikes by B-52 heavy bombers, allowing many Viet Cong and North Vietnamese units to flee the target area before the bombers arrived. According to one Viet

Cong guerrilla, "it was a tribute to the Soviet surveillance technology that we were caught above ground so infrequently."[22] More likely, the fact that the writer and his comrades escaped with their lives is evidence of unimaginative U.S. tactics.

With their bombing tactics frustrated by the combination of Vietnamese intelligence gathering, missiles, and guns, the Air Force quickly had to find a better answer.

So the U.S. — unprepared to deal with defenses no tougher than those put up by Nazi Germany — rushed to fit radar warning receivers into aircraft to warn pilots when they were being tracked by radar, as well as fitting hurriedly developed pods on aircraft to counteract Vietnamese radars. These pods were capable of jamming the Fansong and Firecan radars, especially if several aircraft flew closely together in formation. Aircraft also dropped chaff bundles to confuse radars.

The jamming pods were complemented by EB-66 aircraft carrying jammers to blind Vietnamese radars and perhaps cut communications between missiles and their ground-based radars. Although successful, the EB-66 squadrons suffered very heavy losses from Vietnamese surface to air missiles (SAMs).

The Air Force and Navy also learned to use EP-3 and EC-121D aircraft flying over the China Sea to eavesdrop on Vietnamese radio conversations. The radio intercept crews were frequently able to track the movement of Vietnamese SAMs and aircraft, allowing them to warn many U.S. pilots of impending attacks by missiles and Vietnamese Air Force fighter aircraft. Electronic intercept was also used to find ground targets for the bombers.

Besides traditional electronic warfare techniques, the Air Force also began attacking and harassing defenses to help ease the bombers' paths to the targets. These aggressive tactics are called Suppression of Enemy Air Defenses.

Initial Air Force suppression attacks on SAM-2 missile sites showed that ordinary bombers were inadequate for the task: "Strike missions were flown against targeted SAM sites with disastrous results. The aircrews had great difficulty locating the camouflaged sites, and when they thought they had found them, they encountered intense antiaircraft and small arms fire. When pressing for an attack, other sites would fire missiles from blind sides. The aircrews finally did bomb one site, suffering considerable losses. The site was later found to be a carefully prepared dummy."[23]

But the attacks on missile sites became much more successful when carried out by specially trained and very skilled crews flying aircraft equipped with sensitive radar warning and direction finding receivers plus the short-range Shrike antiradiation missile. For extra firepower, these Wild Weasel aircraft usually were accompanied by another aircraft carrying a heavy bomb load.

Usually arriving at the target several minutes before the fast-flying F-105 Thunderchief bombers, the Wild Weasel crews became very proficient at closing down and suppressing missile sites in advance of the bombers' arrival. By January 1968, the Wild Weasels claimed eighty-nine sites destroyed and many others suppressed.[24]

The story of one raid is told by a backseat Wild Weasel crewman: "One day in December of 1966, we were leading the second strike force on a strike at the Thai Nguyen rail yards. Our tactics dictated that we ingress about 20 miles in front of the strike forces to engage the surface-to-air missile defense before the others arrived ... We knew it was going to be a busy day because the audio from the [radar] warning receiver was buzzing as if it were filled with hornets. As we crossed the Red River, I isolated signals from at least five Fansongs [radars] and several guns [with Firecan radars]. As we approached the target areas, I lined us up on a site south of the target and the pilot lofted a Shrike [antiradiation missile] from several miles out. I called out [SAM missile] launches as two sites fired their SAMs at us, and then as another site fired ... After visually acquiring the SAM site adjacent to the target, we maneuvered hard to dodge the first covey of missiles, then broke to our right to deliver cluster bombs on the site ... We passed through black layers of flak before releasing weapons. We rolled up and watched the cluster bombs sparkle as they detonated around the site, and then again as the wingman's bombs obliterated the radar and command van. As the strike force departed, we lined up and fired a Shrike at a Firecan [radar] because the SAMs were staying off the air. Only one Thunderchief was lost during the mission, to ground fire over the target."[25]

Bomber pilots held the Wild Weasel crews in very high regard, and not just because of their higher than normal casualty rate. "There never was a Wild Weasel crew that could buy their own drinks at our airbase," one pilot told this author almost twenty-five years later.

Eventually, remembering the strategic bombing raids against Nazi Germany twenty years before, top generals combined the attacking aircraft into powerful "attack packages" of more than 100 aircraft. The packages included radar-jamming aircraft, eavasdropping air-craft, Wild Weasels, and fighter aircraft, all supporting the bombers.

For example, following the North Vietnamese invasion of the South in early 1972, the U.S. responded by sending an attack package to bomb a bridge and a railyard near Hanoi in North Vietnam. The May 10 package included 32 bombers protected by 28 fighters to ward off Vietnamese interceptors, 15 Wild Weasel aircraft to suppress the SAM-2s, 8 bombers carrying chaff, 4 EB-66 radar jamming aircraft, one RC-135 electronic intelligence aircraft, plus 4 reconnaissance aircraft, 7 aircraft to rescue shot-down pilots, 20 refueling aircraft, and one command aircraft. Despite the large numbers of antiaircraft guns and the 41 SAM-2s fired at the aircraft, only two fighters were lost on the raids, both well north of Hanoi, victims of surprise attacks by Vietnamese MiG-19 gun-armed interceptors.[26]

Despite the low U.S. casualty rate, it would be well to note that the Vietnamese air defenses were successful in forcing the U.S. to make a huge effort to attack only a few targets. Thus during the 10 May 1972 air attack on Hanoi, the Air Force was forced to use 64 fighter and electronic warfare aircraft, plus 20 air refueling aircraft to help 32 bombers hit two targets, despite the relatively simple Vietnamese air defenses. Worse still, thirteen days later another huge effort of 119 aircraft was needed to escort helicopters on their way into northern Vietnam to rescue one of the pilots shot down in the 10 May raid. Total: Two days used, two aircraft destroyed and 239 aircraft sorties expended to hit two targets and recover one pilot. On longer ranged strikes, up to 250 aircraft would be used to support only sixteen bombers. "Jamming, anti-SAM, the Wild Weasel Stuff, the chaff dispensing, the MiG CAP [fighter escorts] — ate up tremendous quantities of air operations just trying to keep a small strike force alive," said a top Air Force leader, General John Vogt.[27]

Moreover, the damage inflicted by the raids had a minor effect on the war. For example, the Paul Doumer bridge in Hanoi was slightly damaged on May 10 but was quickly repaired by women and old men, even as supply trucks crossed the river on submerged bridges and ferries.[28]

After the war, the Air Force continued development of electronic combat technology, and deployed improved jamming pods and chaff systems to blind radars, as well as infrared flares to fool heat-seeking missiles. These systems are still the basis electronic defense for each combat aircraft.

The EB-66 jamming aircraft were replaced by much more advanced EF-111 Ravens carrying powerful jammers that automatically intercept and jam enemy signals. In combat, these Raven jamming aircraft would either escort a strike force all the way to the target, or stand off behind friendly lines trying to jam radars.

Electronic intelligence was continually improved with new RC-135s and radio-intercept pods carried by fighter-bombers.

Improved Wild Weasel aircraft were gradually developed, and by 1990 the Air Force had about 100 F-4G Wild Weasel aircraft equipped with Vietnam-era Shrike and Standard missiles plus 1980s HARM antiradiation missiles. Also, it is possible that the Air Force's secret force of up to 59 F-117A Stealth fighters would take advantage of their stealthiness to sneak up on and destroy radar sites.

Although there was some jamming of enemy communications systems during the Vietnam War, it was Israeli successes against the Arabs in the 1973 Yom Kippur War that caused the Air Force to develop specialized aircraft for command, control, and communications countermeasures. Delivered in the early 1980s, the sixteen EC-130 Compass Call jamming aircraft are intended to delay and disrupt the exchange of information between radar, missile sites, and air defense fighters, so helping to break up the integrated defense systems into bite-sized chunks small enough to be jammed by aircraft-mounted jamming pods and EF-111 Ravens, or destroyed by roving Wild Weasel aircraft. According to a senior Department of Defense official, William Perry, "We have come to realize that if you jam the enemy, you take out only one weapon. But if you jam out C^3 systems, you disrupt an arsenal of weapons."[29]

With the deployment of the sixteen EC-130 Compass Call aircraft, the Air Force gained the capability to carry out the three elements of electronic combat — electronic warfare jamming and eavesdropping, suppression of air defenses, and command, control, and communications countermeasures.

Also, a host of new electronic combat systems were developed by the Air Force, including improved receivers to tell pilots what radars are watching them, improved target-detection sensors, night vision equipment, new computer systems to help planners quickly attack newly detected targets, improved jamming pods to fend off enemy weapons, and new encryption equipment plus "Have Quick" frequency-hopping radios to defeat enemy eavesdropping and jamming. The increased availability of laser-guided bombs also offers the opportunity of accurately striking targets from altitudes too high for light flak guns to endanger aircraft. Moreover, the limited amount of improved night vision equipment could allow the Air Force to accurately strike targets with laser-guided weapons at night, when the light flak is rendered virtually useless. The Air Force has also developed a powerful smart missile able to use its internal radar to home in on enemy aircraft at long ranges. If it survives budget cuts, the million dollar Advanced Medium-Range Air-to-Air Missile will greatly help U.S. pilots to break up enemy air attacks and defeat superior numbers of enemy aircraft.

Certainly, the greatest improvement was the introduction of the E-3 Airborne Warning and Control System (AWACS) — a Boeing 707 carrying a radar on its back and several expert aircraft controllers in its belly. With the controllers and a radar that can see 640 km (400 mi), the E-3 is a combination of a radar, communications network, and command system of the type that helped the Royal Air Force defeat the Luftwaffe during the 1940 Battle of Britain. But the E-3 is even better. It is mobile, difficult to destroy, hard to jam, and can be used to carry the offensive into the enemy territory. The success of this almost revolutionary system in air-to-air warfare is clearly shown by the Israelis, who used a similar airborne radar (designed by the U.S. Navy at the same time as the AWACS) system to destroy eighty-four Syrian aircraft for no losses in the 1982 Bekaa Valley air battles.

This new equipment has been accompanied by greatly improved training for U.S. aircrews. For example, electronic combat, bomber, and fighter crews can take tours learning to fly through the "Red

Flag" exercise area where they are attacked by aircraft and simulated missiles, even as they search for targets. Budget cuts permitting, more improvements are on the way, including a computer that simulates a complete air defense network for an aircraft's electronic combat systems as the pilot flies on a training mission.

Problems

The Air Force's new electronic combat technology and doctrine were demonstrated in the 1986 U.S. air raid on Libya. Aided by the Soviets, who did not air or even pass on any warning of the impending attack to their Libyan allies, and covered by the night and by Navy aircraft that fended off fighter interceptors, jammed communications and fired antiradiation missiles, Air Force F-111 bombers attacked targets with laser-guided bombs dropped from very low altitude. Only one aircraft was lost, and most of the targets were damaged — except for Libyan leader Khaddafi, who escaped the harm that was to be visited upon him.

But only if judged narrowly in terms of preventing a Libyan missile hitting an American aircraft was the electronic combat effort successful. The threat of the Libyan missiles forced the bombers to fly very low, helping ensure that most bombs missed their targets — killing some innocent civilians in the process. Also, one F-111 seems to have flown into the sea while trying to stay below Libyan air defenses.

So the question now is whether the Air Force is actually ready and able to carry out this doctrine in a war against a lesser power like Syria or Iraq, let alone against a Soviet army. Is the doctrine adaptable to lower intensity conflicts? And, most importantly, is there a better option than the use of many manned aircraft organized into huge attack packages?

According to the former chief of Pentagon electronic combat programs, "If there is an integrated doctrine, it is pretty well hidden" when the Air Force makes plans for spending money. The problem, he said, is that the electronic combat "people are the tail-end Charlies running along with little influence" on the spending of money. Often, procurement of electronic combat systems is governed by managers of aircraft development programs without reference to the numbers or types of systems needed to carry out the electronic combat doctrine.

Moreover, too much money is given to development of new aircraft, rather than the electronic combat systems needed to carry out missions. Thus the Air Force tries to spend vast sums of money on traditional manned bombers such as the B-2 and fighters instead of the jam-resistant radios, guided missiles, passive sensors and other electronic combat technology that it really needs.[30]

The central problems are the Air Force's belief that airpower can win wars without interference by the Army and Navy, and that manned aircraft are the best means of exercising air power.

The delusion that Air Force strategic bombing can win wars on its own has survived repeated failures. After failing to live up to claims that bombing could win World War II, the Air Force seized on the nuclear bomb, but international nuclear deterrence has greatly reduced the possibility of nuclear weapons ever being used. Conventional bombing was tried in the Korean War and the Vietnam War, but failed both times to bring the benefits claimed by the Air Force. And in September 1990, Air Force General Michael Dugan claimed that bombing could single-handedly win any war against Iraq. Amazingly enough, this claim was also repeated by various other flying officers. Of course aircraft are a powerful hammer, but without an anvil of ground forces to hold the victim in place, airpower cannot win significant victories, except against the most fragile of political systems.

The utterly unfounded idea that air power can conquer all, leaving the infantry to mop up, is almost identical the tragically mistaken belief held by French artillerymen in the First World War that "the artillery conquers, the infantry occupies."

The Air Force's faith in its chosen strategy flies in the face of reality and history. But it has not stopped the Air Force from acting as if it were true, thereby minimizing cooperation with the Army or Navy, as well as wasting vast sums of money in pursuit of an impossible goal. And the best means to carry out this strategy is manned aircraft, according to the pilots of the Air Force.

Thus much effort and money has been wasted by the Air Force in a counterproductive effort to maintain its tradition of manned bombers. Instead of spending money on improving all-round electronic combat readiness, the Air Force betrayed its preference for manned bombers by investing more than $35 billion in two aircraft of doubtful usefulness.

The first is the F-117A Stealth fighter, in which the Air Force invested roughly $5 billion for development and production of fifty-nine single-pilot aircraft. This aircraft's angular shape shows that it is designed to minimize its chances of being detected by radar-controlled weapons, at the cost of carrying only a very few missile or bombs. The F-117A's role and weapons are classified, it is probably intended to sneak — in very small groups — into enemy rear areas to attack enemy bunkers or SAM sites. It was a well-run and relatively cheap program, and the F-117 will be a valuable weapon in combat. But surely the Air Force could have spent the $5 billion somewhat better than on fifty-nine reusable aircraft that perhaps carry only one bomb each.

It is much harder to justify the spending of another $30 billion on the development and production of fifteen advanced but fantastically expensive B-2 bombers. They were originally supposed to strengthen nuclear deterrence by being able to hunt down and kill mobile Soviet nuclear-tipped missiles. However, the Air Force admitted in 1990 that they could not do the job. But if the B-2 can only strike static or semi-mobile targets, what justification is there for the huge price of $100 billion over thirty years for seventy-five aircraft? Surely much cheaper missiles fired from silos in the United States could deter nuclear war, even if they have to be able to destroy hard targets.

The U.S. taxpayer would have gotten a much better return on investment if the $35 billion spent by 1990 had been used to increase the survivability of airfields, as well the purchase of new guided missiles, infrared sensors, better training, new antiradiation missiles, a modernized Wild Weasel aircraft, or stealthy cruise missiles.

The belief in the ability of manned aircraft to win wars is also the source of another problem — the Air Force's reluctance to cooperate with the Army. The Air Force's electronic combat doctrine underlines this, because it is focused on wrecking enemy air defenses, not his military or national C^3I networks. Thus Wild Weasels are intended to locate antiaircraft weapons, not find divisional headquarters. The

Compass Call aircraft are supposed to jam air defense networks, not communications links from a corps headquarters nor the enemy's public television channels. Also, the Air Force's antiradiation missiles home on radars, not on top-level radio transmitters.

Given the lack of attention given to electronic combat — despite the expenditure of $22 billion between 1982 and 1990 — the chief of electronic combat operations in the Air Force staff could only write in 1987 that "the needs of electronic combat are well documented and are *starting* to receive the constructive attention they deserve."[31]

This lack of attention is only worsened by another problem — the improving quality of radars and air defense technology, which has made the task of jamming and destroying the antiaircraft systems used by many countries much more difficult than during the Vietnam war.

For example, the quality of Soviet air defense technology surged ahead of U.S. electronic countermeasures in the 1980s. The Soviet military was equipped with growing numbers of monopulse radars, and the introduction of pulse-Doppler and phased-array radars, modern interceptors able to track low-flying targets, and sophisticated missiles capable of defeating U.S. jammers and capable of homing in on electronic emissions from aircraft radars. According to U.S. pilots, the mid-1980s Soviet SA-10 missile is a "real butt kicker in the same class as the Patriot [missile]," which is the most advanced U.S. ground-based antiaircraft missile.[32]

In the worst case, the density of the Soviet frontline air defense threat in a high-intensity war would be so great that aircraft at 6,000 meters (20,000 feet) would be continually exposed to twenty-five to thirty air defense systems at a time. Even at low altitudes of around 75 meters (250 feet), pilots would have to fend off one to three antiaircraft systems every few moments. Luckily for the Air Force, Gorbachev's revolution should greatly reduce the chance of war with the Soviets — although many other countries are heavily armed with antiaircraft weaponry, as the U.S. discovered in late 1990.

In many possible scenarios, the U.S. Air Force would also find itself facing Western-designed antiaircraft systems, such as the American systems supplied to Iran or the French systems supplied to Saudi Arabia.

For example, Iraq is equipped with a wide variety of Soviet and modern European antiaircraft weapons which use various types of radar, optical and infrared sensors, linked together by a communications network. "The Iraqis were even able to get [French antiaircraft] equipment that was not procured by France's own military," said one expert.[33] Iraq's capture in August 1990 of Kuwait's American-designed Hawk missiles only underlined the threat posed by the worldwide profusion of antiaircraft weapons.

With Syrian, North Korean, and Chinese air defense systems constantly improving, Air Force planners cannot ignore the air defenses of developing countries, even with the collapse of the USSR's imperial ambitions.

Against this background of continued improvements in air defenses, the U.S. electronic warfare programs in the 1980s were a series failures. One expert called the 1980s "an admittedly disastrous decade in electronic warfare"[34] even before the Air Force withdrew from the joint Air Force-Navy Airborne Self-Protection Jammer Program, intended to protect the Air Force's F-16 fighter-bombers from increasingly numerous pulse-doppler radars.

Part of the reason for its failure is a slow and inefficient research and procurement program.

The Air Force's electronic combat technology is greatly superior to the Army's technology, and includes many highly classified systems we know nothing about. For example, the B-2 bomber is a remarkable technical achievement, and is equipped with very secret and very impressive active and passive defense, according to several DoD and industry officials.

But like the Army, the U.S Air Force is very slow in deploying new technology. As a result of very slow development, the Airborne Self Protection Jammer was not ready in late 1990 for deployment to the Persian Gulf, despite beginning development in the mid 1970s. As a result, the latest version of the Air Force's F-16 fighters have no internal electronic jamming equipment nor any provision for using underwing jamming pods — forcing them to rely on EF-111 Raven jamming aircraft for protection against Iraqi missiles.

Aside from a clogged procurement system, a primary reason for the failure of the Air Force's electronic jammer effort was an unwise insistence that each aircraft jammer be able to defeat all the threats it was likely to meet. This ambitious desire only "drove technical specifications very, very, very high," ensuring that the programs usually ran into severe technical and expensive problems and were subsequently canceled, according to one former civilian director of all DoD electronic combat programs. The Air Force chief of electronic combat programs, Brigadier General Noah Loy, said "We had a tendency to think we needed an [electronic warfare] system in our aircraft that was capable of taking on everything in the electromagnetic environment. We are getting away from that."[35]

Moreover, it is very difficult to gather the intelligence needed to design electronic jammers. For example, the Soviets do not export their front-line radars, and their passive sensors do not emit anything that can be heard by American electronic interception aircraft. Thus the developers of jamming pods have long complained that they never have enough information about enemy radars. Worse still, information can only be gathered when enemy radars are deployed in the field. With a few years delay in gathering intelligence, and at least five to ten years to field a jammer, the Air Force's jammers are always years behind the most advanced antiaircraft systems. Thankfully, this problem is not nearly as difficult when dealing with the somewhat dated antiaircraft weapons used by most — but not all — developing countries.

Other problems hobble Air Force preparedness. For example, the Air Force will often sacrifice important electronic combat systems to save money for the purchase of more aircraft. To enhance the survivability of its next-generation fighter, due to enter service in the mid 1990s, the Air Force is trying to combine stealth features, internal deception jammers and improved avionics. But these capabilities are very costly and have caused the Air Force to drop plans to place a passive infrared tracking system on the aircraft. This means the supposedly stealthy Advanced Tactical Fighter will betray itself when it uses its noisy radar to find enemy aircraft, some of which have passive infrared sensors.

Similarly, the Air Force proposed in late 1989 to cancel procurement of an aircraft-mounted identification system called the Mark XV. Although rebuffed by top DoD officials, the Air Force will likely try again to cancel the program. If they do succeed, the Air Force will have additional money to buy B-2 bombers and new fighter aircraft, but, cancelation of the Mark XV will cause the death of U.S. troops when they are misidentified and attacked by friendly and allied weapons during the confusion of a future battle.

Another problem is that the Air Force's focus on radar jammers has deflected attention from the growing threat of infrared weapons that destroyed so many Soviet aircraft and helicopters in Afghanistan. "We have been scared so long by [radar] frequencies, that we have forgotten about the other areas," according to one former high level official. This error is all the greater as the Air Force needs to focus on fighting low-technology armies armed with many infrared guided missiles and few, if any, advanced radar-guided missiles.

Moreover, the Air Force appears to have underestimated the threat posed to its aircraft by their excessive use of radar for the detection of enemy fighters. Instead of having passive infrared detection systems, as the latest Soviet aircraft have, U.S. aircraft have powerful radars that broadcast their noisy signals to all who care to listen. Such radar signals will greatly reduce the chance of shooting down enemy aircraft by surprise — the most successful fighter tactic during World War II, and the Vietnam and Arab-Israeli wars.

These failures have only made the ground-attack pilot's job much more difficult. According to one Wild Weasel officer, "We've had to go lower since Vietnam, often as low as 100 feet... The front seater has no time to look inside [the cockpit]. Make a mistake and in two seconds you are in the ground." Another Wild Weasel officer concluded "The situation is going to do nothing but get worse,".[36]

Despite the growing strength of air defenses, the Air Force has still not given the electronic combat doctrine its proper place in its war plans, development efforts or procurement plans. Thus there are only about 100 Wild Weasels, forty Ravens and sixteen Compass Call aircraft for the entire Air Force — far too few in relation to the number of U.S. fighter-bombers.

Moreover, because of funding cuts, the Air Force had decided by late 1990 to get rid of the F-4G Wild Weasels in the early 1990s — despite the example of Israel's use of up to 24 Wild Weasel aircraft. The Air Force is committed to eliminating this specialized type of aircraft with their highly-trained crews, and relying instead upon antiradiation missiles aimed by general-purpose pilots well trained to dogfight and bomb. Also, because the B-2 bombers and the new fighter are eating every spare dollar in sight, the Air Force could

decide to slash by 90 percent its plans to buy Tacit Rainbow unmanned antiradar drones.

Even while underinvesting in electronic combat aircraft, the Air
Force has also failed to buy nearly enough long-range guided weapons that would allow bombers to avoid many enemy defenses.
Instead, Air Force aircraft are armed with short-range missiles, laser-
guided bombs, cluster bombs useful for destroying unarmored targets, and ordinary "dumb" bombs incapable of destroying tanks.
"Here's where the Air Force has really dropped the ball," according
to former Air Force General John Vogt.[37]

Although many unguided dumb bombs can be tossed with great
accuracy onto static targets from a few kilometers away, and although
several types of modern standoff weapons are in various stages of
development, only inadequate numbers of a few types of short-range
weapons — such as Maverick infrared homing missiles and GBU-15
guided bombs — have entered service. Moreover, the Air Force has
failed to deploy any conventionally armed cruise missiles, despite
their large scale deployment by the Navy. This failure has needlessly
exposed U.S. bombers to antiaircraft weaponry, and so greatly
increased the need for high-quality electronic countermeasures.

In October 1990, this failure was glaringly underlined by the Iraqi
invasion of Kuwait. Even while U.S. diplomats were trying
strengthen the allied coalition by distancing the United States from
Israel, Air Force leaders went cap in hand to Israel asking for modern
Have Nap guided missiles, with a range of 50 km (30 mi). And the
U.S. Navy's conventionally armed cruise missiles were given the task
of destroying a wide series of Iraqi sites before the first Air Force
bomber would strike.

However, there is some good news. When leaving his post as Air
Force Chief of Staff, General Jack Welch said that the Air Force was
planning to greatly increase procurement of the AGM-130 guided
missile, two or four of which might be carried by each F-16 fighter.
But this was before the budget cuts imposed in late 1990, which will
likely cause the Air Force to quickly sacrifice the missiles to keep more
aircraft flying.

When the Air Force eventually receives long-range guided missiles,
the price it pays will be the sacrifice of what it often says is the main
advantage of a manned bomber — the long-cherished flexibility and
judgment of an experienced pilot free to make snap decisions in the

heat of battle. Instead, the computer-controlled missile will be launched by the bomber to guide itself the last 10, 15 or 30 km to the targets. But this raises the awkward question of whether or not to replace at least some of the missile-launching bombers with much cheaper missile-launching trucks.

Another problem for bomber pilots is the need to gather and quickly distribute intelligence about enemy air defense systems and potential targets. In high intensity operations, this need for intelligence gathering is so important that a separate air operation is required to protect all the intelligence gathering aircraft. Thus the Joint STARS, RF-4Cs, TR-1s and RC-135s will all need escorts of fighters, AWACS and electronic warfare aircraft to protect them from enemy fighters and antiaircraft missiles. The great effort required just to gather intelligence about enemy deployments will further slow the rate at which the Air Force could prepare and launch air raids.

And the Air Force is very slow at using the intelligence it does collect. For example, Air Force doctrine calls for a tactical headquarters to control the missions of all the aircraft in a region, such as Europe or the Persian Gulf. At six o'clock every day, the headquarters is supposed to distribute a single "Air Tasking Order" describing the next day's missions of each squadron. But the headquarters only receives intelligence updates once or twice a day, because of underfunded C^3I networks. This extremely slow process — which dates from World War II — ensures that by the time the pilots begin their attack, the intelligence is thirty six to forty-eight hours old.

The Air Force has failed to use modern technology to solve these command and control problems. For example, computers could help the headquarters prepare orders faster, while relatively cheap unmanned aircraft could collect intelligence faster, and at less risk. Clearly, the unmanned aircraft could not replace the wide search of the radar and electronic intercept aircraft. But they do provide a cheap alternative in many missions.

Any difficulties in collecting and distributing accurate and fresh intelligence hinders the Air Force from attacking moving targets, such as tank regiments in battle. After all, a moving armored unit can cover tens of miles in only a few hours, entering new air defense zones and completely disrupting carefully prepared plans for air raids.

Another problem with the Air Force preparations for electronic combat is the vulnerability of its airbases and communications.

According to one U.S. Air Force general who fought in World War II and the Vietnam War: "In Vietnam, when we were going up into the North into heavily defended areas, interdiction missions were very, very carefully orchestrated, bearing no resemblance whatsoever to World War II tactical operations. Interdiction was a precise operation...so precise and so carefully orchestrated that the planning can't be done by the human mind. It has to be done by computers."[38] And if it has to be done with computers linked by advanced communications to long-range sensors, then there is every chance this command, control, communications and intelligence network will be attacked by radioelectronic combat.

At the moment, the Air Force relies upon its own fighter aircraft to defend its airbases and tactical command centers. The aircraft are complemented by Army-manned surface to air missiles like the Hawk and Patriot missiles, which can effectively destroy surface to surface missiles. In action, the fighters will use AWACS radar aircraft and possibly jamming aircraft to attack bombers, and the Army's antiaircraft missiles will use electronic counter-countermeasures to overcome enemy jamming.

But there is only a very limited effort by the Air Force to use deception and concealment to protect its most vulnerable assets — its airbases. In 1989, Air Force budget cutters canceled a $15 million program to construct 900 dummy F-15 and F-16 fighters,[39] intended to induce attackers to waste their bombs on wooden and plastic dummies. This decoy effort was part of a large airfield defense program canceled in 1990 which had called for radar reflectors to make airfields less recognizable on aircraft radars, camouflage nets to hide important buildings, fake runways intended to waste enemy bombs, and rockets simulating surface-to-air missile intended to distract enemy pilots as they made their attacks on the airbases. One notable effort called Comfy Challenge, intended to design a ground-based electronic warfare defense system for airbases, disappeared after being folded into a Army program that was killed because of low priority.

Thus today's airbases — and the vital intelligence, command, and communications centers — are vulnerable to bombers that penetrate the air defense screen, and uncomfortably vulnerable to long-range ground-launched missiles. Clearly, the greatest threat would come from Soviet attacks, but the Air Force seems unconcerned by the threats posed by lesser countries.

The same problem faces pilots in combat, because the conservative Air Force has refused to adopt modern technology that would convert its air command and control network into a modern C^3I system that would allow pilots to be aware of their situation, helping them to make good decisions in combat.

To defeat the jamming and eavesdropping that occurred in the Vietnam War, aircraft were fitted with new Have Quick radios that hop from frequency to frequency. These radios should defeat most enemy eavesdropping and make jamming more difficult, but they are used in combat much the same way that radios were used in World War II — to let pilots call warnings of enemy fighters or missiles to each other, or to redirect squadrons in new directions.

But the Joint Tactical Information Distribution System (JTIDS) offers much more than the Have Quick. It can transmit voices as well as computerized radar data, so the pilot can see on a little TV screen in his cockpit the radar picture collected by far-seeing E-3 AWACS aircraft. This allows pilots to know what is going on around them, greatly reducing the chance of being surprised by the enemy, greatly increasing the ability of pilots to concentrate on weak enemy units, and also allowing pilots to turn off radars as they sneak up on the enemy.

Very little of this information can be passed through the Have Quick radios, because each piece of information must be transmitted by voice.

Also, JTIDS will help pilots identify friendly and enemy aircraft, greatly reducing the rate at which friendly aircraft will destroy each other with long-range missiles. This JTIDS capability is especially important because of the Air Force's reluctance to spend any money on the Mark XV combat identification system, which would reduce the rate at which friendly aircraft are destroyed by accident.

Moreover, the JTIDS system defeats jamming and eavesdropping by hopping from frequency to frequency at extremely fast rates. And with over 100 channels possible per radio, there is little or no danger that the radio will be jammed by shouting voices — as one would expect today with the Have Quick radios.

The problem with JTIDS is its cost: up to $1 million per aircraft. But with modern aircraft costing $30 to $40 million or even more, pilots costing several million to train, and missiles costing up to $1 million each, the JTIDS is well worth the money — providing they are used to improve pilot tactics. This point has been accepted by the U.S. Navy and several European air forces who have decided to use the JTIDS to improve their air combat tactics.

In sum, despite some very effective and far-thinking ideas that have greatly improved its ability to shoot down enemy aircraft, the Air Force has not changed its strategy to cope with current circumstances, nor has it fully exploited available technology that could further improve its ability to shoot down enemy aircraft, and greatly improve its ability to attack enemy ground units.

Comparison with World War II is instructive. Once the *Luftwaffe* had been driven back to protect the cities of the Reich from Allied bombers, American and British fighter-bombers were free to roam over German lines, shooting up any trucks and tanks they could see. Although these attacks were often ineffective and even the cumulative total of the attacks could not deal a death blow to the German armies, they did cost the Germans heavily in trucks and supplies, slowed German movement, and to use Clausewitz's term, greatly increased the battlefield friction faced by German commanders.

But in any future war, modern air defenses — and especially Soviet air defense — would likely be able to emulate the North Vietnamese defenses that prevented any repeat of such general attacks as were mounted against the Germans. Instead, Air Force attacks will probably have to use carefully planned and coordinated attack packages against a few fixed and infrequently mobile targets. Instead of roaming around looking for targets and repeatedly fueling up for another flight over enemy lines, each aircraft could only strike a one or two carefully chosen targets per day, greatly reducing any impact on the outcome of the war.

Thus the doctrine chosen by the Air Force is only suitable for carefully-prepared strikes against fixed targets such as industry, bridges, and supply dumps, or slowly moving truck convoys or command centers. The Air Force has not readied itself for the much more important mission of attacking mobile enemy combat units protected by a constantly changing air defense umbrella.

The Air Force's electronic strategy is a great improvement over pre-Vietnam War techniques, and even seems workable when applied against less technologically advanced countries such as Libya, Iran, or North Korea. But this has been achieved in spite of misguided investment in manned aircraft, unprotected airbases, and poor radios.

Opportunities

There are some good signs: Congress seems intent on limiting the hugely expensive B-2 program to only fifteen bombers, while it continues funding the modern technology needed for electronic combat. With any luck, the sharply reduced size of the B-2 program will deal a fatal blow over the next fifteen years to the Air Force's outdated tradition of manned bombers and the foolish and destructive idea that independent action by the Air Force can win wars.

Also, lower-level Air Force officers are increasingly aware of the importance of electronic combat, while a 1990 Air Force Science Board study concluded that too little effort was being placed on command, control, and communications countermeasures. Most important of all, a former Wild Weasel pilot was appointed chief of the Air Force in October 1990. During his nomination hearings, Gen. Merrill McPeak betrayed the Air Force's unpreparedness for modern war and indicated a good future for Air Force electronic combat efforts, when he said one of the greatest problems facing U.S. forces in the Persian Gulf was the task of suppressing enemy air defenses. Another problem admitted by McPeak was the lack of guided weapons.[40]

However, the Air Force is developing a highly classified guided weapon for production in the mid-1990s — if the Air Force's preference for highly expensive manned aircraft or technical problems don't kill it first. The Air Force also plans to add eighteen unmanned aircraft to its reconnaissance squadrons from the mid-1990s, although skeptics expect this plan will die as the Air Force absorbs the budget cuts expected throughout the decade.

But all these measures are only partial solutions to the the steep increase in cost of airpower. There are many way to skin a cat. What is needed now are new and faster ways to apply cheaper firepower against enemy forces.

This requires that the Air Force find new methods of applying new technology — much as the British combined radar, command centers and Spitfires to win the battle of Britain in 1940 — and a new electronic combat doctrine to support it.

Perhaps these new methods should include much greater reliance upon long-range airborne surveillance, long-range smart missiles launched from the ground, plus cheap, pilotless and stealthy reconnaissance aircraft able to slip through enemy defenses. Of course, manned bombers would be very useful for carrying guided weaponry into range of far-distant targets, backed up by the very useful ground-launched Tacit Rainbow drones, standoff electronic warfare aircraft and manned fighter aircraft — for which no alternative seems even remotely in sight. But most of all, the new tactics require much greater cooperation with the U.S. Army.

ARMY AND AIR FORCE COOPERATION

On June 9, 1982, the Syrian Army's nineteen antiaircraft missile batteries in the Bekaa Valley of Lebanon were destroyed at no loss to the attacking Israelis. The sudden attack came after the Israeli Army and Air Force had spent months eavesdropping on Syrian radar and radio signals, planning and practicing an attack on the missile launchers — which had made the fatal mistake of never changing their locations.

The attack was begun by unmanned aircraft that acted as decoys, convincing the Syrians to fire off many of their missiles. Then followed a barrage of electronic jamming from helicopters, aircraft, and trucks, as well as accurate artillery fire directed by officers using camera-equipped unmanned aircraft as long-range telescopes. This electronic and explosive barrage hid the approach of a wave of antiradiation missiles that destroyed many of the antiaircraft weapons' vital radars.

Next came waves of low-flying Wild Weasels and bombers carrying cluster bombs and guided bombs to destroy the remaining missile launchers and radar vans. The attack was a total success primarily because of close cooperation between the Israeli ground and air units.

The U.S. Army and U.S. Air Force are already very powerful forces. But full exploitation of electronic combat doctrines and the new technology offer a way of winning battles at reduced costs, reduced risk, and in reduced time. Such benefits require the Army and Air Force to grasp the new opportunities and to cooperate more closely than ever before.

Despite their very different doctrines for electronic combat, the Air Force and the Army are becoming increasingly intertwined by the accelerating integration of sensors, long-range weapons, and communications systems.

Although this increasing integration is visible in preparations for low-intensity conflict, it is clearest in U.S. preparations for medium and high intensity conflict against well-armed opponents.

One good example of increased integration is the Army's doctrine for Suppression of Enemy Air Defense (SEAD), which is intended both to protect Army-manned attack helicopters and Air Force-manned bombers. The Army and Air Force SEAD doctrines are similar because they share the same purpose. However, the Air Force plans to use air-launched antiradiation missiles while the Army would use artillery, as well as ground-launched antiradiation missiles and jamming.

More subtle and important is the combined impact of the Army's 280 mile range Army Tactical Missile, new sensors such as satellites and the radar-equipped Joint STARS aircraft, and the computerized intelligence systems to be used by the Air Force and Army. The computer systems used by the Army's military intelligence units will provide commanders with the information needed to quickly aim the long range missiles. But the Air Force will use computer systems to find and allocate targets for its aircraft. Although the two organization could not agree during the 1980s to develop a joint computer system, the sharing of computerized information could allow Army and Air Force commanders to share targets, theoretically allowing a more efficient use of the missiles and bombers.

Increased integration, combined with the growth in technology and the weakness of tactical air power against mobile ground targets, creates a strong incentive to change the Army and the Air Force roles and missions in high-intensity war to better take advantage of modern technology. The change would give the Army's weapons the dominant role in attacking targets up to 50 to 80 km (30 to 50 mi) behind the fluid frontlines expected in modern war. The change would allow Air Force to concentrate efforts on defeating enemy aircraft, blinding enemy sensors, and attacking targets more than 80 km (50 mi) behind the lines.

There are plenty of weapons the Army could use to attack targets behind enemy lines. Currently, the Army's 25 km (16 mi) artillery guns can fire shells carrying several tens of mines or bomblets. Rockets launched from armored vehicles can easily reach 40 km (25 mi) into the enemy's rear. Funding permitted, these weapons will be eventually carry several self-guided antiarmor weapons capable of searching for tanks.

Moreover, there are many more weapons that will be in the armory by the end of the 1990s if current research and procurement plans are not greatly changed by the reduced Soviet threat. For example, the Army could launch massive attacks on many types of targets when it finds the money to field its high-technology stealthy helicopter called the LH, which is to be equipped with electronic jammers, infrared sensors and radar-guided antitank missiles. Another powerful weapon would be the FOG-M missile which uses a 40 km (25 mi) long fiberoptic cable to link the missile's TV camera or infrared scanner to a truck-mounted video console, allowing the crewman to guide the missile as if he were playing a video game.

For longer range missions, the Army Tactical Missile can strike targets with pinpoint accuracy. Current plans call for the missile to carry hundreds of destructive bomblets, although it could also carry many smart antitank missiles that would home in on their targets using infrared and radar seekers.

The Army's small share of the defense budget may stymie the programs. But if money is transferred from less useful Navy and Air Force efforts, the new long-range weapons could be bought.

Of course, these advanced weapons cannot completely replace aircraft, especially fighters. The advantage of the manned aircraft over the missile is flexibility. For example, large and powerful bombers have the space and electrical power to operate laser weapons or control heavy antitank missiles. Also, pilots are smarter and more reliable than any computer that can be imagined now. Aircraft have long been used by corps or theater commanders as quick-response, long range firepower for frontline troops. Although not as effective as the Air Force claims, close air support missions have many times helped ground troops win their immediate battle.

But the long range of modern artillery and rockets allow them to fire along the battle front as well as deep into the enemy's rear. This allows the corps commander with his many multiple rocket launchers and his missiles to very quickly respond to calls from his frontline troops for immediate firepower support.

Naturally, if there is no antiaircraft fire, the artillery and rocket-borne smart missiles and bomblets cannot be as effective as a heavily armed aircraft with a pilot able to size up the situation on the spot. But as was shown in Vietnam, extensive air defenses will prevent a pilot from doing much damage unless he knows the exact locations of the targets. And if the targets locations are already known, then a missile or artillery shell can quickly do the job, regardless of enemy air defenses.

In weighing the relative advantages of missiles and close air support aircraft, the time advantage of the Army weapons is critical. According to one study, it would take an Army missile crew ten minutes from receiving target information to strike a target up to 80 kilometers away. However, it would take the Air Force thirty minutes from takeoff to strike that target, and another thirty minutes to cover another 230 kilometers to the next target. Thus the report says, Air Force strikes take three times as long as Army attacks, not counting the extra time needed by the pilot to plan his attack.[41]

The greatest obstacle facing the Army's use of long range weapons is their reliance on good C^3I. A well-prepared enemy could be expected to increase emphasis on electronic combat to help sever communications networks, blind sensors, deceive intelligence analysts, paralyze command centers, and locate U.S. targets for destruction.

For example, political stability permitting, the Soviet military would probably plan to buy additional long range antiaircraft missiles and REB systems to destroy or disrupt U.S. C^3I systems. One simple measure available to all armies would be use of a radio channel to warn combat units whenever the U.S. Joint STARS radar-equipped aircraft scanned the terrain.

Theoretically, the Army's reliance on C^3I networks gives the advantage to the Air Force pilot, who is said to be able to detect and attack targets as he wishes, supposedly free from reliance on the networks.

But we have already seen that the Air Force's need to combine its forces has created a reliance on large C^3I networks and airbases. Only by ignoring the pilots' planning and support structure can anyone say pilots are independent of C^3I systems.

In high-intensity conflict against well-armed enemies, the Army's missile weapons promise to be cheaper and quicker than Air Force aircraft, with their long planning times, reliance on airfields, vulnerability to air defenses, and poor coordination with Army operations. So the Army weapons hold out the promise of effectively replacing much of the Air Force's shorter range attack missions. Meanwhile, the Air Force could refocus its efforts on the only task it really likes — destroying enemy fighter aircraft. It should also increase efforts to use spacecraft and aircraft to collect intelligence that would be rapidly distributed to soldiers, even while increasing efforts to blind and kill enemy long-range airborne and space-based surveillance systems. Meanwhile, long range Air Force bombers should be used to carry highly accurate cruise missiles to destroy such vulnerable static targets as railroads, bridges, supply dumps, and command centers. If necessary, the bombers could carry short range guided missiles for use against moving targets far inside the enemy's rear area.

Despite increased Air Force concentration on defeating enemy aircraft, the new division of labor — Army weapons out to 80 kilometers, Air Force weapons beyond that — would surely be opposed by the Air Force bureaucracy since it would mean the transfer of huge funds to the Army, and the reduction of the long-held Air Force mission of close air support and the personnel used to support it. The Army would also oppose the redistribution of roles unless it were given adequate funding.

Indeed this fight is already underway, cloaked in the political struggle over which aircraft should replace the aging A-10 close air support aircraft. While the Air Force wants to replace the powerful A-10s with glamorous F-16 fighters, the Army opposes the change, fearing that the F-16s will not be used for close air support in combat, but instead will be used as fighter aircraft. Ominously for the Air Force, Congress seems favorably inclined towards the Army's view.

However, one major problem remains. Most discussion of the value of long range weapons has taken place in the contexts of the Army's AirLand Battle and NATO's Follow-on Forces Attack schemes. In those plans, long range weapons are intended to delay, disrupt, and destroy enemy armored forces moving toward the front line. The deep attack efforts are directed at road networks, bridges, command posts and trucks.

This reflects a long-standing Air Force bias for deep interdiction — which is basically a independent Air Force effort to prevent enemy reinforcements from reaching the battlefield. This policy failed in World War II, Korea and Vietnam.

Interdiction attacks by Army missiles *could* represent the addition of the Army to the Air Force's failed deep interdiction strategy.

Clearly, this use of long-range weaponry and C^3I systems is very different from how the Soviet military envisions the role of reconnaissance–strike complexes. In Soviet eyes, the new technology should be used to selectively destroy important targets behind the front lines — headquarters, C^3I sites, missile units, airfields, supply bases — with the purpose of simultaneously wrecking the enemy defense throughout its entire depth so that offensive action by ground forces can exploit the disruption. However, if the Soviet military is forced to shift to a defensive strategy, it may adopt an approach with more emphasis on slowing enemy movement toward the front lines.

Because of the powerful impact of long-range weapons and long-range sensors on the balance of power, the U.S. should expect very broad enemy countermeasures to the weapons. For example, the Soviet military will accelerate procurement of reconnaissance–strike complexes aimed at American C^3I systems and long-range weapons. Even broader countermeasures can be expected. The Soviets have already begun to stir up Western political opposition to the new weapons, saying they increase the chance of war breaking out. Not surprisingly, Soviet development of similar systems is ignored by the Soviet military and many observers. Also, the Soviets have begun to prepare new arms control initiatives to limit the West's long-range weapons systems.[42]

Despite some claims, a strategy emphasizing use of C^3I systems and long-range weapons is not a specialized technological wonder that can be defeated by a straightforward set of countermeasures. Some critics cite France's development in the 1890s of highly specialized cheap and unarmored torpedo boats to sink the heavily armored and expensive battleships of the Royal Navy. Sadly for the French, the specialized torpedo boats were quickly and easily checkmated by the Royal Navy's adoption of searchlights, quick-firing guns, and fast-moving destroyers. Thus it is demonstrated that simple countermeasures can defeat highly specialized (and inflexible) enemy weapons.

But no simple countermeasure can defeat a strategy emphasizing use of long-range weapons and C³I systems, because the countermeasures will have to defeat many types of surveillance sensors linked by many types of communications systems that help control many types of weapons, tipped by many types of guidance sensors and directed by clever soldiers. Moreover, these weapons would be fired at many types of targets, including heavily armored tanks, lightly armored artillery guns, semimobile headquarters and maintenance centers, vulnerable supply trucks, and exposed supply dumps.[43]

Long-range weapons and C³I systems are not intended to win the war single-handedly. Instead, they would work closely with the tried and tested heavily armored combat units — still the main force of any high-technology army — much as artillery now is used to suppress and disrupt enemy units in front of advancing armored columns.

Adoption of long-range ground-launched weapons and reshuffling the Air Force and Army roles constitutes only a small step toward proper exploitation of the new technology and electronic combat systems. What is needed is better coordination between the Army and Air Force to apply a C³CM strategy across an entire theater to wreck an enemy offensive.

While the Soviet's REB doctrine and reconnaissance–strike complexes are planned for use by the Soviet General Staff as well as theater, front, army and divisional commanders to support campaigns, theaterwide offensives, and even nuclear wars, the U.S. Army's C³CM strategy is only designed for use by divisional and corps commanders. The Air Force's concern for C³CM is even narrower: protecting its aircraft from enemy attacks.

Although much about electronic combat is secret in the United States, and there has been much progress in recent years, it does seem that the U.S. military has a much narrower conception of electronic combat than the Soviets. This relatively narrow conception may help the U.S. win battles, but it will hinder much more important goals — the winning of campaigns and wars.

Army and Air Force commanders must learn to view the battlefield and the entire theater of war in a very different way from when they viewed destruction of enemy hardware or seizure of ground as their most important missions.

According to Dale Larson, former commander of the Air Force's Electronic Security Command, "Using the command, control and communications countermeasures strategy, a battle manager looks across the battlefield and sees not an array of tanks, artillery, troops, and airplanes, but the enemy's command, control and communications network, his central nodes, its Achilles heel exposed, vulnerable to disruption by the timely application of the right countermeasures tool."[44] With aggressive and successful application of C^3CM, friendly mechanized and airborne troops would face a disorganized enemy unable to quickly mass forces or firepower to stop attacks, unable to protect command centers and unable to defend supply points from being destroyed.

For example, the Air Force's EC-130 communications jamming aircraft could greatly help an Army commander delay and disrupt an enemy armored attack. Skilled software experts might break through the software defenses of an enemy computer network to steal information or disrupt the enemy command and control system. Attacks by Army weapons on the enemy's frontline antiaircraft systems could free Air Force electronic combat aircraft to help attack rear area air defenses. Bombers and mechanized units could to take advantage of the confusion as they pressed their attacks on headquarters, C3I networks, combat units and supply points.

This is much more than just long range attacks. It incorporates the disrupting enemy organization, slowing movement, delaying decision making, confusing targeting, and most importantly, reducing the enemy's political will to continue the war.

This approach seems to be increasingly accepted by the military. During the American buildup of forces in Saudi Arabia in late 1990, U.S. commanders frequently declared their intention to quickly smash Iraq's military and political command and control networks if war were to begin.

Of course, electronic combat is not a wonder weapon able to effortlessly deliver a death blow to enemy plans. But the advantages gained by such attacks make subsequent attacks by U.S. aircraft, tanks and infantry much more devastating.

Electronic combat is best suited for use against highly organized, high-technology enemies, where it could unravel the enemy's plans and organizations, better allowing the traditional weapons — infantry, tanks and aircraft — to destroy the enemy's military strength and political plans.

Thanks to the collapse of communist ideology and the USSR's economy and political system, the chances of high-intensity war seemed very low — until Iraq invaded Kuwait.

It has been difficult imagining the U.S. military voluntarily getting involved in wars against well-armed and armored opponents, similar to the Iran–Iraq or Arab–Israeli wars. But it is the military's duty to ready themselves, just in case their political masters give the word, as President Bush did in late 1990.

To some extent, a mid-intensity war against a heavily mechanized but technologically unsophisticated opponent would be much more suitable for the Army and Air Force than either a low-intensity or a high-intensity war, because most of their advanced weaponry is optimized for the quick destruction of enemy mechanized forces. Also, the experience of Army-Air Force cooperation that was expensively learned in Vietnam would be applicable. Moreover, the Pentagon's relatively narrow view of C^3CM is wide enough for war against a small power without nearby allies, long-range weapons, or a powerful ideology.

In a defensive war between U.S. forces and heavily-armed Iraq, Syria, Libya, South Africa or North Korea, a few wings of aircraft and a few Army divisions might be able to combine their forces to destroy anything electronic that emits and anything hot that radiates, without having to face the most modern enemy weaponry. Indeed, U.S. forces should be able to wreck the enemy's military organization, forcing him into a defensive and manpower-intensive infantry or guerrilla war. This would hopefully end an offensive military threat for some time, theoretically allowing the U.S.'s local ally to recover.

In such a conflict, expertise in electronic combat will be particularly advantageous, because a poorly developed country will lack the skills to resist the sudden impact of jamming, eavesdropping, integrated C^3I and computerized weapons systems. To paraphrase Hilaire Belloc: Whatever happens, we understand electronic combat and they do not.

According to the authors of three 600-page books on the lessons of three modern wars, "like the Arab-Israeli and Falklands conflicts, [the Iran-Iraq War] indicates that superior C^3I and Air Control and Warning technology and organization can be a key asset for Western and friendly local forces in future low-level wars ... the West should exploit its technical lead as much as possible. This exploitation will be particularly important because of the West's matching lead in Identification Friend or Foe, Electronic Support Measures, and Electronic Warfare."[45]

Of course much is uncertain — especially in an offensive — because war is confusing and chaotic. Also, clever enemies will find ways to combat advanced technology. Use of rapid movement, radio silence, or the cover of fortifications, cities, and jungles are merely some of the military measures an enemy might take. In any Persian Gulf war, one side may be able to minimize the effectiveness of light-intensification equipment by blocking out the light of the stars with smoke from burning oil wells. Similarly, tracer bullets and burning vehicles will reduce the effectiveness of infrared night vision equipment while cheap ground-based radar decoys will reduce the value of airborne radars.

Political constraints will rightly limit military activities, as they did in Vietnam, where Air Force military priorities were overridden by high orders from Washington that prevented attacks on much of the North Vietnamese air defense system. Thus the full capability of the new weapons will be hobbled. It is to be hoped that soldiers and officers will quickly find new way to use their skills and weapons to attain the desired political goals in every new situation.

Despite the Kuwait crisis, it is far more likely that U.S. forces will find themselves involved in low-intensity conflicts, rather than medium intensity conflicts, over the next several years.

In such low-intensity conflicts, U.S. soldiers would likely be called upon to quickly remove an unpopular government, resist guerrilla attacks, or covertly support a guerrilla campaign against an entrenched government.[46]

The use of electronic combat in such scenarios is sharply limited, partly because lightly equipped, loosely organized, mobile guerillas can elude advanced sensors and weapons by hiding in rough terrain or among the civilian population.

There is an endless variety of possible low-intensity operations.

The model for the future may be the December 1989 invasion of Panama. This swift and relatively cheap operation underlined the traditional military virtues of powerful force suddenly applied, with the extra advantages of well-used electronic combat.

Prior to the surprise invasion, the U.S. Army used traditional spies and electronic eavesdropping to map out the Panamanian organization and command and control arrangements. careful planning showed each unit what it had to do, and also mapped out the complex C^3I arrangements for the attack. Once the invasion began, well-trained U.S. soldiers violently destroyed the Panamanian command structure and military organization by seizing the key barracks, buildings, and personnel. This was all done in the dark of night when the U.S. forces had maximum advantage of their superior night vision, surveillance, and communications technology and better training. Airborne command posts, manpack satellite radios, 700 radio nets, a huge amount of U.S. satellite communications capacity, and EC-130 jamming aircraft all played roles in ensuring that U.S. forces were organized and the enemy was disorganized. The overall effect was neatly summarized by one captured Panamanian soldier: "They decapitated us." Thus military victory was swiftly won at relatively low cost.

The success is clearer when compared to two debacles that happened in 1983.

Overcontrol by micromanagers equipped with good C^3I networks caused the first disaster, when U.S. political leaders directed commanders in Germany to attack some hostile groups based in Lebanon. The order for a quick attack flowed from Germany to an aircraft carrier off Beirut. With only an hour to prepare, and crippled by detailed attack instructions prepared by the far-distant commanders in Germany, the Navy pilots attacked one at a time, in broad daylight, at medium altitude, and without the benefit of support attacks on antiaircraft sites. These were perfect conditions for the defenders, so they shot down two multimillion dollar aircraft. Not surprisingly, the military bureaucracy made sure no one was publicly punished for the fiasco.

The U.S. Navy-led invasion of Grenada took several days to defeat only a few hundred communist resisters. Despite a very unpopular government and overwhelming U.S. firepower, the U.S. military was humiliated by its non-existent planning, poor tactics, poor communications, poor intelligence, and a terrible attack plan that directed U.S. forces to land and slowly march to the enemy centers of government. Instead of decapitating the enemy, U.S. forces tried to nibble them to death, with predictably heavy losses on all sides. Again, no one took responsibility for this military farce nor was any blame assigned. Instead, medals and promotions were handed out to all who participated.

But however badly the Grenada operation was executed, the difficult postwar reconstruction of Grenadian democracy effort succeeded. Perhaps military success in Panama will be crowned with the political success of building a stable economy and a democratic political structure.

This points up the difficulty of low intensity conflict. However hard it is to track down and destroy enemy troops, it is much, much harder to build nations and democratic governments. Usually it is impossible. Where it works, it is usually because preexisting conditions were very favorable. And the most important conditions are an unpopular local government and popular support for the attackers.

Given the overriding importance of political issues, the role of electronic combat in low-intensity conflict is limited. But electronic combat will still be a vital tool of soldiers seeking to create conditions for the establishment of a peaceful society.

Whether trying to support or to defeat insurgencies, the U.S. must build, or preferably strengthen, a political base of support. In this effort, "the informational instrument of U.S. national power (public diplomacy, public affairs, and psychological operations) supplements and reinforces traditional diplomacy ...[because] low intensity conflict is a political struggle in which ideas may be more important than arms."[47] The tools of this struggle will be political pressure, economic aid, military aid, and even military support. Other tools include "political indoctrination, disinformation and propaganda."

But this "informational instrument" will also be used by the enemy — as Saddam Hussein did in late 1990 — who will have the major advantage of a pipeline into the living rooms of American and other Western citizens. That pipeline comprises the many international television networks, who will compete to broadcast the most dramatic pictures possible. Thus, in low-intensity war, Irish, Palestinian, German, or Italian terrorists and guerrillas create "newsworthy" events to help them achieve international political prominence wildly out of proportion to their political strength or the justice of their cause. And state-sponsored terrorism can be used to needle a much larger enemy, as the Libyans and Syrians have done to the United States. Skillful enemy manipulation of international television could undermine U.S. government policy — which is not necessarily a bad thing, because it helps ensure that the American government does not blunder into another bloody morass such as Vietnam.

When trying to help guerrilla forces, U.S. advisors supply weapons, radios, training, and also intelligence information. The most important weapons are the helicopter-destroying infrared missiles. Clearly, the Afghans use of Stinger missiles dealt the Soviets a major blow by preventing helicopters from aiding Soviet units when they were attacked by guerrilla forces. Similarly, the use of infrared missiles by Salvadoran guerillas greatly restricted the use of helicopters and light bombers by the government forces in 1990.

But the supply of information can also be important for insurgents. There were persistent reports that the U.S. provided to the Afghan guerrillas maps of government fortifications and unit positions drawn from satellite imagery.

When trying to destroy guerrilla forces, "intelligence provides the basis for all U.S. and host nation counterinsurgency plans and operations... As a result, integration of nonmilitary collection resources, and sharing of resultant information as appropriate will collectively constitute principal elements in intelligence support." Whatever intelligence the U.S. can gather by electronic listening posts, spy planes and satellites would be a powerful support. "In most cases, the capability of the host nation military to use signal or imagery intelligence will be minimal."

When attacking guerrillas, instead of destroying large obvious targets after overcoming large integrated air defense networks, the Air Force would have to spend much time searching for a few trucks, a few guns, or a few infantry, while all the time fending off many pinprick attacks from antiaircraft guns and heat-seeking missiles. Similarly, the Army would lack the large, obvious organizations that the powerful mailed fist of its armored forces are designed to destroy.

The Army's high-technology sensors and weapons would have to strain to find a mobile enemy's infantry units hidden in jungles, mountains or towns.

But C^3I is an extremely powerful tool for U.S. antiguerrilla forces. For example, if a small outpost or lightly armed patrol is ambushed, it should be able to use its radios and navigation systems to quickly call in accurate artillery, helicopter and aircraft firepower. Thus C^3I and long-range firepower can partially substitute for the enemy's possession of the initiative. Such episodes were the norm in Vietnam, where U.S. troops used superior communications and firepower to kill many enemy troops for every casualty they suffered.

However, it is unwise to forget that despite repeated military victories in Vietnam, the side the U.S. backed lost the war because it could not match the political strength of Vietnamese nationalism and the Hanoi government's ruthlessness.

In such low-intensity wars, the military technology that would matter would be the Army's radios, encryption systems, and the electronic warfare systems used to protect helicopters from infrared missiles, as well as rocket-tracking radars able to quickly locate enemy rocket launchers for speedy attack. Perhaps most important are night-vision devices, which give U.S. troops an enormous advantage over less well equipped forces.

The Air Force's primary contribution would be Vietnam-era OV-10 observation aircraft, as well as the A-7 and armored A-10 attack aircraft. The OV-10 and the A-10 were designed for conflicts like the Vietnam War, and so they would be very useful because of their combined on-the-spot surveillance and weapon-carrying abilities. Also, spy satellites and other national intelligence-gathering systems would be useful for finding enemy campfires in the jungle, eavesdropping on radio conversations, and detecting movements of enemy supply convoys. However, with its love of high-performance F-16s and other glamorous fighter aircraft, the Air Force has decided to junk by 1995 the very aircraft designed for low-intensity warfare — the A-7, OV-10, and A-10. The money saved will be used to buy fancier ultramodern fighters.

For U.S. commando forces considering a sneak attack on enemy positions in low-intensity conflict, different technologies are required. For example, very lightweight, reliable, and difficult-to-intercept radios are the highest C^3I priority of the U.S Special Operations Command, which consists of several tens of thousands of highly trained troops equipped with night-vision equipment, long-range aircraft, helicopters, and boats. Also, to help plan raids, the command wants to buy trucks equipped with computers able to display pictures gathered by spy satellites and show soldiers detailed computerized maps of their targets. Called "Purple I-Vans," the tri-service intelligence trucks would also be able to display the current status of enemy air defenses, so helping the commando aircraft fly in and out, and also display information about known enemy troop deployments, tactics, and equipment.

Meanwhile, the gathering of signals intelligence by guerrilla forces cannot be ruled out; it occurred in the Vietnam, Afghanistan, and Nicaraguan wars. "Any tendency to consider the guerrilla force too unsophisticated to acquire communications intelligence must be avoided," according to the U.S. Army.[48]

For example, the poorly armed Viet Cong were very adept at eavesdropping on U.S. combat units during the Vietnam War. According to one official report, U.S. troops in late 1969 discovered a twelve-man team of Viet Cong eavesdroppers who had spent several productive years listening to the undisciplined chatter of American soldiers.

By examining the team's notes, U..S. experts realized that U.S. Army radiomen would frequently reveal to the Viet Cong where the next day's airborne assault would take place, what regions were to be bombarded by artillery or B-52s, what the strength of U.S bases were and whether the Americans were going to ambush communist units. "After monitoring a B-52 warning [used to alert U.S. troops to get out of the strike area], the Viet Cong knew that they had between ten and twenty minutes in which to despatch a courier to a nearby radio station [to radio] warnings to other Viet Cong units in the area before huge, 750-pound bombs rained from the sky."[49]

In a gross understatement, the official history declared that, "Undoubtedly many air assault landing were ambushed ... many American operations were compromised and lives lost due to communist exploitation of loose radio procedures."[50]

In military terms, American forces are likely to quickly wreck the armored forces of lesser developed countries. U.S troops are also likely to hold back or defeat guerrilla forces, depending on local political conditions. The question is whether the battlefield victories will be bought expensively with old tactics, or won less expensively with clever tactics that make maximum use of electronic combat and the new technology.

But war is only politics by another means. What really matters is whether military victories can be converted into political success.

NAVY DOCTRINE

The Navy is acutely aware of the central importance of intelligence and electronic combat. They have developed an engagement timeline that establishes how they will conduct electronic combat, and a headquarters organization to promote peacetime preparedness for electronic combat.

Although the Navy has a doctrine for electronic combat at sea, the electronic combat experts in the Navy do not have the money or influence commensurate with their critically important task. Also, the doctrine has almost no connection whatsoever with Air Force and Army operations, especially in low intensity operations. This will ensure confusion and wasted lives when the Navy is forced by combat to cooperate with the other services. Moreover, the doctrine is grievously undermined by the Navy's over commitment to a soon-to-be outdated type of naval vessel — the conventionally designed, independently operating surface warship — which is critically vulnerable to infrared-, visible- and radio-wave guided weapons.

The Navy has failed to quickly combine the fighting power of its ships, nor has it responded to the forward-looking ideas that call for the development of stealthy surface ships that minimize infrared and radiowave visibility. By resisting introduction of these new ships, the Navy is making its sailors needlessly vulnerable to the many thousands of antiship missiles around the world.

ENVIRONMENT

Whether in combat against the Soviet Navy or the technologically sophisticated navies and air defense forces of the so-called developing world, the U.S. Navy will need every scrap of electronic combat capability it can muster.

Although the Soviet threat has greatly declined, the Navy must keep the Soviet Navy in mind because it uses the most advanced technology. Soviet warships carry many powerful antiaircraft, antisubmarine and antiship missiles, all linked to an impressive worldwide C^3I system — including space-based surveillance radars reporting directly to warships — which together form the most advanced reconnaissance–strike complexes the Soviets have yet fielded.

And such Soviet threats can be easier to deal with than the lone Iraqi pilot who suddenly blasted the unwary U.S.S. Stark with two French-built antiship missiles. Although the military threat posed by developing countries is obviously less than that of the Soviets, the low-intensity conflicts are just as complex and confusing. In action, it is difficult to identity friendly, enemy, and neutral among the blips on radar screens. Thus in the confusion caused by a running battle with Iranian gunboats, inadequate sensors, and unfamiliar weather conditions, the cruiser U.S.S. Vincennes misidentified and destroyed an Iranian airbus with almost 200 innocent people on board.

At sea, the Navy's electronic combat efforts have the extra complication of having to combine electromagnetic and sound sensors and communications systems. The low-frequency sound waves used as the primary surveillance means in submarine warfare can detect targets such as noisy warships at ranges of several thousand kilometers and can guide torpedoes to their targets at ranges of thousands of meters. Many of the techniques used in electronic combat are also used under the sea, including noise and deception jamming, noisy decoys, noise-homing torpedos, and ultraquiet stealthy submarines.

Perhaps the most important feature of the underwater arena is that submarines can find and attack ships at much longer ranges than ships, aircraft, or enemy submarines can find them. While ships and aircraft can only detect submarines at ranges of thousands of meters, submarines can strike ships with 95 km (60 mi) range torpedoes and thousand kilometer (600 mi) range radar-guided missiles. This allows submarines the enormous advantage of being able to hunt their targets and then escape after launching a destructive salvo of torpedoes and missiles. The greatest disadvantage submarines face is the need to move slowly to avoid the noise caused by high speed, which can be ameliorated if submarines can use information on enemy locations gathered by space satellites and aircraft radars.

The great importance of sound means that the Navy must build C^3I networks that can combine both sound and electromagnetic signals, a complication that the Army and Air Force do not face.

As evidence of its efforts to deal with these modern threats, and to increase the priority of electronic combat in annual budget battles, the Navy created a Space and Electronic Warfare Branch in early 1990. Supposedly on equal par with the surface ships, aircraft, and submarine communities, the branch centralizes oversight of all shared detection and targeting systems, and helps electronic combat proponents to argue for more money in the budget. It controls such sensors as oceanwide sonar arrays, ocean-surveillance satellites, and electronic-eavesdropping aircraft. Most importantly, it has begun an effort to completely convert the Navy's C^3I system into a series of modern computerized networks that share information to all who are granted access, instead of a series of radios that pass messages from one point to another.

However, the branch faces great resistance when trying to wrest control of electronic combat programs from their traditional owners. It will take many years before the Navy's C^3I, space and electronic warfare community moves up the Navy's pecking order.

Electronic Combat Operations

Like those of the Air Force and Army, the Navy's approach to electronic combat is greatly shaped by what it envisions to be its central wartime mission.

The Navy believes its central mission is forcing the Soviet Navy back toward its bases, until finally Soviet ships, aircraft, and bases are all laid waste by U.S. carrier-based aircraft strikes. Thus its idea of electronic combat is rooted in the Pacific carrier battles of World War II and is oriented to apocalyptic naval surface warfare rather than to the varied circumstances of conflict in the developing world.

However, the Navy learned much from the Vietnam War about air warfare, and its air electronic combat techniques are largely derived from that experience. Thus Navy air raids will be carried out by large strike packages similar to those used in Vietnam.

These modern Navy strike packages would consist of F-14 Tomcat fighters, E-2C Hawkeye radar aircraft, and EA-6B Prowler jamming aircraft escorting F/A-18 Hornet and A-6 Intruder bombers all the way to the point where the missiles and bombs are loosed. The bomber pilots will also have the additional protection of their own radar jamming, chaff dispensing and flare dropping electronic warfare equipment. Some of the F/A-18 bombers will double as anti-radiation missile-carrying defense-suppression aircraft in "Iron Hand" missions, according to Navy parlance. Also, EA-6Bs can jam radars and some radios from long range, while launching antiradiation missiles.

Money permitting, Navy pilots will be greatly aided by the introduction in the mid-1990s of new Airborne Self-Protection Jammer, which the Air Force decided not to buy because of its cost. One of the advantages of this new jammer is that it can be rapidly modified with new software, allowing it to defeat new radars shortly after they are fielded.

Also, Navy pilots in the mid-1990s will have disposable jammers designed to lure missiles away from aircraft. Pilots will also use air-dropped decoy aircraft call Tactical Air Launched Decoys to mimic attacking aircraft, hopefully attracting the enemy's antiaircraft defense weaponry away from the real bombers which would be approaching from another direction.

However, like the bomber pilots in the Air Force, the Navy's pilots have ensured a continued overinvestment by the Navy in development of highly sophisticated — and extremely expensive — stealth aircraft of uncertain value. The Navy's stealth aircraft was the highly classified A-12 bomber, scheduled to enter service in the mid-1990s, and designed to carry two crew and many bombs to their targets. Because of technical problems and high cost, the A-12 was cancelled in January 1991.

Sadly for the Navy, the cost of developing the A-12 sharply curtailed efforts to develop the guided weapons needed to save the penetrating pilots' lives in combat. With few ground-attack guided weapons in service, it is likely that the Navy will find itself in the ludicrous position of attacking targets with 1970s-era guided bombs as well as unguided bombs basically identical to those used by Navy pilots against the Japanese at the Battle of Midway in 1942.

Also, the development of the A-12 aircraft has diverted spending from other valuable programs, such as keeping A-6 bombers, which are failing because of problems with their old wings.

The Navy is well prepared for air attacks on naval targets, and is equipped with many long-range Harpoon missile and several types of short-range guided bombs. But the Navy's naval enemies will be aided by land-based aircraft and hard-to-detect submarines, neither of which can be easily disposed of by aircraft carriers.

For the Navy hierarchy, electronic combat against ground targets is seen as only a subsidiary part of the battle between enemy fleets. The U.S. Navy envisages a campaign beginning with each side groping around the world's oceans to find the other's main forces without betraying their own location. As soon as possible, each side will prepare and launch a massive strike, much as was done during the Battle of Midway where the outcome was critically effected by greatly superior U.S. intelligence gathering.

Prior to that battle, skillful American decryption of Japanese naval codes allowed the U.S. to mass its only three aircraft carriers to ambush the Japanese fleet as it blundered toward the island of Midway. During the confused battle, several U.S. bomber squadrons were able to pull off an amazingly unlikely coordinated strike after they almost simultaneously stumbled upon the Japanese fleet. Thus U.S. dive bombers and torpedo aircraft fell upon the Japanese fleet and destroyed three out of four Japanese carriers in only a few moments.

Given this Midway model of apocalyptic naval warfare where offense is much stronger than defense, and where the key to victory is landing the first powerful blow, the speedy gathering of intelligence is vital for the Navy. "The contest for information is going to dominate naval warfare," said Rear Adm. Roland Guilbault, deputy director of the Space and Electronic Warfare Branch.[51]

Electronic combat will play a central role in the gathering of intelligence by the Navy and the slowing of the enemy's intelligence gathering. According to the Navy, "A principal task of electronic warfare is to disrupt or destroy the enemy decision maker's sensors and communications, thereby delaying or deterring his achievement of the end game" which is the delivery of crushing attacks on each side's ships and airbases.[52] "Electronic warfare is seen as a way of both buying time and suppressing enemy defenses," according to the Navy.

With the Midway scenario in mind, the Navy has developed a naval engagement timeline showing how a naval battle develops to its climax and conclusion.

This engagement outline, once rounded out by electronic warfare techniques and tactics, is called the electronic warfare battle timeline, and consists of seven stages:

1. Preengagement planning.
2. Surveillance and reconnaissance to find enemy task forces and other assets.
3. Acquisition and tracking of enemy targets, needed for the next stage.
4. Targeting of weapons at various enemy ships and bases.
5. Weapons direction and guidance toward enemy targets.
6. Homing of weapons to impact, and successful fusing of explosives.
7. Postbattle damage assessment to see how much damage was done to the enemy and who emerged the winner.

Movement from each of these stages by the Navy — or its enemy — to the next is a critical decision point that can be delayed and disrupted by electronic combat, according to Navy sources. The timeline reflects both U.S. and enemy needs, and the primary objective of both attacker and defender "is to arrive at the weapons employment point before the adversary."

The engagement timeline helps the Navy manage its defensive and offensive operations. In defense, the effort will be to slow enemy

ENGAGEMENT TIMELINE

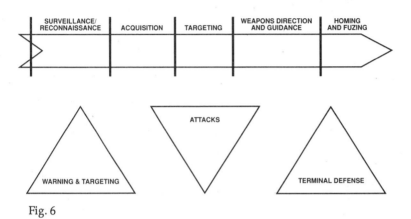

Fig. 6

movement along the timeline. On the offensive, the effort is to speed-ily move along the timeline to the weapons guidance and fusing stages.

Navy electronic warfare operations are not only concerned with degrading enemy use of the electromagnetic spectrum and protecting friendly use of the spectrum, but also with exploiting enemy signals for intelligence and target location. Thus the Navy apparently does not have many command, control, and communications countermeasures systems, because although such countermeasures are considered valuable, there is a much greater emphasis on gathering intelligence from enemy communications networks than from disrupting them, according to one admiral who helped formulate the Navy's doctrine. Also, physical attacks on enemy command, control, and communications networks are subsumed under strike warfare, rather than the Navy's version of C^3CM, according to a Navy official.

As the naval battle progresses along the timeline, so the electronic warfare operations accelerate in tempo. According to one former senior Navy admiral who helped develop the Navy's electronic warfare policy, the early stages of surveillance and reconnaissance consist of long range intelligence gathering, the "getting ready kind of

NAVAL ELECTRONIC WARFARE TIMELINE

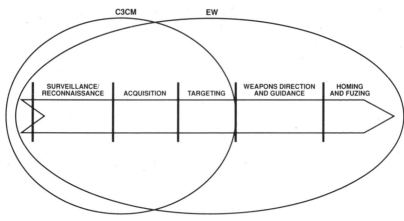

Fig.7

things." At this stage, with the existence and the location of the friendly task force hopefully unknown to the enemy, deception of enemy sensors and leaders is more important than degradation of enemy sensors.

"We believe that surveillance on a global dimension is going to become commonplace. ... whether by satellite or different means. One of the things we feel we have to do is to ensure that we use whatever passive or deception techniques we can muster to deny [knowledge of] where we are, our intentions or force composition," said Guilbault.[53]

Thus the Navy's East and West Coast Deception Groups would try to hide the location and course of U.S. task forces by using merchant ships masquerading as warships, unexpected routes for radiosilent carrier task forces, as well as the jamming of enemy sensors. For example, the Soviets use ocean surveillance satellites equipped with radars and radio-location equipment. But jammers mounted on aircraft or ships located far from a task force could be used to jam the radar satellites while fleets of cheaper radar-decoying rafts and convoys of smaller warships or merchant ships might be used to create a dummy carrier task force. Meanwhile, radio silence would be used to blind the radio-location satellites.

As the campaign progresses, increasing amounts of information flow into command centers. Gradually, the enemy commander becomes more sure of his target's location and he readies himself to launch his strike. Thus he will accelerate his intelligence gathering to pin down the location of the continually moving task force. Once the enemy detected the approaching carrier, the Navy would try to create confusion over the location and course of the task force to "dilute the target area," according to the admiral. After all, if the enemy fires his missiles at an empty piece of ocean, he will be leaving himself vulnerable to a quick U.S. counterstrike.

At this stage, different types of jammers and deception efforts are required to deceive the enemy, largely because the enemy would be using a different type of sensor to precisely locate the U.S. ships — for example the Soviet Tu-95 Bear-D maritime reconnaissance bombers equipped with radars and radiolocation systems. At this stage, hard-kill weapons such as the Navy's F-14 Tomcat jet interceptors and S-3 Viking antisubmarine aircraft would join the fray by searching for aircraft or submarines.

Once the enemy commander is confident that he knows the location of the Navy ships, he can begin the weapons guidance and homing phase of the engagement timeline.

As this happens, the Navy's emphasis will shift from deception to degradation techniques such as jamming and off-board decoys in an effort to make antiship missile miss their targets. The electronic systems that the Navy relies on to help its ships avoid incoming antiship missiles include shipboard deception jammers like the SLQ-32, towed rafts carrying radar jammers, rocket-propelled infrared decoys, and other traditional short-range electronic warfare techniques as well as defensive missiles fired from ships.

The Navy is now trying to extend the range of its electronic combat systems and to better integrate them with firepower, according to Dr. John Davis, chief scientist for the Navy's Space and Electronic Warfare Branch. Also, by extending its electronic warfare operations out to the maximum range of its sensors, the Navy reduces the need to destroy incoming antiship missiles with expensive (and relatively scarce) antimissile weapons, Davis said. The earlier the electronic countermeasures can attack an approaching reconnaissance aircraft, bombers, or incoming antiship missiles, the greater is the time for, and likelihood of, defeating the threat by electronic combat and the less need there is to fire expensive antimissile weapons. Extending the range of electronic combat systems is probably most easily done by using more deception systems to disguise the locations of the U.S. fleet.

Also, the Navy is trying to better combine its last-ditch electronic combat "soft-kill" systems with traditional "hard-kill" guns and missiles. This is especially important to the Navy, because it is very difficult to tell if an enemy antiship missile has been fully defeated by a ship's short-range electronic defenses — unless the missile obligingly smashes itself into the sea. If not, the sailors must worry that the missile will find a new target, or keep reattacking until it hits a ship or runs out of fuel.

Future antiship missiles will be smart enough to reattack until they run out of fuel. So unless the short-range electronic combat defenses can destroy the incoming missiles, their role will be reduced to continually diverting the missiles until they can be killed by the hard-kill defenses. Meanwhile, the crew will be praying that some number of missiles do not overcome the short-range electronic combat defenses and suddenly swamp the last-ditch, hard-kill defenses.

To support the intelligence-gathering efforts needed to progress along the timeline faster than the enemy, the Navy has built and continually upgraded a global intelligence collection effort aimed at keeping continuous track of all potential targets. The increased area of observation is driven by the need to monitor an ever-larger area of the world to give the Navy as much time as possible to respond to long-range, very fast bombers and antiship missiles. One of the more important sensors are the several White Cloud satellites, reportedly equipped with radio direction-finding equipment to track shipping during peace or war.

The Navy is also trying to upgrade its global communications networks to better transmit information gathered by underwater sonars, airborne radars, shipboard radars, ground-based radio direction-finding centers and over-the-horizon radars, as well as satellite information.

The communications networks feed the information to centralized command and intelligence centers worldwide. These command centers include five shore-based Naval intelligence fusion centers, plus regional commanders in chief in Hawaii, Virginia, and Naples, and also eleven to thirteen aircraft carriers. Together, these constitute a C^3I network that has helped shift the focus of leadership from ship commanders (who will often be restricted by the need for radio silence), toward theater commanders directing fleets and aircraft spread across the entire Atlantic or Pacific.

Moreover, the Space and Electronic Warfare branch is preparing to completely overhaul this C^3I network. Instead of radio communication links passing a confusing deluge of written, voice, and data messages from radio to radio, the Navy will establish a series of worldwide computer networks. Intelligence information will be constantly fed into the networks, allowing Navy officers to easily see on their computer screens the latest information they need.

Such networks will be similar to the Joint Tactical Information Distribution System (JTIDS). When JTIDS is deployed on radar aircraft and fighters in the mid-1990s, the information gathered by many intelligence systems will be automatically fed to small television screens in aircraft cockpits, allowing pilots to see the information they need to complete their mission without getting killed.

Of course, if an enemy manages to break the complex encryption scheme that protects the computer networks from eavesdroppers, he will be able to see much more information than by eavesdropping on a single radio link. However, the new networks will greatly increase the ability of U.S. naval officers to coordinate their forces so they can fire the first effective shot in battle.

The strengthening of C^3I networks runs directly against Navy tradition which sanctifies the authority and independence of the at-sea naval task force commander. Authority has shifted from the at-sea ship commander toward the task force commander, and perhaps is shifting to the land-based admiral overseeing the oceanwide battle with the help of computer networks feeding information into his underground bunker. Moreover, warships are slowly being linked together, so that a task force commander's ship will control the missiles and radars of other ships. Despite stiff resistance, this trend toward cooperative engagement will further reduce the independent authority of ships' captains.

In an effort to counter this slide toward centralized authority, the Navy has installed compact command centers, called Tactical Flag

Command Centers, in many of its larger ships. These computerized centers allow admirals commanding task forces to combine intelligence from ships, aircraft, satellites, and other sources without having to rely on the shore-based command centers. This helps restore authority to the admirals at sea, who have the advantage of being in the midst of the action and are ready to make quick decisions, despite the loss of some communications.

Even while the Navy uses its electronic combat doctrine to prevent, misdirect, fend off, or defeat an enemy attack, the Navy intends to launch its own attacks. Naturally, the Navy will try to pass through the various stages as quickly as possible, in an effort to get its blows in before the enemy. Armed with the timeline, Navy officers will plan to defeat enemy radio silence, deception, maneuvering, jamming and physical attacks as well as all the other tricks the Navy plans to use.

Problems

How successful will the Navy's electronic combat doctrine be in combat? How relevant is the Navy's vision of electronic combat and apocalyptic Midway battles?

The answer to these questions are impossible to determine, not least because the Battle of Midway will no more occur again than the Battle of Gettysburg.

Whatever the fortunes of war may turn out to be, the most important issue that affects the value of the Navy's vision of electronic combat is the military strategies chosen by the warring sides. Next in importance is the Navy's intellectual and financial commitment to electronic combat, which determines the quality of the deployed technology. In this case, it is easier to start from the least important question and work our way up to the most important.

The Navy spends far too little money and places too little importance on electronic combat, especially for protection of surface ships. The effects of this failure are clear even to the casual observer. For example, the Navy has no infrared warning systems that could be used to detect low-flying stealthy antiship missiles. The Navy's radar-equipped ships are needlessly vulnerable to antiradiation missiles, partially through lack of decoys, Tomming systems, or mutual-protection techniques. The Navy's land-based intelligence fusion centers are needlessly vulnerable to long range attacks because the lightly constructed buildings have no defenses.

Navy ships rely on a few hand-loaded 1970s-era mortars to launch chaff and infrared flares needed to deceive incoming missiles. The last-ditch defense of radar-guided Sea Sparrow missiles and Phalanx guns are also inadequate to defeat modern sea-skimming missiles. All these failures contributed to the death of thirty-six sailors when the U.S.S. Stark was hit by two Exocet missiles before any defense could be activated. These failures are only slightly ameliorated by the defeat of several twenty-five year-old Styx antiship missiles fired by Iranians at American ships shortly after the Vincennes accidentally destroyed the Iranian Airbus.

Blithely ignoring the lesson of the Stark, the Navy decided in the late 1980s to save a few million dollars by delaying installation of an electronic jamming capability on the new $800 million DDG-51 Arleigh Burke class destroyers. Further money was saved by not giving the ship helicopters that could be used to carry jammers and electronic intercept devices. A primary source of this problem is that electronic warfare systems are very low on the priority list of the naval officers responsible for the design and construction of new classes of warships. Their primary concerns are to get the ships launched without falling too far behind schedule or spending more money than budgeted.

The sad state of affairs is recognized by some Navy officials. "We have not done a good job in either soft kill, passive electronic warfare or offensive electronic warfare," admiral Guilbault said, adding that the Space and Electronic Warfare Branch is intended to focus attention and money on the problems. But so far, the money not spent on needed electronic combat technology has been claimed by other portions of the Navy and spent on purchases of additional under-armed and underprotected weapons, such as the Arleigh Burke destroyers.

Nor does the Navy have any means of destroying Soviet ship-detection satellites, largely because the U.S. Congress does not want to provoke increased Soviet military activity in space. However, as the Soviet naval threat declines, radar satellites become much less of a danger than the Exocet antiship missiles possessed by many developing countries.

The problems are compounded by inadequate deception efforts. Although one industry official involved in deception programs told the author that the Navy is "to the point where they are very good at masking ship movements,"[54] other experts strongly disagreed. They said the Navy does far too little to hide the location of its huge surface fleets from radars, radiointerception, and infrared sensors.

The next problem is the advent of stealth technology. Even as the Navy tries to extend the range of its electronic combat systems, stealth missile and aircraft technology steadily reduces the effective range of ships' sensors and self-defense weaponry. Because stealthy missiles are harder to see and effectively shorten the range of each ship's sensors, each ship will have less time to defend itself against an attack. Also, the reduced ranges of sensors means that ships might not be able to swiftly come to each other's aid.

Also, between the high-level guidance embodied in the electronic combat timeline and the low-level instructions passed out to electronic-warfare technicians, naval officers are not trained to combine the aircraft, ships, satellites, ground facilities, and submarines in a coordinated electronic combat effort. However, progress is being made, partly stimulated by the Navy's need to study this area in order to program shipboard computer systems. For example, the computerized Electronic Warfare Coordination Module is to be used in the early 1990s by task-force commanders to coordinate the electronic-warfare operations of ships and aircraft.

But a more serious problem is that the Navy has made little effort to coordinate its electronic combat effort with the Air Force or Army. The inability to cooperate partly stems from the Navy's possession of its own air force and its own ground force — the U.S. Marine Corps.

This problem will be clearly exposed in a war in the Gulf. The Navy and Air Force will fight separate wars, and will find it difficult to share aircraft or electronic combat assets. Ideally, strong central control by the local commander will ensure all three services fight a coordinated war, although it should be expected that naval aircraft "strike packages" will try to destroy Iraqi naval assets while helping Marine Corps amphibious landings, even as the Air Force aircraft try to destroy the Iraqi air force. Hopefully, the Navy and Air Force aircraft will annihilate their preferred targets quickly so they can help the decisive land battle.

Better cooperation could ensure that Navy cruise missiles strike antiaircraft weapons prior to Air Force attacks, while Air Force Joint STARS aircraft find targets for the Navy, and Compass Call communications jamming aircraft help disrupt C^3I networks before Navy bombers attack.

But all these shortcoming are largely subservient to a deeper and tougher set of problems, caused by the Navy's view of its traditions, roles, and missions.

In the Navy's eyes, the chief and primary enemy is the Soviet Navy, which is considered the only worthy adversary for the Navy's mighty armada of aircraft carriers, ships, and submarines. Thus the Navy's electronic combat doctrine is oriented against the Soviet threat. No doubt, it will take several years, if not decades, before the doctrine recognizes what is surely the collapse of the Soviet naval threat in the 1990s.

Let us accept the Navy's assumption about the Soviet threat, and examine how the Navy plans to deal with high intensity warfare and electronic combat.

During the early 1980s the Navy proudly asserted its maritime strategy of "forward defense" in which an aggressive offensive would be immediately launched to seize the initiative and force the Soviet fleet to defend itself and its home bases instead of attacking NATO convoys. This offensive is built around the Navy's carrier task forces, which include aircraft carriers, destroyers, cruisers and submarines.

Moreover, this independent Navy offensive is expected to have war-winning consequences. For example, during the early 1980s naval officers talked confidently of deterring a Soviet invasion of Western Europe by threatening to launch amphibious raids on the Soviet Far East or even Cuba. Such wildly optimistic faith in the ability of one's own service to gain decisive victories repeats the mistake of Air Force officers who believe their service acting on its own can win land wars.

In comparison, the main purpose of the Soviet Navy would most likely be to protect its missile-carrying submarines by forming protected bastions against the U.S. Navy. Its secondary purpose would be to sever the trans-Atlantic link created by thousands of merchant ships.

This defensive stance has two advantages. First, by remaining on the defensive to protect its submarines, the Soviet Navy can combine the strength of land-based aircraft, short-range ships and an extensive shore-based support structure. Second, the subsidiary mission of denying use of the sea is much easier than the U.S. Navy's task of ensuring that merchant ships continue to cross the Atlantic without too great loss.

These two advantages are well integrated into the Soviet Navy's preferred style of naval warfare, which emphasizes centralized coordination of sensors, land-based command centers, and aircraft- and ship-launched missiles. Thus the Soviets have stressed long-range sensors carried by land-based aircraft and satellites, linked by theater-wide C^3I networks to land-based command centers. The command centers then direct the deployment and firing of many missile-launching aircraft, ships, and submarines, in the hope of causing the target fleet to be simultaneously struck by hundreds of missiles approaching from many directions.

The weak link of this Soviet style of naval warfare is its reliance upon the coordination between the sensors, command centers, and weaponry needed to find the target and get all the attacking forces into the right position at the right time.

This is the link that the U.S. Navy's electronic warfare doctrine is supposed to shatter. If Soviet coordination can be disrupted, then their attacks will be weak and ineffective, so leaving their ships at sea, land-based aircraft and command centers vulnerable to attacks from the aggressive carrier task forces. Correspondingly, if Soviet intelligence gathering and command and control is not seriously disrupted, then the U.S. fleet will find itself involuntarily replaying the Japanese role in the Battle of Midway.

Arrayed against the Soviet centralized C^3I and mission of sea denial, are the two advantages of the Navy's carrier forces. First, the carriers' high mobility helps prevent the enemy from pinpointing their location. Second, the carriers have their own long-range striking force, greatly simplifying the task of coordinating forces to deliver a devastating blow at just the right moment.

But does the carrier's advantages over land-based forces of mobility and coordination still exist fifty years after Midway? Is it not possible that Soviet sensors, communications, and long-range homing missiles can detect the U.S. carriers and launch well-coordinated attacks from far-distant bases?

If Soviet C^3I can overcome the carrier's traditional advantages in mobility and coordination, then surely the carrier's importance in naval warfare has declined in comparison to the Soviet combination of long-range bombers and long-range sensors controlled by a central headquarters. If so, U.S. admirals will sink into Davy Jones' locker with their prized carriers.

It seems the U.S. Navy believes that aircraft carriers no longer have the defensive capability that caused the slaughter by several U.S. aircraft carriers of several hundred Japanese aircraft during the "Marianas Turkey Shoot" in 1944. During the 1980s, the Navy devoted more and more of the carrier task forces' efforts to defend themselves from Soviet attacks. Currently, a single carrier has only ten all-weather bombers, supported by a rough total of twenty-four F-14 fighters, and twenty-four F/A-18 fighter-bombers, several units of jamming, radar, and refueling aircraft, and ten antisubmarine aircraft, plus several antiaircraft cruisers and several antiaircraft destroyers.

Of course, when faced with a minimal antiship threat, the Navy can do as it did during the Kuwaiti crisis, when it loaded the carriers with more bombers and radar-jamming aircraft than usual, partly to support possible amphibious landings by the U.S. Marine Corps.

A deeper question now presents itself: Even if the U.S. Navy *can* defeat the Soviet Navy, so what? In wartime, the USSR would be a self-contained power, immune to pinprick attacks on its useless ports and barren coastlines, well-prepared to defeat an invading force of overconfident Marines, and with plenty of land-based nuclear weapons to compensate for the loss of some missile-carrying submarines. With conventional weapons, the U.S. Navy cannot affect large-scale military operations on land to any significant extent except by transporting large numbers of soldiers to battle. In sum, the only way the U.S. Navy could try to seriously *win* a war by itself would be by using nuclear weapons — a potentially suicidal move for the Navy's prized carriers, and for America as a nation.

Moreover, given the collapse of imperial Soviet ambitions, how important or relevant is the Soviet naval threat? Surely the American

Navy should better prepare itself for sudden contingencies around the world?

For example, the Navy had only six lightly armed ships in the Persian Gulf and an aircraft carrier several days away when the Iraqis invaded Kuwait in August 1990. Such ships had no capability to beat back the invasion, and little or no ability to cooperate with Air Force or foreign units — even if Iraqi leader Saddam Hussein had believed the U.S. would oppose his invasion.

Given the collapse of Soviet naval power, the increased importance of conflicts in the developing world, the vulnerability of carrier forces to missile attacks, and the risks of tactical disaster, the Pentagon and the Navy should cast about for a new approach to naval power.

Opportunities

Despite the comparative advantages of the missile-armed attacker against surface ships, the carrier task force remains the most powerful defensive naval force available because it can defeat threats from aircraft, submarines and electronic combat. Thus the carriers and their aircraft will continue to play a vital role in protecting task forces and convoys for the foreseeable future. Also, carriers are very valuable floating airfields, ready to move airpower quickly to distant locations.

But modern C^3I networks, electronic combat techniques, advanced missiles, and innovative ship designs offer a host of new possibilities for carrying out offensive and defensive missions at sea.

In the short run, C^3I networks allow the Navy to create a fleet of ships and aircraft each able to perform a few missions very well. They can compensate for each other's weaknesses and share each other's strengths when linked together by a C^3I network. For example, antiaircraft cruisers cannot attack enemy submarines well, while antisubmarine frigates cannot defend themselves from aircraft. But both can work as a team when combined by an effective C^3I network.

The Navy leads the other services in this regard, because of its commitment to C^{3}I networks like the Joint Tactical Information Distribution System, which is capable of democratically and automatically sharing information among hundreds of aircraft and ships dispersed over hundreds of miles in all directions, despite enemy jamming and eavesdropping.

Improved C^{3}I networks will allow the Navy to continue down this road. For example, the Navy could design small ships armed with self-defense weapons, unmanned aircraft and a long-range radar that would control antiship, antiaircraft and ground-attack missiles launched from a large missile-carrying ship. Thus a few ships could control the weapons carried by many other ships.

But then, why not try to use land-based radar-equipped surveillance aircraft to guide the missiles? Surely aircraft or satellites could find targets for land-based aircraft, or even missiles launched from the back of trucks that could be quickly airlifted to a crisis. Alternatively, stealthy reconnaissance cruise missiles might find the targets for a closely following swarm of conventionally armed smart cruise missiles.

The same logic applies under the oceans. Why not combine submarines with swarms of computer-controlled mines and underwater drone robots to hunt down and sink any enemy submarines or surface ships that make an appearance. Because submarines are so hard to detect, yet can gather information by sonar or by radio from global surveillance networks — despite the jamming and the chaos of warfare — they have the ability to strike without too much fear of enemy return fire. When armed with cruise missiles, the submarines gain the ability to strike land targets.

And if submarines are hidden so well by the oceans, why not build ships that have some of the stealthiness of submarines? As chief of surface naval operations in the mid-1980s, Vice Admiral Joseph Metcalf urged the Navy to begin a "revolution at sea" by building stealthy warships that were bare of superstructure. Using advanced technology to reduce crew size and absorb electromagnetic radiation, and with a willingness to eliminate the traditional features of ship design — navigation and signal bridges, tall engine exhausts, and gun turrets — the Navy could build ships that were hard to detect and carried more firepower than ever before.[55] Such stealthy ships would also be easier to hide if the Navy released large number of small, computerized decoy boats to create many false targets for enemy sensors.

But if stealthy ships are to be built, might they not be given ballast tanks so they can submerge to minimize visibility and vulnerability to nearby antiship missiles? The use of ballast tanks would greatly reduce their vulnerability, but it would also affect their ability to use sensors and communications networks to control the air and sea around them.

To a greater or lesser extent, all these schemes would have the happy result of reducing the workload for the aircraft carriers, helping them to use airpower offensively or defensively.

Such schemes are useful against many types of naval and air threats that are presented by the increasingly dangerous forces of the developing countries.

Moreover, this innovative approach would allow the Navy to launch new types of ships better suited for the variety of low-intensity conflicts it is likely to face in future years — for example, fleets of small and fast stealth ships able to combine their strength with each other, as well as with long-range fighters, radar aircraft and distant missile launchers. Thus they would be ready to destroy naval and ground targets without the risk of losing aircraft and having captured pilots paraded before TV cameras as in the past.

But the obstacles to reformation of the present U.S. Navy are very strong. The first obstacle is institutional inertia. The Navy has a huge financial investment in surface warships and aircraft carriers. More important, it also has tens of thousands of careers poured into the traditional way of doing things. Indeed, it will launch two new aircraft carriers in the 1990s for $7 billion, expecting them to serve until the 2040s. The suggested wholesale shift to underwater and stealthy warships and land-based aircraft would negate the billions and billions of dollars and many careers already invested in surface warships.

Even a gradual shift would be troubling for the Navy's bureaucracy, which only designs and launches new ships and submarines at a excruciatingly slow rate. For example, the Navy's newest surface warship is the general-purpose DDG-51 destroyer, which costs much the same to buy and operate as the older Aegis class cruisers but carries fewer weapons. Yet the Navy planned the first upgrade of the DDG-51 class with new jamming equipment and electronics in the mid-1990s, after it had begun construction of thirty-three ships. Only because of intervention by the Office of the Secretary of Defense in 1990 was the upgrade moved to 1992, when construction of the eighteenth ship is scheduled to begin. Even so, the Navy still does not plan to equip the ships with helicopters until after the twenty-ninth ship!

One frequently aired Navy argument against specialized ships and C^3I networks is that the variety of naval operations is so great that some circumstances require a general purpose fleet. But the Navy can always maintain adequate numbers of self-sufficient general-purpose ships for missions such as war against the Soviet Navy, while building the specialized ships and their vast C^3I networks.

The Navy's conservatism threatens to derail the much-needed "revolution at sea," according to Metcalf. "This is both a warfighting and 'religious'. issue. To many naval officers, young and old, the [ship's] bridge and [signal] flag bag are fundamental traditions of the service. ... We can plan, write papers, and conduct studies, but if we cannot execute, the revolution will stall and drift in an inconclusive direction. Will the threat wait or move on while we struggle to build a 6,000-ton warship with more than one gun?"[56]

This institutional conservatism is reinforced by tight budgets. After missing the opportunities granted by the big budget increases in the early 1980s, Navy officials will be reluctant to set aside the cash for new ideas in the 1990s.

But the greatest obstacle to increased use of C^3I networks is a fear that they would reduce the Navy's hallowed tradition of the independent role of the commander at sea. For example, U.S. submarine commanders are loath to see their beloved submarines converted to missile boats aimed by others, just as Soviet giant cruise missile-carrying Oscar submarines are really underwater missile platforms controlled by central shore-based commanders. After all, the submariner's traditional style of warfare is sea patrols by independently operating submarines commanded by skilled captains waging war against enemy ships, just as their grandfathers did against Japan in the 1940s.

The tradition of independent command at sea is partially justified by the perfectly reasonable reluctance to place too much faith on the survivability of a C^3I system. Clearly, if the U.S. increases its reliance on C^3I to link increasingly specialized ships, the enemy will increase their efforts to wreck C^3I. Without good C^3I, antiaircraft ships could not call for help when threatened by submarines and antisubmarine ships could not call for help when attacked by bombers. Also, at-sea naval officers are loath to give up control, partly out of fear that no amount of C^3I networks will allow the shore-based commander to really understand what is going on.

But some uncharitable souls also suggest that the Navy's greatest concern is that loss of independent command at sea would erode the dignity and authority of the ship's commander. This is a matter of no small import to a tradition-bound organization like the Navy, which remembers well the great commanders of history, such as Admiral Nelson or Admiral Dewey. With a telescope placed over his blind eye, Nelson ignored orders that would have halted his destruction of the Danish fleet in the battle of Copenhagen. Similarly, Dewey destroyed the Spanish fleet in Manila without any instructions from Washington. It is not surprising that over many centuries the practice of decentralized command has hardened into a principle.

Despite these obstacles to automated cooperation and worldwide C^3I, top-level admirals have always wanted to exercise authority over their subordinates. However, they have always been frustrated by poor communications and sensors, and most importantly, by the chaos of war. Thus, for lack of a better alternative, control has always been distributed or decentralized to the commanders at sea.

Yet this principle is now an obstacle to military progress. It is being steadily chipped away by greater realization of the value of twenty-first century C^3I networks, sensors and weapons. The tradition will be undermined even more when land-based admirals push to gain some measure of wartime control through vast C^3I networks, despite the confusion and chaos to be expected in naval warfare.

The issue is not a crude alternative between land-based and sea-based control, but rather the balance between central authority and local commanders. While there are strong arguments for a centralized system and perhaps equally strong arguments for a decentralized system, complete reliance on either is a sure recipe for defeat.

Thus the Navy must learn how to deploy new world-wide sensor systems and C^3I networks that allow local commanders the freedom to make on-the-spot decisions *and the ability to call up friendly support from vast distances,* while ensuring that top leaders can execute a plan and coordinate firepower.

CONCLUSION

The role of electronic combat is not just to sever communications. Its role is to bewilder, blind, confound, complicate, confuse, disrupt, disorganize, perplex, and paralyze the enemy at tactical, operational, and strategic levels so that the political goals can be won at minimum cost in lives, money, and bitterness.

High-technology war is fast becoming a race to destroy an enemy C^3I networks before one's own networks collapse under the impact of chaos, explosives, and jamming.

Despite some forward thinkers, recent progress and good technology, the U.S. services have not yet fully understood the potential of electronic combat in high- or low-intensity operations. Indeed, the U.S. service bureaucracies remain behind the Soviet military in understanding.

The Army seems to have done reasonably well. Previously content with a few radios and air defense radars, the Army is preparing plans to cooperate with their Air Force in exploiting the expected long-range sensors and long-range weapons. To its credit, the Army has also cut back on production of its most prestigious and traditional weapons — tanks, helicopters, and armored personnel carriers — to better develop the new weapons and electronic combat technology by the late 1990s. But there are many gaps, as we have seen.

Although the Navy is hard at work developing new C^3I networks and electronic combat systems, it remains wedded to its independent strategy, the surface warship, and the aircraft carrier in an age of superstealthy submarines, global sensors, and long-range missiles. The Navy's fixation on a Soviet threat and its tradition of independent command undermine its electronic capability.

Meanwhile, the service that prides itself most on its superior technology is also the most backward, despite the efforts of some smart officers. The Air Force remains wedded to its vision of an independent war-winning role for airpower, its massive investment in manned aircraft and fixed air bases. While it struggles to field working electronic warfare technology and to build multibillion dollar — but obsolete — Stealth bombers, the white scarved pilots of the Air Force are doing their best to ignore the wider impact of sensors and missiles. The only brights spots are the Air Force's refinement of the AWACS and Joint STARS aircraft, and some younger officers trying to push the Air Force into the present.

Perhaps the Air Force has done poorest at coping with the impact of electronic combat. Air warfare is being changed rapidly by technological advances, in contrast to land warfare where army units can mitigate the impact of new weapons by hiding in the ground, cities, jungles, or hills. In air warfare there is nothing but clear sky between an aircraft and a new missile. In such a clear "frictionless" environment, technological advances change the technology, techniques and tactics of war so quickly that no organization as large as the Air Force could evolve rapidly enough in the calm of peacetime. It is easier for the Army because in the confused environment of ground warfare, the impact of electronic combat causes much slower changes in technology and tactics, allowing ground soldiers to stay reasonably abreast of the latest developments.

The services' failures are underlined forcefully by the lack of commitment to space systems. Despite a massive investment in spy satellites, there is an inadequate effort by the Pentagon chiefs to properly harness these superlative observation and communication systems into the worldwide reconnaissance–strike complexes that the Soviet military hopes someday to build. The unwillingness of intelligence agencies to share the satellites is a primary obstacle yet to be overcome. Worse still, the service chiefs chip away at the space research program, which offer the only means of exercising U.S. military influence in space — even if the ambitious Strategic Defense Initiative cannot defeat incoming nuclear weapons.

Similar failures are seen in the service approaches to low-intensity war. The twin possibilities of high- and low-intensity warfare require the maintenance of two types of Armies and Air Forces, each with its own C^3I and electronic combat capabilities. Thus the Army has its heavy armored corps, its lightly equipped infantry divisions and its commando forces. The Air Force will have its Stealth fighters and bombers, but very few unglamorous C-130 gunships, OV-10 forward air control aircraft or the A-10 armored bombers that are so useful in low-intensity conflict.

Although Army and Air Force cooperation has improved in recent years, there is still a long way to go before the services cooperate adequately, or even possess common communications systems needed to share information. Perhaps the Navy is the worst offender in this regard; the fact that this chapter could discuss Navy electronic combat doctrine without reference to the Air Force or Army is condemning enough. The Navy does not feel the need to cooperate with the Air Force or the Army because it intends to fight its own war, and has the U.S. Marine Corps available just in case soldiers are ever needed. But many Air Force officers, and especially those from the strategic bomber units, are also guilty of the same error of believing that they can win a war on their own. Such ideas are very difficult to root out; the Air Force failed to win the war on its own as it claimed it could in World War II, Korea, and Vietnam.

Clearly, such parochial biases are dangerous for the interservice cooperation needed to fight and win on the extended, fast moving and violent battlefields of the future. Modern warfare and electronic combat require that a very high degree of well-practiced technological, tactical and operational cooperation be established well before war breaks out. To cite a few examples, in order for the services to cooperate in combat they must have common communications technology and well-practiced arrangements for allocating radio and radar frequencies. They must have common techniques for electronic combat, radars that won't jam another service's radars, and common computer systems to ensure the services do not all attack the same targets while leaving other untouched. Most important, the services need a shared strategy to ensure they do not fight their own wars, as the Air Force did with its endless, costly and ineffective bombing of northern Vietnam.

This shared strategy is apparently being hammered out, not by the services, but by chairman of the DoD's Joint Staff and the regional commanders in chief of U.S. forces deployed around the world. The chairman and commanders were given extra authority and more influence over DoD budgets by the Goldwater-Nichols Act of 1986, and have used it to ensure improved coordination between the services. The improvements could be seen in the early stages of the Kuwaiti crisis when the U.S. commander controlled all the forces in his area, and seemed to coordinate them well. However, it will be many years before the improved coordination is reflected in improved electronic combat efforts by the services.

Despite all the talk of technology and technique, the most important military tools are skilled soldiers and a wise strategy. If armies win wars without these attributes, it is because their enemies were even more incompetent.

The U.S. has the skilled soldiers, although the rapid defense builddown begun by the 1991 defense budget may drive dedicated men and women out of the services. More ominously, intelligent and skilled people may opt for civilian rather than military careers — especially if a military career is poorly paid.

But if we judge by public statements about the future of warfare and by examination of future spending plans, the Army, Navy, and especially the Air Force, have inadequately studied how electronic combat and the new technology will affect warfare above the tactical level. No matter how much Congress tries to suppress fraud, waste and abuse, no matter how much the U.S. improves its appalling record of technological development, this failure will waste billions and billions of dollars over the next few years. Worse still, in future conflicts, the Pentagon's intellectual failure may cause its defeat.

Money is not the answer to the Pentagon's inertia unless it helps speed the introduction of new thinking and new technology into the services. What is needed is a strengthened central planning staff — perhaps even a forward-thinking general staff able to impose its will on the services and subordinate communities. But most of all, the U.S. needs a decision by top-level leaders to discard the past and seize the future — whatever wrenching changes may be required. As Admiral

Metcalf wrote: "resistance to change is the enemy ... [officers should] lead, follow, or get out of the way."[57]

Notes

1. *Electronic Combat Report*, 20 July, 1990, p. 7.
2. *Aviation Week and Space Technology*, 27 August, 1990, p. 23.
3. U.S. Department of the Army, *FM 34-10; Divisional Intelligence and Electronic Warfare Operations* (Washington, DC: Government Printing Office, November 1986), p. 1-1.
4. Capt. Ralph Peters, "The Age of Fatal Visibility," *Military Review*, August 1988. pp. 51-52.
5. Dept. of the Army, *34-10; Divisional Intelligence*, p. 1-4.
6. Ibid.
7. Ibid.
8. Ibid., p. 5-22.
9. Ibid., p. 5-14.
10. Ibid., p. 5-22.
11. U.S. Department of the Army, *Field Manual 11-92* (Washington, DC: Government Printing Office), p. 2-2.
12. U.S. Department of the Army, *Final Draft, Army Command and Control Master Plan* (February 1990), p.3-20. Given to the author by Caleb Baker, a reporter at *Defense News*.
13. Dept. of the Army, *Field Manual 11-92*, p. 2-4.
14. David C. Isby, *Weapons and Tactics of the Soviet Army* (London and New York: Jane's, 1981), p. 353.
15. Peters, "Age of Fatal Visibility," p. 50.
16. Ibid.
17. Ibid., p. 56.
18. *Army Times*, 5 March, 1990. p. 16.
19. U.S. House of Representatives, Defense Appropriations Subcommittee hearings, 1987, p. 125.
20. Col. Richard Atchison, director of electronic combat operations in the Air Force staff, in *Journal of Electronic Defense*, April 1987, p. 66.
21. See Christopher Robbins, *The Ravens* (New York: Pocket Books, 1987), and Marshall Harrison, *A Lonely Kind of War: Forward Air Controller, Vietnam* (Novato, CA: Presidio, 1989).

22. Truong Nhu Tang, *A Viet Cong Memoir*, (New York: Vintage, 1985), p. 170.

23. *Defense Electronics*, September 1988, p. 54.

24. Larry Davis, *Wild Weasel: The SAM Suppression Story* (Carrollton, TX: Squadron/Signal Publications, 1986), p. 38.

25. *Defense Electronics*, September 1988, p. 59.

26. Jeffrey Ethell and Alfred Price, *One Day in a Long War* (New York: Random House, 1989), p. 50.

27. Gen. John Vogt in Richard H. Kohn and Joseph P. Harahan, eds., *Air Interdiction in World War II, Korea and Vietnam*, U.S. Air Force Warrior Studies (Washington, DC: Office of Air Force History, 1986), p. 87.

28. Ethell and Price, *One Day in a Long War*, p. 185.

29. William Perry, *Electronic News*, 13 February, 1978.

30. Senior DoD official in interview with author, February 1990.

31. Col. R. Atchison in *Journal of Electronic Defense*, April 1987. p. 70, my emphasis.

32. *Jane's Defense Weekly*, 6 January, 1990, p. 20.

33. *Los Angeles Times*, 13 September, 1990, p. 10.

34. James Canaan, *Air Force Magazine*, August 1989, p. 41.

35. *Air Force Magazine*, August 1989, p. 38.

36. *Air Force Magazine*, June 1989, p. 52.

37. In Kohn and Harahan, eds., *Air Interdiction*, p. 92.

38. Gen. John Vogt in Kophn and Harahan, *Air Interdiction*, p. 31.

39. *Defense News*, 25 April, 1988.

40. *Aviation Week and Space Technology*, 29 October, 1990, p. 17.

41. Eugene Boyle and Bruce Jackson, "Follow On Force Attack: Intelligence and Operations, Processes and Constraints," in Clarence McKnight, *Control of Joint Forces: A New Perspective* (Fairfax, VA: Armed Forces Communications and Electronics Association, 1989), p. 203.

42. *Defense News*, 16 July, 1990.

43. For more analysis of NATO deep attack efforts, see *New Technology For NATO*.

44. *Journal of Electronic Defense*, June 1985, p. 37.

45. Anthony Cordesman and Abraham Wagner, *The Lessons of Modern War; Vol I, The Iran-Iraq War* (Boulder and San Francisco: Westview, 1990), p. 458.

46. Gerry Thomas, "C^3I in Unconventional Warfare," in McKnight, *Control of Joint Forces*. Also, James Rawles, "Marine Corps SIGINT is Lean But Mean," *Defense Electronics*, April 1990, p. 43.

47. This and the following quotes are taken from the final draft of *Joint Chiefs of Staff Publication 3-07; Doctrine for Joint Operations in Low Intensity Conflict*. (Washington DC: Government Printing Office, January 1990).

48. U.S. Department of the Army, *Field Manual 100-20: Low Intensity Conflict*, quoted by Thomas, "C^{3}I in Unconventional Warfare," in *Control of Joint Forces*, p. 183.

49. John D. Bergen, U.S. Army, Center for Military History *Military Communications: A Test for Technology* (Washington DC: Government Printing Office, 1985), p. 403.

50. Ibid., pp. 403, 408.

51. Interview with *Defense News* staff, 18 April, 1990.

52. U.S Navy Public Affairs Office, Pentagon, Washington DC, in response to questions from author. 12 December 1989.

53. Interview with *Defense News* staff, 18 April, 1990.

54. Steve Rosa, director of marketing for TVI Corp., Beltsville, MD, in *Defense News*, 30 October, 1989, p. 12.

55. Vice. Adm. Joseph Metcalf, "Revolution at Sea," *Proceedings*, January 1988, p. 36. For another version of the future, see *Navy 21; Implications of Advanced Technology for Naval Operations in the Twenty-First Century* (Washington, DC: National Academy Press, 1988).

56. Metcalf, *Proceedings*, p. 39.

57. Ibid., p. 39.

---◆---

Ten

NUCLEAR WAR AND ELECTRONIC COMBAT

By carrying destructiveness to a suicidal extreme, atomic power is stimulating and accelerating a reversion to the indirect methods that are the essence of strategy—since they endow war with intelligent properties that raise it above the brute application of force.

Basil Liddell Hart, *Strategy*

Nuclear weapons are the colossus of international politics and military affairs. Because nuclear weapons cannot be abolished, the threat of war between nuclear armed powers is greatly diminished, and every politician must find new ways to achieve his political goals beneath their shadow.

The most obvious effect of nuclear weapons is that they frequently deter resort of full scale warfare, so channeling political conflict in new directions.

Thus politicians rely more on diplomacy, economics, propaganda, guerrilla warfare and state-sponsored terrorism to win what they can and defend what they hold. But where nuclear weapons are not available, or where they are too terrible to be used, conventional weapons are thrown into action. The Arab–Israeli wars, the Afghan War, and the Vietnam War, were all fought without nuclear weapons.

How does the potential impact of electronic combat effect the relationship between political conflict and nuclear weapons? Does electronic combat make nuclear war more likely? Can the new weaponry used in electronic combat replace nuclear weapons?

In recent years and months, the threat of nuclear war has drastically diminished to a point where it is utterly incredible. Instead, disarmament treaties are being prepared and western leaders are trying to help the Soviets resolve their internal political problems.

The immediate causes of this happy turn of events are the near-revolutionary changes in the Soviet Union. Indeed, if democracy takes hold in the Soviet Union, global nuclear war between the Soviet Union and the United States will be as incredible as nuclear war between France and the United Kingdom.

However, those who wish to ensure the unthinkable never happens would be wise to examine how such a war would develop when desperate or ambitious leaders turn again to military force, years or decades from now. This knowledge could help prevent misunderstanding and errors that might have truly catastrophic results.

Some would argue that the existence of nuclear megatonnage overwhelms all the military and political factors that might shape nuclear warfare. But this is not so; nuclear-tipped missiles will be aimed at detectable targets by a controlling hand with a certain purpose in mind. It is at those points that electronic combat would change nuclear war, making it less controllable and more dangerous that it already is.[1]

THE ROLE OF ELECTRONIC COMBAT IN EARLY WARNING OF NUCLEAR ATTACKS

The detection and warning of an incoming nuclear strike is an extremely high priority mission for the U.S., China, USSR, and all other nuclear armed countries. It is also an arena where electronic combat could have a critical effect on the likelihood and course of nuclear war.

Because nuclear missiles can destroy anything on the globe in thirty minutes, early warning systems are kept permanently alert for any sign of an impending nuclear attack. A poor warning system could give an attacker hope that he might wipe out his enemy's nuclear deterrent before it could respond.

This problem becomes more critical if a nation possesses only a few nuclear weapons. The United States' nuclear weapons are so numerous and dispersed it is impossible to believe they could be destroyed in one blow. But the much smaller nuclear forces of France, Israel, India, and other countries are vulnerable to sudden destruction because they are stored in so few locations.

To detect incoming attacks, countries will use spies, electronic eavesdropping and radars. The U.S. and Soviets have the most extensive networks of early warning systems, which include satellites and Over The Horizon-Backscatter radars.

Signals intelligence can provide short term warning of an impending attack, or more likely, of a decision to begin limited use of short-range tactical nuclear weapons during a conventional battle. For instance, Soviet signals intelligence sensors would listen for leakages from the vast American organization established to command and control the huge U.S. nuclear arsenal. Soviet eavesdroppers could also monitor the U.S. bomber bases to see if many on-board radar and radio sets were being tested, so giving several hours advance warning of a possible mass takeoff. This technique is no different from that used by the Nazis to get early warning of Allied mass bomber raids, although the modern eavesdroppers rely on satellites.

If a war had broken out in the early 1980s, Soviet signals intelligence specialists would have had the priceless benefit of the information provided by the Walker spy ring. This would have allowed them to decrypt communications between U.S. missile-carrying submarines and the National Command Authority (NCA), which rely on a limited network of only several very low frequency transmitters, about sixteen airborne low-frequency relay aircraft and a limited-range, extremely low frequency radio.

In the same way, U.S. signals intelligence resources would be used to gather any early indicators of an incoming nuclear attack, despite heavy use by the Soviets of land lines and encryption. The U.S. has had some success in predicting Soviet moves: In 1982, the Soviets suddenly test fired several intercontinental missiles and a strategic defense missile designed to shoot down incoming U.S. warheads, causing several seizures in North American Aerospace Defense Command. But command officials became even more displeased once they learned the American eavesdroppers had used signals intelligence to predict the missile tests but had not told NORAD officials for fear the Soviets would discover how much the U.S. knew about their activities. The subsequent bureaucratic conflict resulted in a new communications link being set up to inform the aerospace command of signals intelligence information.[2]

During a war or crisis, the alert level of command and control networks would be increased. Any sudden burst of unfamiliar radio activity on previously unused nets would likely be detected, and so raise the suspicions of even the most complacent analyst.

But the problem is not as easy as it sounds. What signals indicate an incoming nuclear attack, as opposed to a general military alert or an impending conventional offensive? How does one discover the interesting signals in the confusion of war? Will the intelligence analyst be distracted by some other event? Will the top level leaders and politicians listen to the intelligence analyst? Is the evidence of an attack strong enough to take countermeasures?

William Van Cleave wrote that "warning is apt to be inherently ambiguous until too late. Signals indicating the possibility (perhaps even the fact) of a surprise nuclear attack would be those most resisted by U.S. leadership. The realization that an attack is imminent, or underway, would come slowly and reluctantly. The strong disbelief in a surprise nuclear attack makes it likely that warning signals of such an attack would also be disbelieved as long as possible. For [the sixteen nations of] NATO, all these encumbrances would be multiplied."[3]

Given the impact of a surprise nuclear attack, it is possible that one side might use electronic combat to disguise preparation for a nuclear attack, perhaps by jamming signals intelligence satellites, relying on covert communications wires to distribute preprepared orders, and using apparently peacetime routines to disguise hostile preparations.

For example, according to Soviet writers: "To achieve surprise in modern war, an aggressor on the eve of war and in the course of it will evidently take measures to suppress and blind reconnaissance forces and means of the enemy by creating strong interference against radio and radiotechnical means."[4]

Nothing has ever been revealed of any U.S. plans for the use of deception in nuclear war. However, the U.S. has less incentive to use deception because there is no evidence the U.S. political leaders have ever considered preemptive nuclear strikes as wartime options — despite the aggressive bent of the U.S. Air Force, especially in the 1950s.

However, with the Pentagon's acceptance of the possibility of a long nuclear war, further development and integration of electronic combat doctrine in nuclear war strategies are likely. This might result in more extensive American plans for secrecy as well as command, control, and communications countermeasures.

It is important to note that neither the Soviets nor the Americans — or the Chinese, British, or French — have ever placed all their nuclear weapons or command and control systems on full alert — as far as is publicly known — so anything approaching a crisis alert should be relatively easily discriminated from normal routine by intelligence analysts.

An important point raised by Paul Bracken is that the C^3I systems of many countries are closely linked with their respective nuclear weapons and to others' command, control, communications, and intelligence systems. So both sides can monitor the other's actions, and quickly order counteractions.[5] Bracken argues that this close linkage of weapons and C^3I complexes could lead in a peacetime crisis to a series of escalating measures and countermeasures, as each side marched in lockstep to counter the enemy's previous action. In a crisis, this ratcheting escalation could greatly destabilize any military equilibrium and perhaps precipitate a bloody and destructive war.

For example, it is often said that bombers are strategically stabilizing because — unlike missiles — they can be launched from airbases when an attack seems imminent yet be readily recalled to base by radio. But when examined more carefully with the importance of C^3I in mind, this recall capability may fool U.S. officials into thinking there are no bad consequences to the launching of the bombers. Such bad consequences include scaring the Soviets into thinking an attack might be on the way, and taking another step toward actual release of nuclear weapons. It sounds crazy, but in crisis situations what seemed crazy only hours before can seem rational to a scared, poorly informed leader.

Any damage caused to either side's C^3I system by bad luck or conventional war could only increase the possibility of destablization. Thus Bracken recommended that the U.S. improve the stability of its C^3I system, and try to negotiate with the Soviets to establish procedures that reduce the chance of this lockstep escalation. But there is no sign the superpowers are preparing negotiations appropriate to the problem, and even if undertaken, the negotiations would be very difficult to conclude successfully because of their devilish complexity, and because military communications are so inextricably bound up with all military operations — which are very difficult to discuss, describe, or limit in international negotiation.

Some minor successes have been achieved in this area by the signing of a U.S.-Soviet pact on June 7, 1989, which forbade striking either side with lasers or interfering with communications systems in a way that could "cause harm to personnel or damage to the equipment" of either side. The pact also established special procedures to help communications between local military commanders.[6] This agreement might help prevent minor border incidents from flaring into something more dangerous, but does little to prevent each side's C^3I system from driving the other's to ever higher levels of alert, as Bracken suggested might happen.

But with the proliferation of nuclear weapons among developing countries, the problem becomes more difficult. Is it likely that Israel — which could detect incoming missiles only a few minutes before their impact — will agree on crisis procedures with its bitter enemies? And if Israel or Pakistan or other countries deny they possess nuclear weapons, how can negotiations begin?

The broader problem that undermines attempts to create a more stable nuclear balance is military emphasis on nuclear preemption and military advantage.

This issue has never been dealt with in arms control negotiations, and would be extremely difficult to resolve because it cannot be quantified in charts or photographed by satellites, and it will not fit in a newspaper's headlines. It is an issue that depends on unilateral actions on all sides, and most importantly on a recognition that shooting first is more dangerous that being hit by an enemy attack.

CONTROLLING NUCLEAR WAR

What makes nuclear war irrational is the extreme difficulty of controlling war between two nuclear armed powers. If a nuclear war were to tumble out of control, it would destroy peoples, cities, countries, religions, ideologies, leaders — everything that was being fought for. How can actual launch of nuclear weapons be rational (by the standard of peacetime Western democracies) if there is even a small chance that such action would destroy everything?

This is not to say that use of nuclear weapons is irrational when the enemy cannot respond. After all, the destruction of Hiroshima and Nagasaki was deemed rational by U.S. decisionmakers.

Nor does the difficulty of controlling nuclear war make irrational the possession of nuclear weapons and preparation for their use. It would seem the events of the last fifty years — and especially those of 1989 and 1990 — demonstrate that nuclear weapons have a stabilizing influence in international relations. Like sharks circling an overloaded rowboat, nuclear weapons ensure a certain civility between the many heavily armed nations crowded onto the earth.

Because nuclear war cannot be reliably controlled, it is futile to try and think of any credible events that might cause a nuclear war. Anything that could be expected to cause such an irrational event would be itself rightly dismissed as irrational, unreasonable, and ridiculous.

For example, a seer's prediction in mid-1990 that the U.S. would one day find itself leading a huge multinational alliance against Iraq would have only earned him the ridicule of his audience.

Nuclear war is not impossible; history is full of irrational events large and small, most of which were judged irrational only after their failure. Think of Hitler's decision to invade the USSR, or the

Confederacy's decision to secede from the United States in 1861, or the Tibetan peoples' struggle against China, or the bloody fighting in Timor. After an extraordinary forty-five years of peace, it is difficult for Westerners to imagine how changed circumstances could refract the light of rationality in very strange and unfamiliar ways.

Despite the irrationality and improbability of nuclear war, the appalling destructiveness and death that it would ensure requires us to examine the unthinkable. If you want peace, understand war.

However, lack of reasonable causes immediately casts us loose in a sea of competing possibilities, because the purposes and nature of wars are inextricably linked with their causes.

Nonetheless, it is safe to say that the ghastliness of uncontrolled nuclear war would ensure that each side would want to control the nuclear war, and that they would choose nuclear strategies that make wartime control somewhat easier. Thus city-destroying "spasm" attacks that abandon any attempt to control wars would be the least rational strategy of all. Such attacks would be mindless destruction instead of military strategy, sure to be regarded as criminally irresponsible and insane by all Soviet or Western soldiers and politicians.

It is also safe to say each side would seek advantages to help win the original objective it went to war for, partly to justify the pain and bloodshed, partly to prevent another war occurring later. However, the destruction might cause each side to increase its ambitions, making the chance of controlled warfare even less likely.

An important factor promoting control of nuclear war is that the nuclear war will probably have a relatively small beginning, such as a small number nuclear bombs destroying towns in allied countries.

It is often said good C^3I systems will help keep control of nuclear wars, because they will help each side understand what is happening, and help each side negotiate a reasonable solution. But even during conventional war or limited nuclear war, C^3I systems will be thrown into confusion or destroyed, command centers will be eliminated, and political organizations will be fragmented. Just as important, war is very frightening, chaotic, bloody, and emotional. It is very unlikely that leaders or military organizations would operate in the same way as they did in peacetime. A wartime leader may make decisions that seem perfectly rational in battle, but that he would have regarded as quite insane only a few peaceful days earlier.[7]

The comparative ease with which C³I systems can be destroyed by nuclear war is critical: "Once deterrence fails, it fails completely; the rudimentary design and short endurance of our nuclear command, control, communications, and intelligence system nullifies the whole conception of multiple, time-phased counter-force [nuclear] exchanges. The pursuit of bargaining advantages by means of limited attack is a purely academic construct that has little or no relevance to present circumstances."[8]

This danger prompted the U.S. during the 1980s to greatly upgrade its strategic C³I networks with new satellites and low-frequency radio systems, extra command aircraft, and improved communications relay aircraft.

Even if C³I systems do survive, there are other powerful factors that make control of nuclear war very difficult.

These factors include the continued existence of the problem that started the war. Unless the problem was resolved during war, each side would have a strong incentive to push for unilateral advantage to seize the political prize that started the war.

Also, each side will be fighting the war in different ways for different objectives.

For example, a smaller nation such as Pakistan might be using nuclear weapons to fend off the invading forces of India, which could have invaded because of internal Indian strife. Moreover, outside powers such as the U.S. and USSR would be trying to stay out of the conflict while forcing an end to the war.

Another factor militating against the control of conventional and nuclear war is that each side will try to justify and compensate for the ghastly price of war by acquiring some political benefit. Thus the Soviets might initially be concerned with shoring up their position, but might decide occupation of Eastern Europe is needed to build a defensive wall to help prevent another war.

The various factors working against control of nuclear war are both a source of hope and terror: hope because they reduce the chance that any country might try to use nuclear weapons in desperate circumstances; terror because even limited use of nuclear weapons will probably escalate to global catastrophe.

Politicians and generals will try to make their way, limited on side by the desire for control and on the other by the desire for some kind of advantage.

ELECTRONIC COMBAT AND NUCLEAR WAR

Having assumed that a nuclear conflict has begun, the question is how electronic combat would affect the course of the nuclear war.

Whatever nuclear strategy is chosen in a nuclear war, electronic combat will have a very important role to play.

If a disastrous war begins, politicians will desperately seek to end it as soon as possible.

But military organizations will seek to destroy enemy nuclear weapons, partly to minimize the chance that such weapons will be used against their soil.

This counterforce strategy is favored by the U.S. military, but especially by the Soviet military who remember how the Nazi invasion of the USSR in 1941 killed 20 million Soviets. It is unclear whether other nuclear-armed powers in the future will also follow this counterforce strategy.

If the counterforce strategy is followed, the problem for strike planners is one of finding and tracking targets, such as nuclear bombers, nuclear missiles, and nuclear submarines. If they cannot be destroyed, the next best thing is to make the enemy nuclear attacks as disorganized and ineffective as possible.

With good satellite intelligence or radio eavesdropping units, the task of finding the nuclear bombers is not impossible. Of course, if an antisatellite system or a secret means of jamming satellite sensors is developed, then tracking the bombers will become much more difficult. But even if the location of the bombers were unknown, a massed surprise attack using very small nuclear warheads might quickly destroy many of the well-known airfields, before any bombers hiding there had time to escape.

Bombers are much more difficult to track than submarines. However, this situation bears monitoring; it seems that radar-equipped satellites can use sophisticated computer processing of radar echoes to find submarines by detecting their wakes' wave patterns on the surface of the ocean. According to *Aviation Week and Space Technology*, the Soviet Almaz satellite is capable of detecting submarines hidden 300 meters underwater. If closely linked to weapons and command centers, the Almaz satellite could be the primary sensor for a Soviet reconnaissance-strike system capable of destroying U.S. submarines. Although the U.S. countermeasures could include dispersing submarines over vast areas of ocean, diving submarines deeper, or moving them very slowly, the advance of technology will ensure that Soviet radar satellites and associated signal processing are only going to get better and better.[9]

But the most intractable problem for a planner would be a land-based, mobile missile force. For example, the Soviet military plans to possess by the end of the 1990s a land-based armory of at least 400 road-mobile, one-warhead SS-25 missiles and 100 rail-mobile, ten-warhead SS-24 missiles. Tracking such a quantity of missiles — despite deception and the chaos of war — would be an extremely difficult task, even for the U.S.

Faced with the invulnerability of many land-based nuclear warheads, one option is to weaken nuclear retaliation by wrecking the enemy command and control system.

Evidence of this Soviet desire to destroy command and control systems was strong enough for Major General Van Doubleday to firmly testify before Congress that "Soviet strategic doctrine indicates Soviet strategic targeting specifically includes U.S. command, control, communications, and intelligence."[10] And Bruce Blair wrote: "by all indications, Soviet planners have long believed that exploiting command, control, communications and intelligence deficiencies is the only route to significant damage limitation. The high priority assigned to command suppression in Soviet military writings strongly suggests that Soviet strategy has been designed to fracture the command system and disorganize counterattacks rather than to deter U.S. commanders from ordering a counterattack."[11]

Well before REB was developed, Major General I. Annureyev of the Soviet General staff echoed its themes: "The measures applied for combating radioelectronic means worsen the quality of his control system, which leads to a decrease in the coefficients for distribution of nuclear means, a reduction in the probability of surmounting the defense, and an increase in the probability of enemy carrier destruction at launch. Well-organized measures for combating enemy radioelectronic equipment will lead to a sharp increase in the correlation of forces in our favor."[12]

This is strong stuff; there is no pussy-footing around with American-style discussions of intrawar deterrence or efforts to avoid destruction of cities, but just an aggressive effort to destroy the enemy's C^3I systems. If successfully done, this could ensure that the confused U.S command systems would fire nuclear warheads on already destroyed, low-value, or useless targets, leaving fewer warheads to do terrible damage to Soviet cities and military forces.

The implications of an aggressive attack on command and control sites are staggering. According to Western analysts, such an attack would remove any possibility of a negotiated end to a nuclear war, and would make war more likely because less effort would be spent on avoiding conflict by prewar diplomacy.

Seemingly quite robust, the U.S. command system has several critical vulnerabilities to such an attack, including reliance on too few vulnerable aircraft and communications nodes. This has led one former commander of the Strategic Air Command, which controls the missile and bomber retaliatory forces, to conclude, "If the enemy struck first—barraged Washington, Omaha [Strategic Air Command headquarters], et cetera — we would never recover, recover control, recover anything."[13]

A critical area of vulnerability is the reliance upon the back-up communications relay and command aircraft. This back-up aircraft command network is critically vulnerable to a Soviet missile strike, which could destroy the aircraft on their airfields before they have time to escape. With missile flight times ranging from twenty-five minutes when launched from the Soviet Union to only five minutes when launched from missile submarines hiding off the U.S. coast, there is very little margin for error.

However, this vulnerability is greatly reduced if there is any truth to occasional reports that the U.S. has another wartime command network housed in trucks, able to use the vast road network to hide from prying satellites and destructive nuclear weapons.

Another area of vulnerability for the command system is the danger of electromagnetic pulses caused by nuclear weapons. If an attacker were planning a strike of C^3I networks, they could use a high-altitude nuclear explosion to create an extremely powerful electromagnetic pulse capable of destroying electronic components, especially computer chips, across an entire region as large as the U.S.

Despite the expenditure of billion of dollars on electronics hardened against electromagnetic pulses, the U.S. cannot be sure that its nuclear command and control systems — or its missiles and B-52 bombers — would not be knocked out by an electromagnetic pulse.

The cumulative impact of the electromagnetic effects of nuclear explosions are staggering. It is conceivable that several medium-sized nuclear weapons exploded high over the U.S. could knock out tens of thousand of military communications, weapons, and sensors systems. The early warning radars and other sensors supposed to detect an incoming nuclear attack are especially vulnerable simply because they are deliberately designed to collect electromagnetic radiation. If the radars and other sensors were knocked out, the U.S. would be blinded and potentially vulnerable to an enemy first strike.

Similarly, a single nuclear pulse could destroy electronic systems throughout much of the Middle East, including Israel.

Great effort is poured into understanding the electromagnetic threat and to shielding friendly systems from destruction, but no one can be sure anything would operate as expected in wartime. Predicting the full effects of a nuclear explosion is basically impossible; there are too many electrical systems, each with peculiar vulnerabilities to particular electromagnetic threats that reinforce each other's effects in unpredictable ways. But unpredictability cuts both ways; no one can be sure their electronics would survive an enemy attack, and no one can be sure their nuclear weapons could destroy enemy electronics.

Aside from electromagnetic-pulse-induced faults, nuclear explosions can disrupt the ionosphere, greatly disrupt radio communications, especially high-frequency radio, and largely preclude radio communication or radar scanning through the "blackout" zones. However, the higher the frequency used by the communications system, the quicker normal operations are restored. Thus ultrahigh frequency signals are only blacked out for a hour or so from a region a few hundred miles in diameter.

In addition to nuclear strikes and electromagnetic pulse effects, attack planners could also count on various other electronic combat measures to disrupt and disorganize the enemy. For example, the French government relies on four communications-relay aircraft to transmit retaliatory orders to its seven nuclear submarines. These links could be jammed by extremely powerful transmitters, perhaps for enough time to prevent a response before the launchers are destroyed.

Thus a 1970 article in the Soviet Navy's *Morskoy Sbornik* argued that any delay in the receipt of a missile launch order by a missile-carrying submarine "could have, if not a decisive effect, at least a very considerable effect on the outcome of the combat operations."[14] Blair notes the range of the U.S. aircraft relied upon to relay orders to submerged submarines would suffer "severe range limitations" if the low frequency transmitters were jammed.[15]

During the 1960s, 1970s, and 1980s, "In all likelihood, Soviet strikes against C^3I systems would have severely impaired and possibly blocked U.S. retaliation ... the ability of Soviet forces to deliver a crippling blow to U.S. C^3I systems long ago created strong incentives on both sides for launching a first strike or for launching a U.S. second strike on warning [of an incoming Soviet attack], incentives that have undermined crisis stability," according to Blair.[16]

It is unlikely that U.S. forces would carry out such counter-force attacks in wartime, largely because of tight civilian control. Also, the rise of modernizers led by Gorbachev might end the Soviet military's willingness to carry out such attacks. However, unless military forces have been trained in peacetime not to strike enemy C^3I networks, it would be very difficult to prevent them doing so in the chaos and confusion of war. It is clear that such strikes are what the Soviet strategic forces train for, and what they will most likely do in a war. And many historical examples show just how difficult it is for the politicians to control military operations in war.[17]

ELECTRONIC COMBAT AND SPACE-BASED STRATEGIC DEFENSES

Nuclear-related electronic combat will become more important if the U.S. joins the Soviets in deploying a limited strategic defense system.

Most predictions of an early version of a U.S. strategic defense system assume it will be more advanced than any Soviet system, and suggest that it will rely on ground-based weapons linked to space-based sensors.

Observers envisage the U.S. weapons gradually moving into space as directed energy weapons are developed. From space, these energy weapon systems could destroy Soviet missiles early in their flight when their rocket exhaust provides a bright signature for infrared sensors — and before the nuclear missiles have time to dispense their many nuclear warheads and before they have time to implement radioelectronic measures such as decoys, chaff, and jamming.

The Soviets will not sit around claiming peaceful intentions while the U.S. deploys its defense system. One can already see diplomatic offensives backed up by propaganda barrages and concealment of similar Soviet strategic defense efforts. The chief military means of defeating the U.S. defense system will be REB, with jamming, deceptive commands to destroy and paralyze strategic defense satellites, as well as physical attacks by lasers and interceptor rockets.[18]

The future response is indicated by past Soviet practice. The Soviet response to U.S. strategic defense plans in the 1960s was described in a typically circumspect fashion by Major General N. Vasendin and Colonel N. Kuznetsov, who wrote around 1970 that "ways are being sought for the missile warheads to effectively overcome the antimissile defense. In particular, special plastic or metallic shells of warheads covered with a radioabsorbent coating can be used. This decreases their capacity for reflecting [radar] radiowaves and considerably reduces their range of detection in trajectory. At the same time, means of active and passive interference of the antimissile radar system, as well as dummy targets, are installed in the missile and the warheads. ... It is proposed that special space apparatuses be used to create active interference for the antimissile radar system."[19] Many other possibilities exist, such as secretly planting computer viruses, jamming communications links, using nuclear blackout zones to blind sensors, or bypassing defense with ground-hugging nuclear-tipped cruise missiles.

Although the future cannot be predicted reliably, it is safe to say neither side would spare efforts to weaken each other's strategic defense systems, simply because nuclear weapons are of life or death importance to the U.S. and the Soviets.

But there is always the possibility that a Moscow government might cooperate with the U.S to deploy some type of thin defense system that could defeat the missile of smaller powers, such as Islamic countries, India, China or Iraq. Theoretically, such a defense could be deployed after suitable modification of the 1972 Antiballistic Missile

Treaty, and would be too weak to undermine nuclear deterrence between the Soviets and the United States.

CONVENTIONAL WEAPONRY
AND NUCLEAR WAR

Can conventional weapons such as long-range, highly accurate cruise missiles, be used to augment or even replace nuclear weapons?

Conventional weapons cannot replace nuclear weapons because nothing can match their destructiveness — which can range from the equivalent of 1,000 tons to 10 million tons of high explosive.

However, long-range, highly accurate weaponry might be used to augment nuclear weapons. Why blow up a target with a nuclear weapon when a highly-accurate cruise missile could do the job? Thus some countries might be strongly tempted to use conventional weapons to attack an enemy's nuclear weapons or strategic C^3I network during conventional war.

This destabilizing problem become sharper in countries which lack the ability to hide a nuclear deterrent from the accurate missiles, or an advanced air defense system needed to defeat the conventional missiles. Also, smaller countries might rely on ordinary bombers to carry their nuclear weapons; the threatened loss of the bombers in conventional air warfare may increase the pressure on leaders to use nuclear weapons.

The use of conventional weapons to hit strategic targets would bypass limits established on the number of nuclear weapons by international arms control treaties. Their use — instead of nuclear weapons — would also reduce the escalatory risk for countries already intent on a counterforce strategy of striking the enemy's nuclear weapons and C^3I.

For example, if the U.S. command center were hit by conventionally-armed smart missiles, the U.S. leaders would be much less likely to retaliate with nuclear weapons. Thus one side could radically change a nuclear balance by using conventional weapons to destroy the other side's nuclear weapons and C^3I networks during a conventional conflict. If such a conventional conflict could be kept under control — and prevented from escalating into nuclear war — then the side whose nuclear deterrent had been wrecked might feel it had no choice but to accede to the other's demands.

The Soviets fear this possibility. Thus Marshal Sergei Akhromeyev, the chief of the Soviet general staff before he became one of Gorbachev's closest military advisers, revealed Soviet military thinking in 1985 when he wrote: "In recent years our probable enemies, recognizing the unavoidability of a retaliatory strike and its catastrophic consequences ... are modernizing the methods of unleashing *strategic* military action with the use of *conventional* means of destruction, primarily the new types of controlled and automated modes of high-accuracy weapons."[20]

Luttwak's vision of reconnaissance-strike complexes as strategic weapons may be the direction that the Soviet military wishes to go. Also, it may be the direction that advanced technology will take Western militaries. But there is no sign that such advanced weapons can replace nuclear weapons in their role as the greatest terror weapon ever invented.

It is unlikely that arms control treaties will restrict the development of such destabilizing "dual-use" conventional technology. It would seem only traditional military measures — such as good air defenses and good electronic combat skills — can minimize the impact of these weapons.

CONCLUSION

Electronic combat affect the likelihood of nuclear war breaking out, the way in which nuclear war is conducted, and whether nuclear war can be controlled.

Electronic combat will improve or degrade warning of nuclear attacks, preserve or destroy C^3I systems, and strengthen or weaken strategic defenses. Electronic combat will also affect whether the interlinked C^3I systems on each side will increase the chance of war getting out of control.

Even during nuclear war, electronic combat will be important because soldiers and politicians are not likely to abandon their responsibilities and training in the midst of nuclear chaos. Because both sides will be trying to control the fighting but also to end the war on terms acceptable to them, there will be combat as each side uses whatever means it has to extract what benefit it can from the ghastly situation.

Negotiated arms control agreements are unlikely to provide a solution to these nuclear-related problems. The SALT I, SALT II, and START arms control agreements have been unable to tightly limit nuclear capabilities, so why should arms control be more successful in the much more complex and intractable field of protecting strategic C^3I systems against conventional or nuclear weapons? What kind of arms control agreement would force the Soviets to change their military strategy? What kind of negotiated arms control agreement would prevent attacks on C^3I systems during war?

Unless political harmony among nuclear-armed enemies can be swiftly reached, one solution is to adopt unilateral measures to stabilize nuclear deterrence. This means increased numbers of mobile hard-to-detect missiles, mobile war headquarters, more jam-resistant communications, and protected early warning sensors. Also, the nuclear forces and C^3I networks should be backed up by conventional forces to fend off all non-nuclear threats, such as cruise missiles.

Notes

1. See Bruce Blair, *Strategic Command and Control: Redefining the Nuclear Threat* (Washington, DC: The Brookings Institution, 1985); Desmond Ball, *Can Nuclear War be Controlled?* Adelphi paper 169 (London: International Institute of Strategic Studies, 1981); Paul Bracken, *The Command and Control of Nuclear Forces* (New Haven and London: Yale University Press, 1983); William Arkin and Peter Pringle, *SIOP: The Secret U.S. Plan for Nuclear War* (New York and London: W. W. Norton, 1983).

2. Related to the author by a top-level command official.

3. William Van Cleave, "Surprise Nuclear Attack," in Brian Dailey and Patrick Parker, *Soviet Strategic Deception* (Palo Alto, CA: Hoover Institution, 1987), p. 454.

4. Ibid.

5. Bracken, *Command and Control of Nuclear Forces.*

6. *Washington Post,* 7 June, 1989, p. 1.

7. John Steinbrunner, *The Cybernetic Theory of Decisionmaking* (Princeton, NJ: Princeton University Press, 1974).

8. Blair, *Strategic Command and Control,* p. 4.

9. *Aviation Week and Space Technology,* 8 October, 1990.

10. In Roman Kolkowicz, *The Soviet Calculus of Nuclear War* (Lexington MA: Lexington Books, 1986), p. 54.

11. Blair, *Strategic Command and Control,* p. 216

12. Maj. Gen. I. Anureyev, "Determining the Correlation of Forces in Terms of Nuclear Weapons," in Stephen Cimbala, *Soviet C³I* (Fairfax, VA: Armed Forces Communications and Electronics Association, 1989), p. 133.

13. Gen. Bruce Holloway, former commander of Strategic Air Command, interviewed by Daniel Ford and cited in *Our Nation's Nuclear Warning System:, Subcommittee of the House Govt. Operations Committee,* September 1985, p. 11.

14. Cited by Capt. Floyd Kennedy, "The Radioelectronic Struggle: Soviet EW Doctrinal Developments," in Cimbala, *Soviet C³I,* p. 293.

15. In *Our Nation's Nuclear Warning System,* p. 183.

16. Ibid,. p. 4.

17. Even Raymond Garthoff, long regarded as holding an optimistic view of Soviet strategic thought, concludes, "Soviet operational doctrine for waging a general nuclear war does not appear to spare the enemy leadership." See Raymond Garthoff, "Conflict Termination in Soviet Military Thought and Strategy," in Cimbala, *Soviet C³I,* p. 404.

18. Office of Technology Assessment, *Strategic Defense Research: Technology, Survivability and Software* (Washington, DC: Government Printing Office, 1988).

19. Maj. Gen. N. Vasendin and Col. N. Kuznetsov, "Modern Warfare and Surprise Attack," in Cimbala, *Soviet C³I,* p. 335.

20. Phillip Petersen and Notra Trulock, "A 'New' Soviet Military Doctrine: Origins and Implications," in Clarence McKnight, ed., Control of Joint Forces: A New Perspective (Fairfax, VA: Armed Forces Communications and Electronics Association, 1989), p. 55, my emphasis.

Eleven

ELECTRONIC COMBAT AND WAR

Only the dead have seen the end of war.

Plato

Even while the shadow of nuclear weapons remains dominant over international politics and military affairs, electronic combat is continuing to change the conduct of warfare and political conflict.

In the well-developed countries of the world, nuclear weapons are helping redirect conflict toward less destructive diplomatic and economic battles.

But the strains of economic and political change ensure continued conflict in the developing world. To help minimize the damage of such conflict, U.S. policymakers and soldiers need to understand the nature of modern warfare.

It is clear that electronic combat is becoming more important than ever. But we cannot be sure how electronic combat would affect warfare, largely because there have been such revolutionary technological changes since Hiroshima.

Some things are obvious. Electronic combat has created its own technology, such as antiradiation missiles, and its own tactics, such as jamming. Electronic combat is also continuing to change the nature of any future campaigns and theater offensives. Electronic combat, or more broadly, the struggle over the collection, manipulation and distribution of information, may also yet change the nature of warfare. Will the manipulation of national or international public opinion by satellite television be more important that several aircraft carriers? Will U.S. national security depend less on military power, and depend even more on the wise combination of the government's psychological, economic, political and military powers?

The nature of the changes wrought by electronic combat are uncertain, and serve to compound the normal uncertainty of war.

The uncertainty is a danger and an opportunity — a danger because unexpected failures may cause disaster, an opportunity because the nation or alliance that best understands electronic combat will have a major advantage in conflict.

Electronic combat changes more than the techniques, technology and tactics of warfare; it changes higher levels of warfare, including military organization, operational campaigns and strategies.

The increased role of electronic combat first effects offensive and defensive technology.

Radios must be upgraded to include features designed to defeat enemy interception, jamming and eavesdropping. Sensors must be combined to defeat enemy jamming. Identification systems must be designed to allow earlier identification of approaching targets. But improved jamming devices must be built and combined by C^3I networks with other jamming devices to defeat or deceive a wide range of sensors and communications systems.

Electronics systems must be hardened against powerful electromagnetic pulses or lasers, while scientists must pursue the development of more powerful directed energy weapons.

Computerized weapons need to be protected against viruses, even as more effective viruses need to be produced to damage enemy computerized systems.

This cornucopia of electronic combat systems also changes tactics in high- and low-intensity warfare.

At the tactical level, radio-direction finders and unmanned robot aircraft can be used to find targets for increasingly long-range weapons. Sensors can be blinded by laser weapons. Soldiers must disperse over more ground than ever, yet combine their strength faster with the aid of C^3I networks.

Mobility, dispersion, stealth, and electronic countermeasures become the keys to survival.

For example, when threatened by missiles carrying infrared, radar, and passive guidance systems of unknown technical design, a wise course is to forgo reliance on a single defense, but to combine electronic countermeasures and stealth to blind the enemy, high mobility to sidestep attacks, and aggressive physical and electronic attacks to destroy enemy weapons and C^3I networks.

In aircraft to aircraft combat, the very high quality of infrared technology will allow missiles to strike home despite the escape maneuvers of their targets. Thus the dogfighting skills of individual pilots decline further in importance, while cooperation, speed, passive surveillance range, and long-range identification capability become vital. Such desiderata argue for close linkage between fighters and radars, identification systems, and ground-based long-range antiaircraft missiles. Indeed, this C^3I integration was precisely the technique used by the Israelis in their lopsided 84 to 0 air battle with the Syrian Air Force in 1982. But organized networks of flying machines only increase further the role of electronic combat and the expense of military preparations.

Control of the air and space will be more important than ever because it greatly determines the ability of warring armies to find targets and transfer information. If one side can prevent reconnaissance by the other, but gather information for itself using aircraft and satellites, then it will have won an advantage that can be used to help destroy targets, including the enemy's vital C^3I networks.

But against well-armed opponents, the price of aircraft survivability is becoming too great to bear, and is forcing greater use of unmanned space satellites, unmanned reconnaissance drones, and unmanned cruise missiles.

The role of manned aircraft is being restricted to fighter aircraft and various forms of electronic combat aircraft, whose well-trained pilots cannot be replaced by relatively inflexible computers, no matter how powerful. Such changes in technology and tactics will combine to cause changes in military operations.

For example, the high ground of space will become increasingly important for gathering and distributing information.

Although the U.S. has better space technology than other countries, the military effort is crippled by a lack of commitment to space by top staff who learned their trade in tanks, aircraft or aircraft carriers. It is also crippled by a lack of congressional or administration appreciation of the importance of space. Indeed, Congress seems determined to suppress any attempt to ready the Pentagon to extend U.S. military influence into space, aside from the use of supposedly peaceful spy satellites.

At sea, modern weaponry is making surface ships less survivable, while the price of defensive systems is driving the costs of ships to great heights. It seems clear the U.S. Navy is heading for a major reduction in size during the 1990s — ensuring the remaining ships will have to cooperate even more through the use of advanced C^3I networks.

Moreover, the threat of electronic combat will force ship designers to build stealthier ships, and ultimately, to seek the safety granted by water's absorption of radio and infrared signals. This trend may drive naval aircraft ashore and funnel more money into construction of submarines able to cooperatively control huge volumes of air and sea by the use of long-range missiles, unmanned minisubs, and unmanned robot aircraft. In effect, large submarines could become underwater versions of aircraft carriers, complete with the carrier's former ability to avoid attack and its good C^3I that allows the concentration of coordinated firepower.

Despite the growing role of submarines, carriers have many years of useful service yet as midocean defensive airbases for relatively short-legged fighters and surveillance aircraft. Carriers are also an excellent means of bringing tactical airpower close to distant low-technology enemies and useful as majestic big sticks in "show the flag" exercises.

If modern weapons can clear the sea's surface of shipping, that would be a major loss for the Western world, which relies heavily on free use of the sea to transport oil, minerals, and manufactured goods. Perhaps any future high-technology naval war may split merchant navies into a two-level fleet composed of large numbers of small, cheap cargo ships and some number of fast-moving cargo aircraft that use a cushion of air between the sea and their large wings to carry heavy loads.

Electronic combat can cause similar changes in the nature of land warfare. The last time a new military revolution was in 1940. The next revolution will become obvious over the next few years as the new technologies are combined in unexpected, powerful, complex, and unfamiliar ways.

For example, indirect-fire weapons such as artillery and long-range rockets carrying bomblets and smart missiles will become more important because of their ability to reach out and kill at 40 km (25 mi) or more. The better these long-range weapons are tied to long-range sensors by good communications, the swifter they can reach out and destroy someone. Moreover, instead of forcing their way through the thick defense of the front line into the enemy's rear area, modern weapons allow invaders to attack frontline, rear-area, and enemy homeland simultaneously, so increasing the chance for a quick victory.

The new technology that created long-range sensors and fast-flying missiles is extending the depth of combat. Just as each war has been limited by the distance that the participants could see, shoot and talk to each other, so will high-technology war expand until what was formerly the frontline will eventually expand to hundreds of kilometers width — the range of airborne sensors and long-range missiles. Thus military effectiveness rests ever more on the effective use of electronic combat to preserve one's own sight, reach and organization, while blinding, limiting and disrupting the enemy.

It might be argued that a clash between huge masses of the modern armies in a small region would prevent them from using C^3I systems to disperse in order to avoid attacks. The crush of forces would instead convert the battlefield into a vast cauldron where units would be pulverized and replaced in hours, and where sheer weight of numbers would win the day.

However, NATO and the Soviet Union are reducing the size of their armed forces, partly to invest in modern weaponry. Indeed, the U.S. looks ready to reduce its mechanized forces to only three corps of two armored divisions each, which happens to be the same number of infantry divisions that the British sent to France in 1914. The reduced size of armies only underlines the overall trend — the accelerating enhancement of manpower by machines and the replacement of massed guns by long-range, fast moving, well coordinated firepower.

The advent of long-range conventional weapons and sensors, especially spy satellites, also blurs the distinction between offensive and defensive forces. Now, both defenders and attackers do not even need to leave their bases in order to mass destructive fire onto enemy units.

Indeed, the defender can seize the initiative by striking first. But who is the attacker if both armies commence destroying and disrupting each other while still parked on their separate exercise grounds? The increased importance of long-range concentrated firepower over massive tank armies means that the attacker can now concentrate firepower for his onslaught even while remaining in what were formerly regarded as dispersed, defensive positions.

Moreover, because the initial effect of electronic combat attacks on enemy networks and organizations is their temporary disruption, military logic calls for a complementary mechanized offensive to take advantage of the enemy's confusion and paralysis. As in all military affairs, the combination of different weapons creates much greater power than the sum of the parts. Without an offensive to destroy or capture what has been disorganized, the enemy will simply repair himself and return to the attack.

Thus the trend toward attack — and the advantage of surprise — is strengthened by electronic combat. Sadly, this logic will only increase the chance of a crisis escalating to war, and also will make control of wars more difficult.

This trend is fortified by arms control treaties. Although intended to promote stability by reducing the forward-deployed offensive forces of both sides, such as tank battalions and bomber squadrons, these treaties only channel military efforts into new areas. Without resolving the political conflict, the generals and politicians on all sides will just seek new ways to strengthen military power. Indeed, politicians and generals try to use treaties to limit the enemy's technological developments and military deployments. Thus any arms control treaty that limits the traditional weapons of World War II — tanks and bombers — will probably cause armies to accelerate development of what will be the weapons of World War III.

The fewer the traditional combat units permitted by treaties, the more important electronic combat becomes. The remaining units must be able to see further, move firepower faster, and strike at longer ranges. Thus, for perfectly rational military reasons it is likely the Soviet military will increase its emphasis on reconnaissance–strike complexes and the Western militaries will increase the role of long-range weapons to compensate for the negotiated loss of tanks and bombers. The increased use of such long-range, quick-strike weapons will effectively reduce the stabilizing benefits of the arms control treaty.

This destabilizing end might be delayed for a while if arms controllers press on to ban long-range missiles and longrange artillery such as the Soviet's 70 km (46 mi) range multiple rocket launchers. But then military logic would just lead armies to bypass these arms control limits by accelerating adoption of antitank missiles guided by fiberoptic cables whose range could be easily and quickly increased to 50 km (32 mi)in a crisis.

Only deep political reform — indeed, a political revolution — of the USSR can help reduce the ideological and great-power conflicts between East and West. Such reforms would allow the radical arms control measures needed to ensure crisis stability. Ironically, such a political revolution would also make such arms control agreements irrelevant because the various nations would rapidly start disarming without any agreements. Happily, it does seem that Gorbachev's reforms are leading to such an overdue political revolution.

Much easier to imagine are controls on the movement of advanced technology. Such multinational arms control efforts became much more attractive after the danger of Iraqi missiles were realized in late 1990. However, the controls are bound to be opposed by the countries they are aimed at, such as Iraq or Pakistan, which are seeking to build atomic weapons.

To be effective, such controls will have to be very extensive, and include provisions that will deter third countries from acting as a transit point for such technology. For example, rocket technology might be barred from export to Libya, but not to businessmen in Western Europe, who would be willing to pass the technology to Libya for a profitable fee. Moreover, the controls will have to address not only the movement of hardware, but also the movement of software and the education of foreigners who may return home with knowledge of military value.

The power of the new weaponry undermines arguments for schemes intended to ensure adequate defenses without appearing to create an offensive capability. Proponents of such defensive schemes envisage light infantry militia forces equipped with powerful antitank weapons and antiaircraft weapons, backed up by minefields and bunkers and possibly by a small mechanized force. Additionally, these defensive forces would have much electronic combat capability to blind, jam, and deceive the new long-range sensors and weapons. The scheme's lack of offensive capability is expected to reassure the other side that no attack is possible, helping prevent political crises from escalating into war.

Unfortunately, the growing importance of reconnaissance–strike complexes and fast-moving forces united by extensive C^3I systems helps the attackers concentrate their strength into sudden narrow thrusts at critical points. Also, the attacker's electronic combat would hinder the defender's attempts to mass defensive forces in front of the rapidly moving attackers. Moreover, reconnaissance–strike weapons can simply fly over the infantry, much as the B-29 bomber sailed over the Japanese infantry on the way to drop its nuclear bomb on Hiroshima.

Thus the improved ability to concentrate offensive firepower — combined with greatly improved tank armors that can defeat antitank missiles small enough to be man-portable — effectively buries proposals for nonprovocative defense forces.

It might be argued that adoption of the new technology will strengthen the defender more than the attacker, because the defender can concentrate his long-range firepower as the enemy concentrates for an attack. Also, the survivability of the defender's C^3I systems might be helped by remaining on the defensive because he can use extensive and well-prepared networks of military and civilian communications.

But this is only partly true in Western Europe, where large armies would be massed and where the German civilian communications system could be utilized by Western forces. Even in Europe, the argument does not carry enough strength to give any confidence that the new technology will significantly help the defender more than the attacker.

The importance of electronic combat means that if soldiers want to win, they must take the offensive to wreck the enemy networks as fast as possible, and before the enemy wrecks their own networks. Like Machiavellian diplomats disassembling the enemy's alliances, soldiers must try to disassemble the enemy's organization by wrecking his C^3I networks.

War is a two-sided business, so both sides will be racing to wreck each other's C^3I networks. This means that each side has less and less time to wreck the enemy before they are wrecked themselves.

Whereas in the past soldiers, commanders, armies, and even nations had time to recover from enemy surprise attacks, now frontline troops and small nations will not have a second chance to recover from defeat by fast-flying missiles, swift helicopters, and rapidly moving mechanized corps.

The best possible use of time is more crucial than ever because the tempo of war is faster. According to Sun Tzu, "The value of time — that is, being a little ahead of your opponent — has counted for more than either numerical superiority or the nicest calculations with regard to [logistics] commissariat."[1]

The accelerated pace of combat caused by long-range weapons has raised the importance of first strikes, especially when nuclear weapons are used. Twice blessed is he whose cause is just, but thrice blessed is he who gets his fist in first. This means that surprise and deception will be more important than ever before.

Indeed, the pace and violence of conventional war may combine with the increasing interwining of nuclear and conventional forces so that conventional war may be nearly impossible to control, especially when electronic combat is waged. For example, to protect its fleet from Soviet antiship missiles, the U.S. Navy needs to destroy or sever the Soviet links to their ship-detecting satellites. But such antisatellite operations blur the gap between conventional and nuclear forces because any attack on space-based systems could be as dangerous to a nation's nuclear forces as to its conventional forces.

This could mean that any high-technology conventional war between nuclear powers, especially the U.S. and the Soviet Union, could become as uncontrollable and as dangerous as nuclear war itself.

The uncertain effect of the new weapons and electronic combat on the nature of future war may increase or decrease the chances of war, depending on whether leaders think they add to the certainty of victory or add to the uncertainty of war.

The complexity of the tactics and technology of electronic combat, and the potentially very broad impact it can have on battle might cause some leaders to hesitate before placing faith in the ability of their force to win a quick victory. But if leaders trust the military's confident claims that electronic combat will help them win a quick, bloodless victory, they might be more willing to risk war in a crisis. Thus while the unpredictability of electronic combat has the happy effect of making war more risky, it also leaves room for political and military miscalculations.

Some observers argue that effective use of electronic combat would reduce casualties and the cost of war, much as the Panzer divisions captured France at minimal cost in World War II compared to the bloody casualties of inconclusive battles in World War I. However, this would be true only if electronic combat can be waged effectively — despite the uncertainties — and actually helps to win the war, not just a single campaign in a long war.

Would electronic combat help achieve lopsided victories in battles and campaigns? Perhaps so, but only when used by skilled soldiers in high-technology mechanized warfare. For example, the Israeli army has several times achieved lopsided results against Arab enemies, although it has not been able to create a permanent political solution.

Perhaps electronic combat will bolster the arguments of the maneuver school who suggest that Blitzkrieg warfare can allow inferior forces to beat superior forces and that military skill can prevent wars from degenerating into bloody tests of endurance by attrition. Perhaps so, but only if the political aims of the war can be achived in a single leap by virtue of incompetent and politically weak opponents or limited war aims. Otherwise, the immense resources of modern states will be harnessed for war and bled away into the mud.

Electronic combat cannot be seen as a cheap war-winner when an enemy has the great benefit of strong political support at home or abroad, or when the enemy is armed with ballistic missiles capable of carrying nuclear, chemical, and biological warheads back to friendly cities. Nonetheless, trying to fight such a enemy without the advantage of soldiers skilled in electronic combat would be courting disaster.

The technology and tactics needed to fight a low-intensity war differ greatly from those needed in a high-technology war, forcing armies to create, train, and equip two distinct types of ground and air forces.

Electronic combat and modern technology have only limited uses in low intensity wars between insurgents and governments. Spy satellites are not very useful for tracking urban guerrillas.

But more than ever, rebel forces need the technological gifts of a friendly government to win — unless they are fighting such a corrupt and unpopular power that it can be kicked down like a rotten door. For example, the revolts in Romania and the Philippines succeeded not just because of popular demonstrations, but because they helped or even prompted local military and political leaders to stage a coup d'etat.

Unless the military can be won over, insurgents will be at a severe disadvantage because modern technology enhances the advantages of firepower and organization, which have long been in governments' favor rather than insurgents. Even the acquisition of some advanced heat-seeking missiles does not change this greatly; neither the Afghan *mujaheddin* nor the Salvadoran rebels have yet prevailed against helicopters, missiles, and tanks protecting the governments.

The improving technologies of developing countries are not as impressive as they look on paper, because the users often lack understanding of how to best use the technology or the technical knowledge to quickly upgrade, maintain, and repair the equipment. Indeed, mastery of these two areas is the war-winning quality that the Israelis bring to their battlefields.

This difference in quality will continue for the foreseeable future, regardless of any advanced weapons bought by the developing countries. Moreover, the increased demands of future advanced military technology upon the limited pools of military or civilian skills in the developing countries, will only increase the advantage of technologically advanced countries, with their huge reserves of military skill and scientific expertise.

But do not believe that the armies of advanced countries understand how to best use the technology just because it exists. Just as it is much easier to build a bridge over a raging torrent than to cross a field against a few clever enemy soldiers, so it is much harder to fully understand the impact and effect of new technology than it is to build the technology.

After all, the nature of technology is very different from the nature of war. Technology is rational and predictable, while war combines emotion, intellect, responsiveness, and chaos. Therefore, to get the best use from technology, soldiers must not try to twist war into a shape that suits the technology, but must twist the technology to suit the needs of combat. When cutting wood, it is always better to go with the grain than against it.[2]

Not the least aspect of quality is the skill with which large groups of soldiers cooperate in vast combined efforts, with the aid of extensive C^3I networks. The reach and speed of modern weaponry requires soldiers to think in larger terms than how to use a brigade, division or even a corps. Just as no one could expect infantry platoons to fight the Korean War by themselves, so no one can expect corps, air wings, or fleets to fight modern high-technology wars by themselves. If they do try, they may well doom the entire enterprise to a bloody, destructive, and wasteful end.

Instead, ground, air, and naval forces must be welded together by a common goal, a shared theaterwide strategy for winning a war, which must match publicly supported political aims. This strategy must use the strength of each military arm to complement the others, and must use them as efficiently as possible to generate the maximum effective firepower and disruption as quickly as possible.

The same trends that call for increasing cooperation between the various services also call for increasing cooperation between the various national security arms of a state or an alliance.

Political agreement on the goals of a conflict must be forged between various nations and the arms of each government, and must match the wishes of the people.

Military, economic, and political intelligence must be quickly shared throughout government, so that threats can be deterred before they are answered with bloody and uncertain force.

Military, political, psychological and economic actions must be coordinated by the occupant of a strengthened post of Presidential national security advisor, rather than by a well-connected secretary of state or a charismatic secretary of defense.

Government agencies must endeavour to control the flow of military-related exports. This requires much better cooperation between the DoD and the Department of Commerce, which oversees trade matters, than in the past. One possibility is that the government might install computer viruses and similar destructive software in computerized weapons before they are exported, so the weapons can be crippled by activating the virus at a later date if the U.S. wishes. Internal security, customs, coast guard and other groups must be coordinated to guard technical and economic information in peacetime as well as to defend vital assets in wartime. It does little good if air defense fighters patiently patrol the borders while enemy commandos explode a nonnuclear electromagnetic pulse generator in downtown New York — possibly causing an economic recession by destroying the computerized assets of many large companies and Wall Street speculators.

Moreover, while an enemy may use information to wreck combat units on the battlefield, he may also use information to wreck domestic support for a war — much as Iraqi leader Saddam Hussein tried to use hostages and the international media to weaken the political will of the multinational coalition arrayed against him in late 1990. Thus the international Cable News Network was used by Iraq as a first line of defense against an American assault.

An enemy can influence international media broadcasts by restricting reporters' movements, silencing dissidents, and by disseminating lies. Meanwhile Western governments are faced by a barrage of questions and second-guessing from media pundits, eager to detect any changes, problems, lies or errors.

This is just too bad; the U.S. government must operate within the American constitution at whatever cost, and American citizens have every right to read, hear, and see information, even if it is a series of lies from start to finish. Public debate is not an impossible obstacle to an effective foreign policy: the American people have shown themselves quite acute in judging such matters. Moreover, a good result of this electronic competition for hearts and minds is that it pressures the U.S. government to clearly articulate a coherent policy, which can only be good for U.S. interests.

These trends suggest the emergence of a fourth generation of warfare, according to an article written by two Army colonels, a civilian, and two Marine Corps officers. The new warfare will tend to replace third-generation warfare of armored divisions and deep attack weapons with thoroughly integrated all-arms teams. Such groups will blur the distinctions between the services, and will include very small groups of commandos able to select and destroy targets with powerful weapons, including directed energy weapons.[3]

But most importantly, there will be greatly increased efforts to wreck an enemy's will, determination and internal strength.

The goal is "collapsing the enemy internally rather than physically destroying him. Targets will include such things as the populations' support for the war and the enemy's culture. Correct identification of enemy strategic centers of gravity will be highly important."[4] Electronically gaining temporary use of the enemy television network to broadcast propaganda that helps divide the people from the government, using viruses to temporarily disable telephone networks, and wrecking radio stations so that they can be replaced by propaganda are some of the means by which the enemy population — rather than the leaders or the military — might be influenced.

Psychological operations "may become the dominant operational and strategic weapon in the form of media/information intervention. ... Adversaries will be adept at manipulating the media to alter domestic and world opinion to the point where skilled use of psychological operations will sometimes preclude the commitment of combat forces. ... Television news may become a more powerful operational weapon than armored divisions."[5]

"The fourth generation battlefield is likely to include the whole of the enemy's society. Such dispersion, coupled with what seems likely to be increased importance of actions by very small groups of combatants, will require even the lowest level to operate flexibly" without tight control by top commanders.[6]

Moreover, much nonlethal weaponry will be very useful in conflict or crisis, even before fourth-generation warfare matures. For example, when the U.S. was trying to exert political pressure on Iraqi leader Saddam Hussein in September and October 1990 without sparking a war, viruses and radio frequency weapons could have been used to damage Iraqi military power without spilling blood. Such bloodless victories would also have the happy result of solidifying international and domestic approval for the U.S.-led coalition.[7]

As countries in the developing world acquire more and more powerful weapons dependent on internal electronic systems and overall C^3I networks, the value of such nonlethal weaponry increases. Thus an attack being prepared by the reasonably sophisticated armed forces of a developing country could be crippled in its tracks by several blasts of a defender's radio frequency weapons. And if bloody combat did continue, then the defenders would be better able to resist the attack.

Also, nonlethal technology such as viruses can be used to paralyse an enemy's C^3I — including domestic telephone networks — prior to a sudden attack, such as the U.S. occupation of Panama in 1989. Immediately after the attack, the telephone network could be made operational again by electronically killing off the viruses. Such systems have the added advantage of causing little damage to the enemy's country, reducing the cost in lives and money.

Moreover, increased use of nonlethal technology might help create a world that would be readier to condemn use of lethal weaponry, thereby edging the world a little closer to peace.

To prepare for use of fourth generation war and nonlethal technology, the U.S. will need to increase research into such weaponry and also build up its Special Operations Command, based in Florida, which is composed of heavily trained Army, Navy and Air Force commandos, equipped with helicopters, aircraft, and submarines.

But whether or not fourth-generation warfare ever appears, future warfare will demand high-quality soldiers able to quickly and intelligently wield powerful weapons to achieve important objects.

And the only way to get high-quality soldiers is to pay and educate them well, in a society that recognizes their value in peacetime, as well as wartime.

It may seem ironic, but the incredible progress and uncertainty of electronic combat technology ensures that what really counts is smart soldiers. As George S. Patton wrote in 1922, "Untutored courage is useless in the face of educated bullets."

A critical peacetime task for soldiers is to develop new technology and to learn how it is best used. Even a brief look at military history will show many military organizations that have failed to adapt to new technology. The Saxon Housecarls could not adapt to the offensive power of the Norman knights and bowmen in the eleventh century, the French knights could not adapt to the defensive power of the English bowmen and infantry in the fourteenth century. Equally, the Allies could neither understand the offensive power of submarines nor the defensive power of trenches, machine guns and artillery in World War I. Nor could the Allies understand the offensive power of the Panzer divisions in World War II. The Germans did not understand the defensive power of the British radar network during the Battle of Britain, and also failed to understand the immense defensive power of Russian industry and society.

With such a record of military failures during periods of relatively slow technological change, it would be very surprising if any of the world's militaries fully understood the impact of electronic combat and the new weapons of today.

Some aspects of the changes are fairly easy to accept. For example, new radars fit easily into military organizations that learned their value in World War II, while antiradiation missiles can be accepted by the Air Force as simply another type of guided missile.

But new technologies, or new ways of using existing technology that demand significant changes in the services' routines have much greater difficulty being accepted. For example, the decline of surface ships and manned aircraft are bitterly resisted by the Navy and Air Force. Also, the services are slow to pay attention to issues that cannot be easily quantified, such as target identification, computer viruses, or the increased return on investment in C^3I systems compared to investments in new aircraft or ships.

Much advantage will belong to the military and the nation that do the best job of understanding the new electronic combat technology, and of harnessing it to their purposes. The advantage of understanding the new technology is greater than having faster computers, better sensors, or more reliable software. After all, the Allies had better and more tanks when the Germans overran France in 1940. Indeed, an advantage in understanding may be the decisive factor in a war so short that the ignorant army has no time to learn the lessons it needs to survive.

Thus high-quality soldiers of the U.S. and other NATO countries — aided by academics, scientific researchers, professional analysts — must study in peacetime how best to use the new technology.

This study must give the military the intellectual and technological tools they need to cope with the complexity and uncertainty of modern warfare. Knowing how to best organize and fight with the technology requires extensive prewar study. How will the enemy fight for what goal and what will best deter and defeat him? What kinds of weapons and tactics will your allies support? What will result when thousands of antiradiation missiles and myriads of eye-damaging lasers are used for the first time on the modern battlefield? How best to prepare troops for the destruction of their own C^3I networks even while training them to make use of those same networks? How will those networks survive the stress of combat? What will happen when the enemy unveils his secret weapons? What are those secret weapons? How much faith should be put in the secrecy of one's own weapons? How can the enemy population or government be most influenced?

This improved understanding would underpin and motivate military research into the most important technologies. Without a better appreciation of military needs, the U.S. research bureaucracies will continue to plod along wasting vast amounts of money, talent, time, and possibly lives. Instead of using technology to find innovative ways to meet military needs, the research bureaucracies are content with building superb versions of World War II weapons such as tanks, surface ships, and manned aircraft, just as the Polish Army bred wonderful cavalry horses until overrun by the blitzkrieg.

So soldiers must aggressively explore what they want, and find out if new or existing technologies can meet their needs. Then they must light a fire under the developers so that the new equipment is quickly designed, fielded, and absorbed by military organizations willing to change when technologies offer new ways of achieving political objectives.

But whatever the quality of military thought, some quantities of the extraordinarily complex and costly weaponry and C^3I systems must be developed, built, and maintained at the expense of other national priorities.

This means the U.S.'s appalling procurement systems must be thoroughly reformed — even at the risk of the media subsequently exposing some scandals that embarrass the administration, the DoD, and Congress.

The equipment must also be kept ready for war, and ruthlessly tested by troops so they know how to use it, and more important, so they find new and improved ways of using new equipment. This requires large and expensive training exercises in which electronic combat techniques and technology are tested and improved. But these exercises must somehow hide technical secrets from orbiting enemy electronic intelligence satellites.

Also, much effort must be poured into establishing civilian and military technological expertise, so that in wartime the military is capable of rapidly rewriting software, speedily designing and building new weapons, and quickly repairing damaged weapons. Equally, this technical expertise and its fruits — military software, sophisticated machine tools, powerful computers — must be carefully managed so they can help civilian industry but cannot be used by the country's enemies.

Combat readiness requires more that a collection of C^3I and electronic combat technology. More than ever, given the violence, tempo, uncertainty, and revolutionary changes in warfare, combat readiness needs determined leaders, a flexible organization, good training, and brave and smart soldiers using the best equipment they have in the best possible way against the enemy's weaknesses — one hopes for a good political cause. These requirements argue for a professional force, backed up by well-trained reserves — a situation toward which the Soviets seem to be moving.

The breadth and scale of preparations needed for modern high-technology war represents a very heavy burden on civil society, although it can be accomplished with much less than the 9 percent of gross national product invested in defense by President Kennedy or the 5.6 percent that was invested by President Reagan.

Rightly, much effort has gone into seeking ways to avoid the heavy financial burden involved in preparing for high-technology war. Partly this is motivated by the desire to redirect U.S. defense spending toward domestic spending on worthwhile antipoverty programs. Less worthwhile is the desire to fortify middle-class entitlements such as tax relief on mortgages.

Some experts have argued that the U.S. should cut back its global military commitments because of reduced chances of Soviet aggression, thus reducing its military burden. Others argue that the global role of the U.S. helps stabilize world politics and could be preserved with a reduced military burden by the building of fewer but more powerful weapons animated by extensive C^3I systems.

Some argue that new weapons should be designed and then placed on the shelf for wartime production instead of being expensively produced in peacetime. But others respond that such a design-then-shelve scheme would be a waste of money, because soldiers would never learn how to properly use the new weaponry, and after only a few years had gone by, industry would be unable to build the now technologically obsolete weaponry largely because the civilian electronics industry is changing so rapidly. Whatever means by which military burdens, strategic plans, and civilian priorities are matched, the tail of military plans and preparedness must not be allowed to wag the civilian dog. Civilian goals must control military preparations; the military and technological demands of modern war must not control political goals or society. But equally important, politicians must not ask more of the military than can safely be provided or than the government is willing to spend.

Is there a gleam of light to end this dark tale of military uncertainty and effort? It is possible that the technology that brings us C³I systems may also bring the world together in a global village, tolerant of others' wishes. But this author suspects that the people of the world are too diverse for such neat solutions. More realistically, C³I technology might shrink the world into a New York City complete with crime, ghettos, and middle-class suburbs and — one hopes! — a well-organized, democratic government to ensure the common welfare and a police force to ensure order.

Notes

1. Sun Tzu. *The Art of War*, trans. James Clavell (New York: Delacorte, 1983), p. 13.
2. See Marin L. Van Creveld, *Technology and War* (New York: Free Press, 1989).
3. William Lind, Col. Keith Nightengale, Capt. John Schmitt, Col.. Joseph Sutton, Lt. Col. Gary Wilson, "The Changing Face of War; Into the Fourth Generation," *Marine Corps Gazette*, October 1989. p. 22.
4. Ibid., p. 23.
5. Ibid., p. 24
6. Ibid., p. 23.
7. *Defense News*, 1 November, 1990, p. 1.

Index